THE ALA GUIDE TO RESEARCHING MODERN CHINA

ALA Editions purchases fund advocacy,
awareness, and accreditation programs
for library professionals worldwide.

The ALA Guide to Researching Modern
CHINA

美国图书馆协会
现代中国研究指南

Yunshan Ye

Supported by a Carnegie-Whitney Award
from the American Library Association

an imprint of the
American Library Association
Chicago   2014

Yunshan Ye is the academic liaison librarian for anthropology, East Asian studies, and political science at Johns Hopkins University in Baltimore, Maryland. He is also serving as chair of humanities on the Collection Development Council of the Sheridan Libraries and Museums of Johns Hopkins University and is editor-in-chief of the *CALA Occasional Paper Series*, a peer-reviewed journal published by the Chinese American Librarian Association (CALA). Both on local and national levels, Mr. Ye has taught workshops for scholars and librarians on the topic of researching modern China. This book project won the Carnegie-Whitney Award from the American Library Association in 2008. Mr. Ye earned his master's degree in education at Calvin College, Michigan, and master's degrees in comparative literature and library science at the University of Iowa.

Printed in the United States of America
18 17 16 15 14   5 4 3 2 1

Extensive effort has gone into ensuring the reliability of the information in this book; however, the publisher makes no warranty, express or implied, with respect to the material contained herein.

ISBNs: 978-0-8389-1209-6 (paper); 978-0-8389-1953-8 (PDF); 978-0-8389-1954-5 (ePub); 978-0-8389-1955-2 (Kindle).

Library of Congress Cataloging-in-Publication Data
Ye, Yunshan.
   The ALA guide to researching modern China / Yunshan Ye.
      pages cm
   Includes bibliographical references and index.
   ISBN 978-0-8389-1209-6 (alk. paper)
   1. China—Bibliography. 2. China—History—21st century—Bibliography. 3. China—History—20th century—Bibliography. 4. China—History—Qing dynasty, 1644-1912—Bibliography. I. American Library Association. II. Title.
   Z3106.Y4 2014
   [DS735]
   016.953—dc23
                                                     2013042906

Cover design by Kimberly Thornton. Images © Shutterstock, Inc.
Text design by Mayfly Design in the Arno Pro and DIN OT typefaces.

♾ This paper meets the requirements of ANSI/NISO Z39.48-1992 (Permanence of Paper).

To Caiyun, Joanna, Julia, and Jamie, with love

CONTENTS

Acknowledgments ix

About This Guide xi

Modern China: Basic Facts and Figures xv

Chinese History and Culture: A Chronology xix

Chapter 1   Historical Overview of Modern China Studies
            in the United States 1

Chapter 2   Fundamentals of Scholarly Research
            in the Digital Environment 9

Chapter 3   Finding Reference Sources 17

Chapter 4   Finding Books and Dissertations 25

Chapter 5   Finding Articles in English 39

Chapter 6   Finding Articles in Chinese 55

Chapter 7   Finding Related Articles for Literature Review 63

Chapter 8   Finding Government Documents 75

Chapter 9   Finding Archives, Statistical Data, News, and Images 85

Chapter 10 Researching Humanities in Art, Film, and Media Studies 103

Chapter 11 Researching Humanities in Modern Chinese History 119

Chapter 12 Researching Humanities in Literature,
            Philosophy, and Religion 129

Chapter 13 Researching Social Sciences in Anthropology,
Sociology, and Education 141

Chapter 14 Researching Social Sciences
in Economics and Business 157

Chapter 15 Researching Social Sciences in Law, Politics,
and Women's and Gender Studies 173

Appendix A: Guide to Buying Chinese Books and Films 193
Appendix B: Guide to Buying Chinese E-resources 197
Index 205

ACKNOWLEDGMENTS

This book project is funded by a Carnegie-Whitney Award from the American Library Association, awarded in 2008. First of all, my thanks go to the Carnegie-Whitney Award committee for their generous support for this project. I also want to thank Waidner-Spahr Library at Dickinson College and the Sheridan Libraries at Johns Hopkins University for their rich research resources that have informed the project. Also, I want to thank my colleague and friend Mr. Tao Yang, East Asian studies librarian at Rutgers University, for his kind comments and suggestions, and Ms. Margaret Burri, associate director of the Milton S. Eisenhower Library at Johns Hopkins, for supporting my work on the project. I also extend my thanks and gratitude to my former supervisors and friends, Ms. Terri Fishel, director of DeWitt Wallace Library at Macalester College, Ms. Kris MacPherson, faculty librarian at St. Olaf College, and Ms. Theresa Arndt, associate director of Waidner-Spahr Library at Dickinson College, for their kindness and support during the early years of my career.

I presented a portion of this project at the symposium "Scholarly Resources for Research and Teaching on East Asia," held on April 23, 2009, at Dickinson College. I want to thank the 36 participants from 25 colleges and universities for their participation in the event and for their feedback on my presentation. In particular, I want to thank Mr. Kirk Moll, representing ACLCP (Associated College Libraries of Central Pennsylvania), and Ms. Victoria Bestor, representing NCC (North American Coordinating Council on Japanese Library Resources), for their assistance with organizing the symposium and making it a great success.

Last but not least, I want to thank my wife, Caiyun Zhao, and my daughters, Joanna, Julia, and Jamie, for being such a supportive family.

ABOUT THIS GUIDE

Although the content and scope of the project has evolved a great deal during the process of research and writing over the past four years, the primary goal has remained the same: to fill in a critical gap in the existing reference resources on China Studies. This guide is intended to address the changing landscape of scholarly research, especially the predominant role of digital resources, and does not merely list resources but also teaches critical information literacy concepts and skills in the field.

The spectacular economic growth in China in the past decade has generated tremendous interest in the country and drives rapid expansion of China Studies in Western academia, particularly in the United States. Nearly all US colleges and universities now include China-related courses in their curricula, and up to 400 institutions offer degree programs in China Studies or closely related fields (Macmillan Reference USA 2007). Not only does the field continue to expand and grow in large research centers and universities—traditional strongholds for scholarship on China—it has also gradually over the past few decades become a significant presence in many primarily undergraduate institutions. For example, most liberal arts colleges, fueled by popular demand and generous support of charitable foundations (such as the Freeman Foundation), now embrace the study of China or East Asia as a critical strategy to prepare their students for future leadership in the globalizing world (Clancy 2012). Recently, China Studies has even entered the field of secondary education. Recognizing the strategic importance of China in the future US economy, many high schools are now offering Chinese-language courses, some even going as far as mandating Chinese courses for public school systems (Yamashita 2000).

While a record number of students are entering or interested in the field of China Studies, there has been no published reference work to date that can provide a proper introduction to the rich research resources now available for

Chinese studies. For example, a preliminary study using WorldCat shows that out of the 21 existing research guides for China Studies, 12 of them were published prior to 1979 (hence outdated); another three were highly specialized, focusing on very specific topics (such as Sung history); and the remaining six were bibliographies clearly intended for advanced students of China Studies that would not be useful for beginners. More important, none of the works covered electronic resources.

In addition, most of the existing reference works are devoted to the study of premodern Chinese literature, philosophy, and culture. The focus of China Studies as a field, however, has shifted onto modern and contemporary China (see chapter 1 for details). It is common nowadays to find students in China or Asian Studies also double-majored in business, international studies, political science, or other fields of study, with the intention of pursuing future business, government, or NGO careers in connection with China. For this reason, most China Studies curricula now focus on modern and contemporary China, covering not only subjects in humanities but also, perhaps more important, those in social sciences.

In short, the existing reference resources published to date are inadequate to reflect the changing field of China Studies, both in terms of the reality of today's academic research in the digital age and also in light of the growing diverse population of today's China researchers, which encompasses not only scholars and advanced students in graduate schools but also undergraduate and even high school students, people working in private businesses or government agencies, and virtually anyone who may or may not be a China specialist but who needs to conduct research on China. For this reason, the first and foremost goal of this book is to create a high-quality, up-to-date, and practical reference work that guides researchers of all levels to the most important research resources in the field of Modern China Studies. Rather than trying to make a comprehensive list of all the resources available (an impossible task given the explosion of information related to China), the book focuses on the most crucial resources, particularly those in digital format, that are commonly accessible in academic institutions and likely to be useful for any China researcher. At the same time, the book tries to teach the basic concepts and skills of academic research so that the reader can apply the same knowledge and skills to the use of other research resources and tools that are not covered in this book, thereby improving his or her research skills.

Specifically, the book begins with some contextual information about China and Modern China Studies that is intended for those who are new to the field. The contextual information includes basic facts about China and a chronology that covers more than 3,000 years of Chinese history, from around 1000 BC to the present, highlighting the most significant historical and cultural figures and events. It also includes a full chapter coverage (chapter 1) of the history of Modern China Studies as an academic field to show how the field has evolved over the years.

The main body of the book, chapters 2 through 15, is devoted to detailed discussions on researching modern China with the most vital research resources in the field. Chapter 2 covers some of the fundamental concepts about library research. They are the building blocks for later discussions on research resources and strategies. Chapters 3 through 9 cover different types of resources, including reference works, books, articles, and various types of primary sources. The resources and tools covered in these chapters can be used for research in all disciplines in humanities and social sciences. Chapters 10 through 15 take a different approach by focusing on research resources specific to disciplines. Each chapter covers specialized resources, both in print and online, for some of the major subject fields in humanities and social sciences. Again, to benefit readers of different levels, I have included both resources that are for advanced scholars and those intended for beginning researchers. And finally, the appendix sections include information that librarians may find useful, such as different ways to acquire Chinese-language materials, including print books, DVDs, and electronic resources that are currently available on the market.

References

Clancy, Heather. 2012. "Georgia City Mandates Chinese Courses for Public School System." *Smart Planet*. September 10. www.smartplanet.com/blog/business-brains/georgia-city-mandates -chinese-courses-for-public-school-system/26226/.

Macmillan Reference USA. 2007. *Degrees Offered by College and Subject*. Vol. 3 of *The College Blue Book*. 34th ed. New York: Thomson and Gales.

Yamashita, Samuel H. 2000. "Asian Studies at American Private Colleges, 1808–1990." In *Asia in the Undergraduate Curriculum: A Case for Asian Studies in Liberal Arts Education*, edited by Suzanne Wilson Barnett and Van Jay Symons, 23–51. New York: M. E. Sharpe.

MODERN CHINA

Basic Facts and Figures

Map of the People's Republic of China

Government

Official name: People's Republic of China (*Zhong hua ren min gong he guo*)
Form of government: Single-party (China's Communist Party) rule with one legislative house (National People's Congress)
Chief of state: President
Head of government: Premier
Capital: Beijing (Peking)
Official language: Mandarin Chinese (*Putonghua*)
Official religion: None
Monetary unit: 1 renminbi yuan

Independence

The People's Republic of China was established on October 1, 1949. Notable earlier dates include first unification under the Qin (Ch'in) Dynasty, 221 BC; Qing (Ch'ing or Manchu) Dynasty replaced by a republic on February 12, 1912, marking the end of China's 2,000-year dynastic period.

Geography

Total area: 9,596,960 square kilometers. China is the fourth largest country in the world, following Russia, Canada, and the United States.
Cities: Beijing, the capital city, is located in northeast China; other major cities include Tianjin, Shenyang in the northeast, Shanghai and Nanjing in the southeast, Guangzhou and Hong Kong in the south, Chengdu and Chongqin in the southwest, and Wuhan in central China.
Terrain: China's vast terrain includes plains, deltas, and hills in the east and mountains, high plateaus, and deserts in west.
Climate: China has a wide range of climate from tropical in the south to sub-arctic in the north.

Demography

Population (2012 est.): 1,343,239,923
Population growth (annual average, 2002–2012): 0.54%

Median age (2012 est.): Total population: 35.9; male: 35.2; female: 36.6

Gender ratio (2012): Males: 51.2%; females: 48.8%

Fertility rate (live births per woman, 2011): 1.6

Foreign population (% of total, 2010): 0.1%

Urban-rural population (% of total, 2010): Urban: 46.6%; rural: 53.4%

Life expectancy at birth (2012): Total population: 74.84 years; male: 72.82 years; female: 77.11 years

Literacy (percentage of population age 15 and over literate, 2010): Male: 95.7%; female: 87.6%

Ethnic groups (2000 census): China has 56 ethnic groups, of which 91.6% of the population is the Han ethnic group. The other 55 ethnic groups are customarily referred to as "ethnic minorities" (*shao shu min zhu*). The Han people can be found throughout the country, mainly on the middle and lower reaches of the Yellow River, the Yangtze River, and the Pearl River valleys and the Northeast Plain. The 55 ethnic minorities can be found in approximately 64.3 percent of China, mainly distributed in the border areas of northeast, north, northwest, and southwest China. Yunnan Province, home to more than 20 ethnic groups, has the greatest diversity of ethnic groups in China.

Religions: Officially atheist, China's Constitution (1982) states that citizens enjoy freedom of religion and that legitimate religious activities are protected. Since 1994 all religious organizations have been required to register with the government. Falun Gong, a new religious sect that became popular in the late 1990s, is banned as an "evil cult." Major popular religions in China include Buddhism, Daoism (Taoism), Christianity, and Islam, with Buddhism being the most widely practiced.

Languages: Mandarin Chinese, plus many local dialects such as Cantonese

Economy

GDP (2010): US$5.734 trillion (exchange rate based)

Growth rate (annual average, 2005–2010): 11.2%

Per capita (2010): US$6,801 (exchange rate based)

Exports of merchandise (% of GDP, 2011): 30.3%

Imports of merchandise (% of GDP, 2011): 27.8%

Exports of services (% of GDP, 2011): 2.9%

Imports of services (% of GDP, 2011): 3.8%
Government revenue (% of GDP, 2010): 20.9%
Government expenditure (% of GDP, 2010): 22.5%
Inflation rate (% per annum, 2011): 5.4%

Information in this section comes from a variety of sources, including *Countries of the World and Their Leaders Yearbook 2011* (Gale Cengage Learning), *The Statesman's Yearbook 2012, Encyclopaedia Britannica Online* (Academic Edition), and the UN *Statistical Yearbook for Asia and Pacific 2012* (www.unescap.org/stat/data/syb2012/country-profiles).

CHINESE HISTORY AND CULTURE
A Chronology

Traditional China

1046–206 BC, the Zhou and Qin Dynasties

- Confucius (ca. 551–479 BC) edited the *Classics*. His teachings, recorded in the *Analects*, became the philosophical foundation of the Chinese civilization.
- Qin unified various kingdoms of China in 211 BC. Its king claimed the title of "First Sovereign Emperor," Shihuangdi. The excavation of Shihuangdi's tomb, near today's city of Xi'an, revealed more than 6,000 life-size terracotta warriors. Between 220 and 206 BC, Shihuangdi built the Great Wall. Much of what is left today of the Great Wall, however, was rebuilt during the Ming Dynasty (1368–1644).

206 BC–AD 220, Han Dynasty

- Confucianism was adopted as an official ideology to provide universally accepted norms, morals, and ritual and social behavior.

AD 220–581, the Six Dynasties

- By the end of the second century, the rule of the Han Dynasty gradually fell into disarray and China entered a prolonged period of internal divisions, such as the Three Kingdoms (AD 220–280), and external invasions, such as the Sixteen Kingdoms (AD 303–439), a period filled with political strife, diplomatic intrigue, and bloody warfare.

AD 581–618, Sui Dynasty, and AD 618–907, Tang Dynasty

- After nearly four centuries of political fragmentation, China was reunified under Sui and Tang and entered a golden era marked by "good government," economic growth, and cultural prosperity.
- Poetry was the greatest glory among many artistic achievements during the time, with great poets such as Li Bai, Du Fu, Wang Wei, and Bai Juyi. Printing also appeared for the first time in the Tang Dynasty.

AD 907–960, the Five Dynasties and the Ten Kingdoms

- China once again fell into political disunity during the roughly half a century between the Tang Dynasty and Song Dynasty, with short-lived dynasties rapidly succeeding each other in the north (the Five Dynasties), and new independent kingdoms emerging in the south (the Ten Kingdoms).

AD 960–1279, Song Dynasty

- Despite wars with the invading Juchen from Manchuria (northeast China), Song China continued to lead the world in farming, manufacturing, transportation, and culture in general.
- Chinese porcelain attained international fame at the time. Lyric poetry, *ci*, was among the greatest achievements in art.

1279–1368, Yuan Dynasty

- China was ruled under the Mongols, originally a nomadic people in the north.
- Dramatic literature peaked during the Yuan Dynasty, later seen as the classical age of operatic arias, *qu*.

1368–1644, Ming Dynasty

- Zhu Yuanzhang, a Chinese native and founder of the Ming Dynasty, successfully ousted the Mongols and established one of the most stable and long-lasting ruling periods in Chinese history. The new dynasty controlled the whole of modern China and exerted a predominating influence over East Asia and beyond.

- Zheng He, a court eunuch of great influence, was selected by the Ming emperor to command a fleet of 62 ships and 27,800 men on "tribute collecting" missions to "Western Oceans." Between 1405 and 1433, Zheng led seven voyages and visited states of Southeast Asia, the coast of India, the Persian Gulf, the Red Sea, and as far as the east coast of Africa.

- In the cultural realm, the Ming Dynasty is noted for popular fiction in colloquial style and produced universally acclaimed masterpieces such as historical novels, *San guo zhi yan yi* (Romance of the Three Kingdoms), *Shui hu zhuan* (The Water Margin), a supernatural novel, *Xi you ji* (Journey to the West), and a naturalistic novel of love and life of middle-class men and women, *Jin ping mei* (Golden Lotus). Colloquial short stories were also popular at the time, such as *Jin gu qi guan* (Wonders Old and New) by master writer and editor Feng Menglong.

1644–1911, Qing Dynasty

- The Manchus from Manchuria (northeast China) took over China after defeating Chinese rebels who ended the Ming Dynasty and remnant Ming forces and established the Qing Dynasty. The Manchus adopted the Confucian norms of traditional Chinese government.

- During the early Qing period, the Qing government consolidated control over most areas formerly under the Ming and extended their influence to new frontier areas such as Xinjiang, Tibet, and Mongolia.

- During the nineteenth century, however, the Qing was greatly weakened by costly wars against internal rebellions and external challenges from Western imperialist powers. The rebellions, the largest of which was the Taiping Rebellion (1851–1864), brought immeasurable devastation to China and seriously undermined the rule of the Qing. The Qing's abject defeats in the wars against imperialist powers, such as the Opium War (between China and the British, 1840–1842), the Sino-French War (1883–1885), the Sino-Japanese War (1894–1895), and the subsequent signing of unequal treaties that trampled upon China's sovereignty and national pride, effectively spelled the demise of the dynasty.

- *Hong lou meng* (Dream of the Red Chamber), written during the middle of the eighteenth century, has been recognized as the pinnacle of classical Chinese novels.

Modern China

1911–1928, Republican China I: Warlord Era

- 1911, a number of young low-level army officers revolted in Wuhan. Revolution soon spread across the country, resulting in the Manchu abdication and end of more than 2,000 years of dynastic rule.
- 1912, the Guomindang (Kuomintang or KMT—the National People's Party, frequently referred to as the Nationalist Party) was founded.
- 1913, Yuan Shikai, a powerful warlord with no interest in republicanism, took the presidency of the Republic of China.
- By the end of 1915, it became known that Yuan intended to reestablish a monarchy. Widespread revolts ensued. Yuan died of natural causes in 1916, deserted by his lieutenants. Shifting alliances of regional warlords fought for control of the Beijing government. China descended into warlordism.
- 1914, World War I broke out. China declared war on Germany in 1917.
- 1915, Japan set before the warlord government in Beijing the so-called Twenty-One Demands, which in effect would have turned China into a Japanese protectorate. The Chinese government accepted most of the demands.
- 1919, Beijing's sellout became public following the Paris Peace Conference, which confirmed Japan's claim on China. Massive

student demonstrations and protests broke out on May 4, 1919, starting what is now known as the May Fourth Movement.

- 1917–1923, the New Culture Movement, the intellectual environment in which the May Fourth Movement developed, advocated various social and political theories on modernizing China, ranging from complete Westernization to socialism. The movement had profound impact on Chinese intellectuals for generations to come.
- 1921, the Chinese Communist Party (CCP) was founded. By 1922, the CCP had a membership of 300, while the Guomindang had over 150,000 members.
- 1928, after defeating various warlords, the Chiang Kai-shek (Jiang Jieshi)–led Guomindang controlled most of China and established a republic government in Nanjing with Chiang as president.

1928–1948, Republican China II: Guomindang Era

- 1931, the Japanese took over Manchuria, a vital area with vast fertile land and great potential for industrial development in northeast China. In the years of 1932–1935, Japan seized more territory bordering on Manchuria.
- 1931, the CCP established a soviet government, the Jiangxi Soviet, in the rural areas in central China.
- Following Chiang's policy of "national unity before resistance against foreigners," Guomindang armies fought the Communist troops and, between 1934 and 1936, forced the latter on an almost two-year retreat across western China in what is now known as the "Long March." During the Long March, Mao Zedong rose to the top of the CCP leadership.
- 1937, another Sino-Japanese War started. During the eight-year war, the Japanese committed numerous atrocities against the Chinese, the best known of which was the Rape of Nanjing in December 1937 and January 1938. It was estimated that 200,000–300,000 Chinese, most of whom were civilians, were killed.
- 1945, the Japanese surrendered.

- Between 1945 and 1949, the Guomindang and the Communists fought a massive civil war. Despite initial superiority in equipment and human and material resources, the Guomindang was eventually defeated by the Communists and retreated to Taiwan.

1949–1978, Communist China I: The Era of High Socialism

- On October 1, 1949, the People's Republic of China was formally established, with its national capital at Beijing. The Communist Party was under Mao Zedong's chairmanship, and the government was headed by Zhou Enlai.
- 1950, China entered the Korean War. An armistice was reached in 1953.
- As a result of land reform that started in 1947, about 50% of all arable land in China was redistributed by 1952. Former landlords were persecuted. Hundreds of thousands were executed. Starting in 1953, agriculture was collectivized. All land belonged to the state. Private farming became a thing of the past.
- Between 1955 and 1956, industries and commerce were nationalized.
- 1958, Mao Zedong launched the "Great Leap Forward," a radical reorganization of rural production that involved pooling labor of tens of thousands of peasants from different villages into one huge rural unit called the "people's commune" in the hope of dramatically increasing agricultural and industrial production.
- 1959–1961, bad policy plus inclement weather led to massive famine and starvation. The Great Leap Forward ended in national disaster.
- 1966–1976, China saw the 10 years of the "Great Proletarian Cultural Revolution," a catastrophic political movement launched by Mao Zedong that led to the suffering of millions and destruction of cultural institutions, producing cruelty and oppression on a horrific scale.
- 1976, Mao Zedong died. The members of the "Gang of Four," the radical group led by Mao's widow Jiang Qing, were arrested.
- 1978, full diplomatic relations with the United States were established.

- 1978, the Chinese government formally adopted the "Four Modernizations" (modernizations in agriculture, industry, science and technology, and national defense) as the country's highest priority. An official reform policy was announced.

1979–Present, Communist China II: The Era of Reform and Market Economy

- 1979–1982, the collective farming system was dismantled in favor of a return to family farming.
- 1979, one-child policy was adopted to control population growth.
- 1980, "special economic zones" along the southern coast (Shenzhen, just across the border from Hong Kong; Zhuhai, adjacent to Macau; Shantou, home of many overseas Chinese; Xiamen, a major port in Fujian across Taiwan) were established to attract foreign investment. These zones became the engines driving China's tremendous and sustained economic growth in the next decades.
- 1984, China extended free market reforms to industry; 14 coastal cities were opened to foreign trade and investment.
- 1989, college students, joined by many others, took to the streets in dozens of cities, most notably at Tiananmen Square in Beijing, and protested against corruption and demanded political reform and democracy. On June Fourth, the Tiananmen Square Democracy Movement was suppressed by the military with substantial loss of life.
- 1992, Deng Xiaoping criticized the continuing "leftism" in the country and called for renewed effort at economic reform.
- 1997, Deng Xiaoping died. Jiang Zhemin, successor to Deng, continued the pragmatic, reform-minded approach to the economy while maintaining a strong Party control over the government. Jiang gradually relinquished his posts to Hu Jintao in 2002–2004.
- 1997, Hong Kong, a former British colony, was returned to China.
- 2001, China entered the World Trade Organization. Consequently, China's economic growth accelerated.
- 2008 (August), the Olympic Games were held in Beijing.

- 2010, China surpassed Japan to become the world's second largest economy, behind only that of the United States.
- 2012 (November), Chinese President Hu Jintao handed over power to his vice president, Xi Jinping, at the eighteenth Congress of China's Communist Party, marking the beginning of a new generation of leadership in China for the next 10 years.

Sources consulted for this section include *Encyclopaedia Britannica Online* (Academic Edition), *Modern China: A Guide to a Century of Change* by Graham Hutchings (Harvard University Press, 2001), and others.

Historical Overview of Modern China Studies in the United States

This chapter will show you:
- ★ The evolution of the field of China Studies since the nineteenth century
- ★ The effect of accessibility of information on China Studies scholarship

We can trace the beginning of China Studies in the United States back to the work of missionaries in the nineteenth century. American missionaries started to arrive in China around the middle of the nineteenth century. Some of the missionaries spent decades living in China and produced a large amount of literature about China, in the form of newsletters, diaries, personal letters, and memoirs. Some of the missionaries compiled dictionaries and published introductory books about Chinese history, culture, and people. Thanks to these materials, people in the United States for the first time in history started to have some idea about the real China, instead of just envisioning some remote, mysterious place on the other side of the earth. These publications also laid the foundation for later China Studies scholarship, and they continue to be interesting to scholars even today because they record and bear witness to the most significant changes in Chinese history, such as the collapse of the centuries-old dynastic system and the first encounters between China and the West.

While the missionary materials are valuable historical accounts of what life in China was like at that time, they can also be very much biased. For example, Samuel Wells Williams, a missionary who had spent 43 years in China, wrote in his influential work, *The Middle Kingdom* (1883):

> The Chinese would be found to have attained, it is believed, a higher position in general security of life and property, and in arts of domestic life and comfort among the mass, and a greater degree of general literary intelligence, than any other heathen or Mohammedan nation that ever existed.... They have, however, probably done all they can do, reached as high point as they can without the Gospel; and its introduction, with its attendant influences, will erelong change their political and social system. (Williams 1883, 1:48)

One can argue that there is an implied justification for Western (at least cultural) imperialism.

We can easily find similar biases in another major work by an American missionary, Arthur Smith, titled *Chinese Characteristics* (1894). Smith was born in 1845 in Vernon, Connecticut, to a middle-class family with a strong religious background. His missionary work took him and his family to a small village in Shandong Province in 1872, where Smith spent many decades preaching to the poorest in the village society. One would think that his book would give a more or less realistic account of what Chinese people were like. Reading it today, however, one cannot but see blatant racism throughout his book. For example, chapter 11 of the book is titled "The Absence of Nerves," which the author claimed was one of the characteristics that he had observed in Chinese people. Basically, he claimed that from his "observations" he had found that Chinese people had no nerve system in their bodies and so could endure any kind of pain. Historically speaking, Smith did not make this claim out of the blue. There was an influential book at the time titled *American Nervousness* by a Dr. George Beard (1881). In that book, Beard claimed that "civilized" people such as Europeans and white Americans had more advanced nervous systems than "less-civilized" people such as blacks. It is likely Smith had read that book, because in his own book he contributed to this infamous theory by saying that the Chinese had no nerves at all. The implication was that the Chinese were uncivilized and therefore an inferior race to white Americans. Smith's book later became tremendously popular in the Western world. A lot of Western racist stereotypes of the Chinese that exist today can be traced back to this book. This book also became very popular in Japan when it was translated and published in 1897. The Japanese used this book to justify their imperialist ambition as the hegemonic power of East Asia and their claim to being a superior race to the Chinese, something equivalent to the "whites" of Asia (Lui 2002). In short, due to their obvious prejudice, missionary works in the nineteenth century contributed as much to the myth as to any real understanding of China.

The academic interest in China started to grow in the United States around the turn of the twentieth century. A Chinese scholar who visited the United States in the early part of the twentieth century, Kiang Kanghu, wrote a book titled *On Chinese Studies* (1934). The book describes the field of China Studies in the United States in the early part of the twentieth century:

> When I first came to America in 1914, there were only two universities having Chinese departments, namely, Columbia University and the University of California. The Library of Congress had in its Chinese Division only the gifts of the Chinese government and other small private collections. Since my last visit in 1927, during the last four years, there have been instituted about 300 Chinese courses at over 100 universities and colleges. The Library of Congress has special appropriation for the purchase of Chinese books and has now approximately 150,000 volumes. (Kiang 1934, xx)

China Studies at the time was dominated by what we call Sinology, which literally means "examination of Chinese texts." US scholars tended to follow the French school of Sinology and used philology and translation as primary methods in their study of China. They focused on the textual studies of the Chinese classics (mostly philosophy and literature) and sought to uncover the fundamental principles of Chinese civilization. Because of their preoccupation with premodern classics and the philological approach, early sinologists largely ignored what was going on in contemporary China. Without solid scholarship providing up-to-date and objective analysis of China, the overall understanding of China in the United States remained shallow. The situation was ridiculed by a European scholar in 1912:

> Sinology without knowledge of Chinese thrives particularly well also in the United States. It is strong in the magazines, but also abounds especially in the daily press. Information is imparted with the rapidity of the telegraph on the most complicated and profound secrets of the political, economic and social life of the Middle Kingdom—but the sources of this omniscience

unfortunately, as a rule, are only from the bars of the foreign clubs in Shanghai, Tientsin and Hong Kong. (Dorsey 1912)

World War II had a tremendous impact on the field of China Studies. The war brought the East and West into closer contact, and consequently the East was no longer a remote mystery but something more tangible and real. There was a sense of urgency in the United States on the part of both the government and general public to know what was really going on in that part of the world. The books on Sinology proved inadequate in meeting this demand, as Mortimer Graves said in 1937:

> As I see it, we have in the study of China, Japan, India, the USSR, and the Arabic world to create a new (American) attitude, and probably new techniques; we cannot borrow either from academic learning of the 19th century.... For in dealing with these newer civilizations we are not dealing with dead ones, but on the contrary with civilizations that are very much alive...we have to participate, and that means to know what the Orientals are doing and try to do it with them. (Zurndorfer 1995, 34)

Because of this change in attitude, the US academia during the Cold War saw the rise of "area studies," which Schwartz (1980, 15) defined as "an enterprise designed to achieve an encapsulated understanding of the unknown areas of the world in which we suddenly found ourselves engaged." The consequence for China Studies was the creation of Modern China Studies at Harvard in 1946, largely as a result of the persistence and leadership of John Fairbank. What distinguishes the Harvard Modern China Studies program from early Sinology is that the Harvard program combined language with a disciplinary approach, especially social sciences such as history, anthropology, and sociology, to the region where the language was spoken, in contrast to a sinologist's central concern on language itself. Fairbank justifies his new approach this way: "For historians, the problem is to use the language rather than be used by it" (Zurndorfer 1995, 35). The Harvard program clearly marked a breakaway from traditional Sinology and redefined the entire field of China Studies. Now when we talk about China Studies, we are mainly referring to this particular type of disciplinary approach in which problems of Modern China are examined under the light of theories of modern disciplines.

The years between the 1950s and 1970s saw fast growth in the field, thanks to a large infusion of funds from the federal government and private foundations. Millions of dollars were given to institutions of higher education in support of China Studies during the period (Ford Foundation alone donated $30 million). On the one hand, China Studies thrived because of this generous funding; on the other hand, China Studies as a field soon became a target of criticism from scholars both inside and outside the field. For scholars in mainstream disciplines, China Studies was ridiculed as a "nondiscipline," meaning that scholarship in China Studies was too narrowly focused on China and failed to address larger, more general theoretical problems. There was to this point very little dialog between China scholars and their colleagues in mainstream disciplines. After assessing the state of Modern China Studies in the United States up to 1980, Ramon Myers and Thomas Metzger (1980) came to the sobering conclusion: "Between 1958 and 1970 nearly $41 million was poured into our institutions of higher education in support of Chinese studies. Has this investment paid off to produce high quality scholarship and a corps of reliable China experts? No." Myers and Metzger attribute what they perceived as the failure of China Studies scholarship in the United States to US scholars' lack of adequate language skills, restrictive compartmentalized training, lack of deep understanding and appreciation of China's intellectual and political traditions, and so forth.

While all this may be true, we may also add that little or no access to quality information contributed, to a significant degree, to the general malaise of the field during those early years. During the decades between 1949, when the Communist Party took over China, and 1979, when Deng Xiaoping emerged as China's paramount leader and initiated a sweeping economic reform that would change China forever, the country was shrouded in deep mystery and seemingly impenetrable insulation. There was very little information accessible to Western scholars, making it extremely difficult to conduct scholarly research. Andrew Walder of Stanford University thus describes his experience of coping with the paucity of information as a China Studies scholar in the 1970s:

> Few Chinese citizens could travel abroad; U.S. citizens could not freely travel to China. Research by foreigners was impossible; collaborative research was out of the question; scholarly exchanges had yet to begin. The country's publishing industry had yet to recover from the effects of the Cultural Revolution;

only a handful of leading national party newspapers could be obtained abroad; even regional and local party newspapers were off limits to foreigners and were scarce. Government documents that found their way outside China through obscure means were pored over by scholars; the open press was painstakingly read and analyzed; English-language transcriptions of radio broadcasts published by the BBC World Service and the U.S. Foreign Broadcast Information Service were important sources. Interviews of émigrés in Hong Kong was a major component of one's "field" research...almost none of us had ever been to the People's Republic of China. (Walder 2002)

Another China Studies scholar, Harry Harding, describes the crippling effect of the lack of information on the quality of scholarship:

> Limited access to information and the relatively tight controls over Chinese society severely handicapped many areas of American research on contemporary China during this period. There was little work in the humanities.... Anthropology languished from the lack of opportunities to conduct field work in China.... Economics was hampered by the enormous effort required to compile and reconstruct official data so as to obtain reliable statistics on China's industrial and agricultural performance. (Harding 1984)

Without high-quality information, it was impossible for China Studies scholars to apply the rigorous standards required by disciplines in social sciences to the field of China Studies. As a result, they had to content themselves with gathering facts about China and sharing them with a relatively small and tightly knit community of scholars interested in China. Most of the scholarship was published in *The China Quarterly*, which had become the center of this scholarly community. Because of its scarcity, any information could benefit anyone in the community regardless of discipline. Therefore, there were very little disciplinary boundaries in China Studies at the time, hence the label "nondiscipline."

Dramatic changes have taken place since the 1980s. With the normalization of China–US relations and China's open-door policy, travelling to China and gathering firsthand data are no longer a problem. Easy access to information has led to a new kind of scholarship: China Studies scholarship is no longer confined to China alone but tends to frame itself as part of a disciplinary dialog. Its use of theory and methodology is now recognized as part of mainstream scholarship in the discipline. China Studies scholarship starts to go beyond China-specialized journals, such as *The China Quarterly* and *Modern China*, and gets published in US mainstream discipline-based journals. For example, the *American Journal of Sociology* and *American Sociological Review* published no articles on China between 1978 and 1987, five between 1988 and 1992, 15 between 1992 and 1997, and 16 between 1999 and 2003. Similar trends can be seen in other social science fields like political science and economics. This implies that China Studies is finally coming out of the narrow confines of traditional area studies and merging into mainstream scholarship based on individual disciplines. In other words, China Studies now is clearly an interdisciplinary field, with different disciplinary approaches all contributing to a broad understanding of what is going on in China.

Spectacular economic growth in the past decades has brought China to the center of the global community. It has generated tremendous interest in the region and drives rapid expansion of China Studies in the United States. With the thriving of China Studies here, we have also seen much greater interaction between scholars in China and the United States. Besides visiting and collaborating scholars, more and more US students, the future generation of China Studies scholars, are coming to study in China. Between 1979 and 1983, there were about 3,500 US students studying in China; by 2001, the number rose to 50,000. The number of Chinese scholars and students coming to study in the United States has also increased dramatically. In 1978, there were about 50 students from China; by 2009, the number mushroomed to 127,628. Now China has become the leading country to send students to America (Institute of International Education 2012). The increasing number of students studying in the two countries will undoubtedly contribute to more interaction and collaboration between Chinese and US scholars.

Another significant change is that the quality of China Studies scholarship has much improved, both in the United States and in China. In this country, a great number of Chinese students choose to stay after finishing their graduate training and join the China Studies community here. Because they do not have the language and cultural barriers that plagued early China Studies scholars, these China-born scholars are playing an increasingly important role in the China Studies field. At the same time, there are also a large number of Chinese students who choose to return home upon graduation, and many of them become leaders in their fields in China. They channel what they have learned from the United States to the classrooms and scholarly publications in China and help train and nurture new generations of scholars in China. Compared to the older generations of Chinese scholars (such as in the 1950s up to the early 1980s), this new generation of scholars is much better informed. They are well versed in the latest Western theories and well aware of cutting-edge research in their fields. They have overcome the political and ideological barriers that isolated the older generation of Chinese scholars and are fully equipped to engage their Western colleagues in scholarly dialog. As a result, the overall quality of scholarship in China has greatly improved. The implication for China Studies researchers today is that in order to do complete and thorough research on a China-related issue, we can no longer rely on English-language sources alone but have to expand our search to sources from China, including both primary and secondary sources.

References

Dorsey, George A. 1912. "Professor De Groot on American Sinology." *Science N.S.* XXXVI (936): 787–789.

Harding, Harry. 1984. "The Study of Chinese Politics: Toward a Third Generation of Scholarship." *World Politics* 36 (2): 284–307.

Institute of International Education. 2012. "Open Doors Data Fact Sheet: China." www.iie.org/en/Research-and-Publications/Open-Doors/Data/Fact-Sheets-by-Country/.

Kiang, Kang-hu. 1934. *On Chinese Studies.* Westport, CT: Hyperion.

Lui, Lydia. 2002. "Introduction to the 2003 Edition." In *Chinese Characteristics,* by Arthur H. Smith. Norwalk, CT: EastBridge.

Myers, R. H., and T. A. Metzger. 1980. "Sinological Shadows: The State of Modern China Studies in the U.S." *The Australian Journal of Chinese Affairs* 4: 1–34.

Schwartz, Benjamin. 1980. "Presidential Address: Area Studies as a Critical Discipline." *Journal of Asian Studies* XI (1): 15–25.

Walder, Andrew. 2002. "The Transformation of Contemporary China Studies, 1977–2002." *The Politics of Knowledge: Area Studies and the Disciplines.* University of California International and Area Studies Digital Collection. http://repositories.cdlib.org/uciaspubs/editedvolumes/3/8/.

Williams, S. 1883. *The Middle Kingdom.* New York: Scribner's.

Zurndorfer, H. T., ed. 1995. *China Bibliography: A Research Guide to Reference Works about China Past and Present.* Leiden, Netherlands: Brill.

Fundamentals of Scholarly Research in the Digital Environment

This chapter will show you:

★ What constitutes effective research
★ What are a reference (tertiary) source, a secondary source, and a primary source
★ What is unique about researching modern China

Before we launch into a discussion of the rich resources now available for scholars of Modern China Studies, we will start with two basic questions: What makes effective research in the digital environment? Is there anything different or unique about researching modern China?

We all have our own research styles. There is no cookie-cutter model for effective research. That said, we all need to learn some basic lessons if we wish to improve our research efficiency and become effective researchers; that is, we must be able to do thorough, systematic research for high-quality information and do it efficiently. One of the basic lessons is that research is not a random, hit or miss process. For any research topic, there are different types of information available, and each type of information plays a role in the process of research. An effective researcher, regardless of his personal style, would know what information he needs at any point of his research and where and how to find it.

For example, if we are assigned a research topic but have little or no idea what it is about, the first step to take is probably to find some basic overview article about the topic itself. In that case, we need to consult such reference sources (also known as tertiary sources) as encyclopedias or dictionaries to get the background and contextual information. These sources can help us gain a basic understanding of the topic, and we could possibly pick up a few key terms or concepts that could help us narrow down the topic for more in-depth research. For instance, "globalization in China" is definitely too big a topic for a class paper of fewer than 10 pages. To narrow down the scope of the topic, we would have to identify a key issue or aspect of globalization in China, such as how globalization has impacted China's "environment" or "traditional culture." Only after we have narrowed down the topic with a specific problem can we hope to explore the topic in some depth within the space of the paper. A good place to look for such an issue or problem would be what we call "reference sources."

At the same time, we also need to be cautious about using this type of material. Sources like encyclopedias and dictionaries are designed to prepare us for further research, not to be the end of our research. We can certainly use the information we have found in an encyclopedia in our final research paper, but quoting excessively from an encyclopedia is always a sign of shallow, incomplete research.

Once we have developed some basic understanding of the topic and narrowed it down to a manageable scope, then we should move on to the next step: finding secondary literature, which includes scholarly books and articles on the topic. Almost all academic papers include a section called "literature review" or an equivalent. It is essentially a summary of what other scholars have written about the topic to date. This is a most crucial step in any research project regardless of discipline. Scholars do not work in isolation; they engage in a dialog with other scholars through their published works. By invoking the work of other scholars, we are making our way into a scholarly conversation within a community of scholars who share the same interest. In other words, our research is not supposed to start from scratch, but should build on the work that others have already done. The literature review section is therefore the foundation of our project. We build and develop our thesis idea on this foundation and make our own contribution to the body of accumulated knowledge on the particular topic. There are numerous sources for

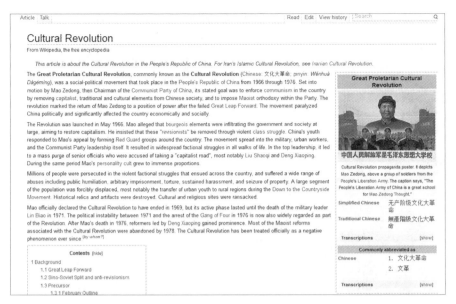

FIGURE 2.1 Result page of *Wikipedia* on "Cultural Revolution"

finding secondary literature, either books or articles, which we will discuss in detail in the following chapters.

Even if we have exhausted all the sources of secondary literature, our research is still not completed yet. For secondary literature only represents what has already been written and talked about on a given topic. It only serves to set the stage for the most important part of the project: our own thesis idea or argument, which is our own voice in the virtual scholarly dialog. To make our argument convincing, we will have to find and use primary sources to support, reinforce, or substantiate it. Primary sources come in many different formats. Any document originated from a historical event or person would constitute a primary source, such as a personal letter, a literary text, a government document, a photograph, an archival collection, statistical or experimental data, and so on. It is an object that we will have to analyze and interpret. We could make a strong argument by quoting from the best scholarship in the field. But ultimately, our argument has to be grounded in an expertly executed (i.e., logically sound and theoretically informed) analysis or interpretation of primary sources.

In sum, to conduct effective research, we should know that there are different types of research resources for any topic, and that each type of resource

FIGURE 2.2 Result page of *Encyclopaedia Britannica Online* on "Cultural Revolution"

plays a role at different stages of the research process. Rather than searching for random pieces of information, we need to assess where we are in the research process and determine what we need (in terms of reference sources, secondary sources, or primary sources) and where and how to find it.

Perhaps even more important, beginning researchers should avoid the temptation of taking shortcuts when they start out with a research project by relying too much on one or two research tools. For example, in today's digital age, with powerful Internet search engines like Google, it is often all too tempting to skip the complicated library system and go straight to Google and *Wikipedia* for information. These free online resources have their own place in the overall research process, but they can never replace the library.

To illustrate this point, let's do a quick comparison between *Wikipedia*, representing free Internet resources, and *Encyclopaedia Britannica Online*, representing library paid research sources. If we do a search on "Cultural Revolution" on both *Wikipedia* and *Britannica Online*, on the surface we have two similar results (see Figures 2.1 and 2.2).

Both entries give us overview articles on the historical event, both with images. However, the key difference is that the *Britannica Online* entry comes with the author's name, Kenneth G. Liberthal, which is prominently displayed at the top of the entry. If we click on the name, it leads to a brief biography that tells us the academic credentials of the author. It says that Kenneth

G. Liberthal is "Professor of Political Science; William Davidson Professor of Business Administration; Research Associate, Center for Chinese Studies, University of Michigan, Ann Arbor; Author of *Governing China* and others." It also tells us that his contributions to the encyclopedia include "China," and "Cultural Revolution." With this knowledge, we are reassured that the information in this entry is of high quality, from someone who is well qualified to write about the topic.

On the other hand, we cannot say the same about the entry in *Wikipedia*, which is contributed by an unnamed author or authors. This is not meant to disqualify *Wikipedia* as a useful source of information; it is just to say that *Wikipedia* as a source of information is designed differently from a library database and serves quite a different purpose. With over three million entries, *Wikipedia* is definitely an excellent source for quick information on virtually any topic. However, *Wikipedia*, by relying on the goodwill of nameless contributors with minimum editorial intervention, is *not* designed as an authoritative source of information for scholarly research. Scholarly research work has to be built firmly on verifiable, authoritative information of the highest quality. It is never a good idea to include unverified or unverifiable information or claims in a scholarly research paper. That would most certainly have negative impact on the quality and integrity of any scholarly work.

In short, to be an effective researcher we need to be able to do at least two things: (1) assess our own information needs at different stages of research and identify ways to acquire the information needed, and (2) exercise critical thinking and distinguish what is "good" information (information appropriate for a scholarly work) and what is not. This is essentially the basic definition of *information literacy* by the ACRL (Association of College and Research Libraries), a branch of the American Library Association (ACRL n.d.). The importance of using diverse sources of information and exercising critical thinking applies to all subject fields, including Modern China Studies.

Now, let's turn to our second question: What is unique about researching modern China? There are many things that make researching modern China different from researching other parts of the world, such as China's unique language, history, culture, population, and so on. But what is most unique is China's political system (the so-called socialism with Chinese characteristics). The most salient feature of this system is the predominant role of the government in Chinese society. China boasts the world's largest and most powerful government bureaucratic system, which has been under the firm control of China's Communist Party since 1949. The government commands all political power and practically all economic resources in the country. This is a crucial background to bear in mind when we try to tackle any China-related topic. It has a direct impact on what China does, where China is going, and also on what kind of information and scholarship is being produced in China.

An obvious example of the impact of the government on information and knowledge production in China would be the issue of censorship. Since the government controls and monopolizes virtually all information channels, from public media (newspapers, television, radios) to academic publishing houses, it has the resources and power (and political will and necessity, too) to bend the process of information production and dissemination to its own advantage. Censorship, as we all know, is one of the indispensable tools for any nondemocratic government to maintain its hold on power. For scholars of Modern China Studies, the implication is that it is absolutely crucial that we exercise critical thinking when dealing with information coming out of China. We cannot just take at face value what is said in a Chinese news report, for instance, on how the one-child policy has worked wonders and successfully controlled China's birthrate and population (which may be true), without fully reflecting on the gaps, absences, and silence in the report on the brutality and enormous human toll the policy has exacted on the Chinese people.

Besides censorship, the power of the Chinese government is also reflected in the process of knowledge production. The blatant examples of this in recent years would be the numerous "scholarly" articles published in China on the so-called theory of the Three Representatives, promoted by former Chinese president Jiang Zemin, and theories of the Scientific Development and Harmonious Society by succeeding president Hu Jintao. But even in nonpolitical/nonideological fields such as the natural sciences, we can still see how information flow and knowledge production are influenced by the government agenda. For example, if the political leaders in China's central government decide that in the next five years China's top priority is to tackle the energy problem, the first information on this issue would come out in government documents in the form of the government's five-year plan, speeches given by key political leaders, followed by editorials in the *People's Daily*, CCTV, and other major government organs. Since all research institutions in China, such as universities and research centers, are funded by the government, the scholarly community is very much attuned to the messages from the central government. Very soon, scholarly conferences on energy solutions would be convened, and scholarship on the topic would start to come out in key academic journals. Following that would be theses and dissertations from a few key universities, which typically enjoy the lion's share of government funding and national educational resources and serve as the government's think tanks and brains. These theses and dissertations would be among the first in-depth studies on cutting-edge topics, often reflecting the national priorities set by the government, before full-length books on those topics are published.

To recap, the overall knowledge production in China is characteristically driven by the government agenda. This model of government-driven knowledge production, as well as the extent to which the Chinese government can marshal its political and economic power to influence scholarship, reinforces the two points that we have made about being an effective researcher: first, we need to use diverse sources of information to get a complete picture on a research topic, and second, and perhaps more important, we need to exercise critical thinking when we research and evaluate information. In particular, when we work with information coming from China, we should always ask the crucial question on how trustworthy the information is and how political power and ideology might be at play behind what information is being disseminated and what knowledge is being produced.

Reference

ACRL (Association of College and Research Libraries). n.d. "Information Literacy Competency Standards for Higher Education." Accessed December 3, 2012. www.ala.org/acrl/standards/informationliteracycompetency/.

Finding Reference Sources

> **This chapter will show you:**
> - ★ How to use the library catalog to locate print reference sources
> - ★ How to use databases to find reference sources
> - ★ How to access Chinese reference sources
> - ★ How to find scholarly reviews

Reference sources are a great place to start if we feel we don't know enough yet about a research topic. Typically at this stage, we only have a very broad and somewhat vague topic, something like "globalization in China," which would be way too big a topic for a 10-page paper. What we need at this point is to find out more about the concept of "globalization," such as what it is about (the definition), what are major issues (key concepts and terminologies), and how they may be related to China (possible topics for our paper). With the contextual information, we should be better prepared to narrow down our topic to a manageable level. In other words, what we need is a reference source that could give us the big picture, an introductory overview article of the topic, so that we can situate our own paper in an established scholarly context.

Locating Print Reference Sources

The question to ask is where we can find such introductory articles. A common mistake of beginning researchers is the attempt to find such entry-level materials through one or two databases they know (e.g., JSTOR) without knowing what the database contains. Most databases like JSTOR include only scholarly articles that are intended for scholars in the fields, with the assumption that readers already have all the necessary background knowledge. Therefore, they tend to be highly specialized and use a lot of jargon intelligible only to those well versed in the field. If we find this type of article hard to follow, it is a sign that we are not ready to tackle the topic as an expert yet. We need to step back and consult a reference source. As we said earlier, a reference source can be an encyclopedia, a dictionary, or a subject-specific research guide. It is designed to provide guidance to a research topic or subject field. Most libraries maintain a collection of print reference sources, usually located near the main entrance of the library building and/or close to the reference/information desk.

The most convenient way to locate a reference book on a research topic is through the library catalog. For example, using the library catalog at Johns Hopkins (called Catalyst), we can do a keyword search on "globalization" and "encyclopedia" and find 56 titles.

Many of the titles deal with special aspects of globalization, such as women's issues, security, or the environment. At least one title, *Encyclopedia of Global Studies*, deals with globalization itself and may contain the information we need—that is, a general introduction to globalization.

If we decide to do a narrower search for "globalization" and "China," the keywords for our research project, Catalyst does not yield any results. That only means that the library does not have a reference work that deals *exclusively* with globalization in China; the library may in fact have reference works that include information on the topic. This is a common problem of using print reference sources. The catalog only searches the "record" of a book (see Figure 3.1), which includes mostly the citation information (title, author, publisher) of the book, plus some subject terms that describe what the book is about. It does not search the content of the book. If our search terms are not included anywhere in the records of the encyclopedias, we will not get any results. It is possible, however, that one of the encyclopedias may

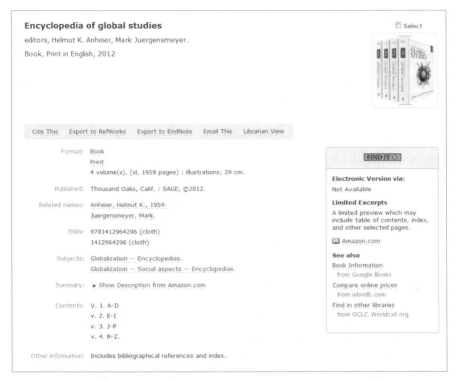

FIGURE 3.1 Example of a catalog record

well contain discussions on globalization in China in one of its chapters. But due to the limitation of the catalog, we are unable to search inside the books and find the information we need. That said, it is still a good idea to consult the library reference collection first when looking for overview articles on a given topic. If we do find such a book (an encyclopedia or specialized dictionary) that deals with the topic, we will get a good jump start on our research project.

Using Online Reference Databases

The good news is that with more and more reference sources being digitized and web-based reference databases growing rapidly in number and popularity, finding reference sources has become so much easier. Nowadays, it is very common for academic libraries to have at least one or two of the following databases specialized in reference sources.

Encyclopaedia Britannica Online

One of the oldest English-language encyclopedias still being produced, *Encyclopaedia Britannica* was first produced between 1768 and 1771. For over 200 years, the encyclopedia has been a staple in the reference collections of public and academic libraries. Under the pressure of the digital age, Britannica ceased its print publication in 2010 and now exists exclusively in the online format.

The major advantage of using the online version of the encyclopedia is that now we can search the full content of the encyclopedia with ease. For example, if we type in "globalization" and "China," we will get a list of entries that contain the two search terms. Even though there is no entry in the encyclopedia devoted to the topic of our interest, we are still able to find many entries that do include discussions related to the topic, a huge improvement over print reference sources. In the entry on "Cultural Globalization," we would find some content about political consequences of globalization on some countries, including China. This information could guide our research to a certain direction and help us narrow down our topic, which is exactly what a reference source is designed to do. Without the convenience of a full-text search capability of the electronic database, it would be very difficult for us to discover such information.

Gale Virtual Reference Library

Instead of a single title like *Britannica Online,* some reference databases include hundreds of reference titles (encyclopedias and dictionaries) and provide full-text, cross-search capability to all the contents. Gale Virtual Reference Library (GVRL) is one such database. Another popular database of this kind is called Credo Reference. Many academic libraries have either or both databases.

Depending on the library subscription, GVRL may contain hundreds of reference titles in 18 subject categories. From the search box on the homepage, we can choose to search one single title or within a subject category or across the entire collection that our library subscribes to. A simple search on "globalization" and "China" produces 469 hits (see Figure 3.2). The left-hand side menu allows for easy navigation through the results. We can further refine the search just by clicking on any of the "facets," the categories by "Document Type," "Publication Title," or "Subjects."

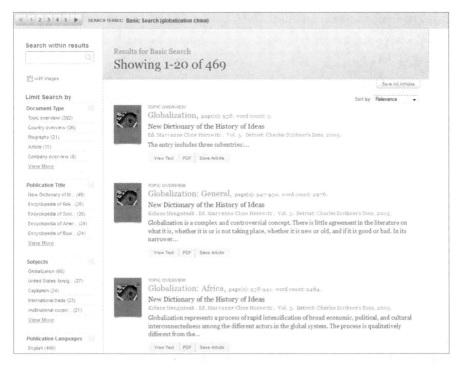

Search within results

🔍

with images

Limit Search by

Document Type
Topic overview (392)
Country overview (26)
Biography (21)
Article (11)
Company overview (8)
View More

Publication Title
New Dictionary of th.. (49)
Encyclopedia of Rel.. (26)
Encyclopedia of Soci.. (26)
Encyclopedia of Amer.. (24)
Encyclopedia of Busi.. (24)
View More

Subjects
Globalization (60)
United States foreig.. (27)
Capitalism (24)
International trade (23)
multinational corpor.. (21)
View More

Publication Languages
English (469)

Results for Basic Search
Showing 1-20 of 469

Save All Articles

Sort by: Relevance ▾

TOPIC OVERVIEW
Globalization, page(s): 938. word count: 5.
New Dictionary of the History of Ideas
Ed. Maryanne Cline Horowitz . Vol. 3. Detroit: Charles Scribner's Sons, 2005.
The entry includes three subentries:...

View Text | PDF | Save Article

TOPIC OVERVIEW
Globalization: General, page(s): 947-950. word count: 2976.
New Dictionary of the History of Ideas
Kidane Mengisteab . Ed. Maryanne Cline Horowitz . Vol. 3. Detroit: Charles Scribner's Sons, 2005.
Globalization is a complex and controversial concept. There is little agreement in the literature on what it is, whether it is or is not taking place, and whether it is new or old, and if it is good or bad. In its narrower...

View Text | PDF | Save Article

TOPIC OVERVIEW
Globalization: Africa, page(s): 938-941. word count: 2464.
New Dictionary of the History of Ideas
Kidane Mengisteab . Ed. Maryanne Cline Horowitz . Vol. 3. Detroit: Charles Scribner's Sons, 2005.
Globalization represents a process of rapid intensification of broad economic, political, and cultural interconnectedness among the different actors in the global system. The process is qualitatively different from the...

View Text | PDF | Save Article

FIGURE 3.2 Result page of Gale Virtual Reference Library

Because of cross-search capability over hundreds of reference sources, databases like GVRL revolutionize our access to reference sources. No longer do we need to be intimidated by the walls of bound volumes that occupy the library reference shelves, not knowing where to start and how to determine where the information we need may reside. Nor do we need to solely rely on Internet sources like *Wikipedia*. The reference databases are powerful, easy to use, and contain only high-quality authoritative information. For beginning researchers, they represent a treasure trove of information that could jump-start any research project.

Finding Chinese Reference Sources

For those who are proficient in the Chinese language and wish to consult a good Chinese reference source, they can always search the library catalog and see if they can find a relevant Chinese reference book in the library collection. They can do the same search mentioned previously for searching print reference sources and limit the language to Chinese. Whether they can find a relevant Chinese reference source, however, totally depends on the library collection.

Another option, and a much better one, is to use one of the Chinese reference databases now available in many US libraries. The most popular one is China Reference Works Online (CRWO), one of the China National Knowledge Infrastructure (CNKI) databases.

This database contains an astoundingly large number of Chinese reference works of a great variety, from all subject fields. As of October 2012, it contained the full text of 5,762 titles, including a wide range of types of reference sources, such as Chinese dictionaries, bilingual dictionaries, specialized dictionaries for different subjects and disciplines, encyclopedias, atlases, medical reference books, literary reference works, biographies, handbooks, chronologies, quotations, and more. The database is distributed by East View Information Services, a company based in St. Paul, Minnesota, and can be accessed directly at CNKI's homepage (www.cnki.net/, and click on 工具书). CNKI offers a free index search, so even if the local library does not have a subscription, it is still possible to search the database and use it to a certain extent.

Finding Scholarly Review Articles

Besides the reference sources already discussed, there is another kind of contextual information that could be very useful for the early stage of research: research-based review articles written by scholars in the field. The difference between general reference sources and scholarly review articles is that reference sources are intended for the general public. They provide basic factual and background information on a topic and tend not to be peer reviewed. In contrast, scholarly review articles are intended for fellow scholars in the same field. They are summaries or syntheses of the existing scholarship on a research topic. This type of article is most often published in peer-reviewed scholarly journals. We may not be able to find such review articles on every topic, but if we do find one it could really boost our research project by giving us the scholarly context of our research topic.

Scholarly review articles could be published in any discipline-based academic journal, which makes it hard to find them. Fortunately, there is one publisher, Annual Reviews, specialized in publishing review articles for the sciences and social sciences, including anthropology, economics, law and social science, political science, psychology, public health, resource economics, and sociology. Publishing since 1932, Annual Reviews has offered timely scholarly reviews of major research topics in the disciplines. These articles are useful for both seasoned researchers and novices alike. They help keep researchers up-to-date about current developments in the field, or serve as an excellent introduction to the major research topics in the disciplines. In addition, these articles are highly reputable scholarly sources. It is perfectly acceptable to cite these sources in a research paper. In fact, Annual Reviews articles are often among the most-cited sources in scholarly publications. If the library subscribes to Annual Reviews journals (most academic libraries do), go to the publisher's website at www.annualreviews.org/ and search for review articles in the disciplines of interest.

In comparison, finding review articles published in Chinese is relatively easier. Most of this type of article includes the wording "综述" (such as 研究综述, 理论综述, etc.) in the title. All we need to do is to search a Chinese article database, such as China Academic Journals Online (see in particular chapter 6). With a keyword search on a research topic, such as "全球化," plus a title search on "综述," we will get all the review articles relevant to our research topic.

We will conclude the chapter with a clarification: the scholarly review articles we discussed previously are not the same as book reviews. The former are summary reports on a research topic, sometimes an entire field of study. They are intended to keep scholars up-to-date about the latest developments in the field. These articles are written by experts and they are research based. Book reviews, on the other hand, are commentaries on a recently published book (or a recent film or any work of art). They are not necessarily research based and do not count as a scholarly source. However, book reviews can be useful for the purpose of research and learning as well. Whether we are preparing for a book report as a class assignment or just reading a book for fun, we may wonder how other people react to the book. If that is the case, all we need to do is find reviews on the book. There are many places to find book reviews. If the book is a scholarly work, you may go to databases, such as JSTOR, Project Muse, or Academic Search Complete, that include reviews on scholarly works (see chapter 5 for a discussion on these databases). We can search the author or the book title and limit our search to "reviews"; however, if the book is a popular reading such as a novel or biography or a film, we should search the *New York Times* (or other similar sources) instead, because the *New York Times* publishes reviews of popular books, films, and other works of art.

Finding Books and Dissertations

This chapter will show you:

★ How to find books in the local library collection
★ How to find books beyond the local library collection
★ How to find Chinese-language books
★ How to find e-books
★ How to find theses and dissertations

When we start out on a research project, before we jump into databases for articles (to be discussed in the following chapters), we need to find out what books are available on the topic. A book-length study of a topic usually gives us much broader coverage than an article could. Also, a well-researched scholarly work typically comes with copious footnotes (or endnotes) and a lengthy bibliography, which could give us important clues as to what other sources of information may exist on the topic. In this chapter, we will discuss various ways to find books, both in Chinese and in English. We will conclude the chapter with a brief discussion on finding theses and dissertations.

Finding Books in the Local Library Collection

The first online tool for finding relevant books is the catalog of our local library. The catalog is the most important tool for accessing resources in the library collections. Besides books, we can also find many other types of library materials, such as DVD films, archives, periodicals, and so on, but *not* articles. To find articles on a topic, we will have to use databases. As mentioned in chapter 3, the library catalog is essentially a database of indexes; it only searches a "record" of a book or any other library item (such as a periodical), but not its "content." In comparison with full-text databases that search the entire content of their sources, index databases such as the library catalog appear to be less powerful. Nonetheless, because the library catalog is designed for accessing local library collections, it remains an important tool for that purpose. In recent years, most library catalogs have much improved, in terms of usability, with many added-on features. For example, in addition to the traditional list of book titles, many online catalogs can now display the images of book covers, tables of contents, and even links to book reviews and the search-inside functions of Amazon or Google Books, all of which have undoubtedly enhanced the usefulness of library catalogs.

Each library may have different names and interface designs for their catalogs, but all library catalogs function in similar ways. Figure 4.1 shows a screenshot of the Advanced Search interface of Catalyst, the library catalog at Johns Hopkins University. Like most library catalogs, Catalyst allows the user to search by keywords ("Any field"), title, author, subject, and so on. For beginning researchers, it is easy to understand what it means to search by keywords or title or author, but they may not know what is meant to search by subject.

Basically, the term *subject* refers to a list of specially defined terms (called "subject headings") by the Library of Congress. They are standard terminologies that library catalogers use to describe what a book (or any other library material) is about when they "process" the book (inputting information about a book in the library catalog database, assigning a call number, labeling the book, and then putting the book on the shelf ready for checkout). Subject headings assigned to a book are typically included in the book's catalog record. For example, the catalog record of the book *China and Capitalism: A History of Business Enterprise in Modern China* displays not only the citation information of the book (title, author, publisher, date), but also a list of subject headings that are assigned to the book when the book is cataloged (see Figure 4.2).

For the purpose of searching for relevant books, these subject headings can be very useful. Because books that share similar topics are often assigned the same subject headings, we can easily find all relevant books in the library

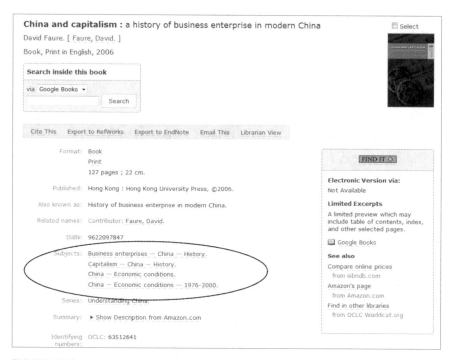

FIGURE 4.1 Advanced Search interface of Catalyst, the library catalog of Johns Hopkins University

China and capitalism : a history of business enterprise in modern China

David Faure. [Faure, David.]

Book, Print in English, 2006

Search inside this book

via Google Books ▾

[_____] Search

Cite This   Export to RefWorks   Export to EndNote   Email This   Librarian View

Format: Book
           Print
           127 pages ; 22 cm.

Published: Hong Kong : Hong Kong University Press, ©2006.

Also known as: History of business enterprise in modern China.

Related names: Contributor: Faure, David.

ISBN: 9622097847

Subjects: Business enterprises -- China -- History.
             Capitalism -- China -- History.
             China -- Economic conditions.
             China -- Economic conditions -- 1976-2000.

Series: Understanding China.

Summary: ▶ Show Description from Amazon.com

Identifying   OCLC: 63512641
numbers:

FIND IT ↻

Electronic Version via:
Not Available

Limited Excerpts
A limited preview which may include table of contents, index, and other selected pages.

📖 Google Books

See also
Compare online prices
  from isbndb.com
Amazon's page
  from Amazon.com
Find in other libraries
  from OCLC Worldcat.org

FIGURE 4.2 Sample book record with subject headings

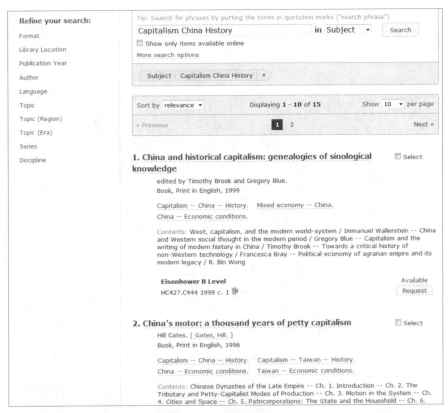

FIGURE 4.3 Search results of subject heading "Capitalism—China—History"

collection just by clicking on the subject heading. Using the previous example, if we decide that we want to focus on the topic of "history of capitalism in China," we can click on the subject heading "Capitalism—China—History." This would retrieve all 15 books on this topic in the library collection (see Figure 4.3).

Finding Books beyond the Local Library Collection

The greatest advantage of using the library catalog is its easy access to the books we need. Once we discover a book of interest in the catalog and write down its corresponding call number, all it takes is a quick trip to the stacks (bookshelves) and we will have the book in hand (if it is not already checked out). However, no matter how large our local library is, in all likelihood it

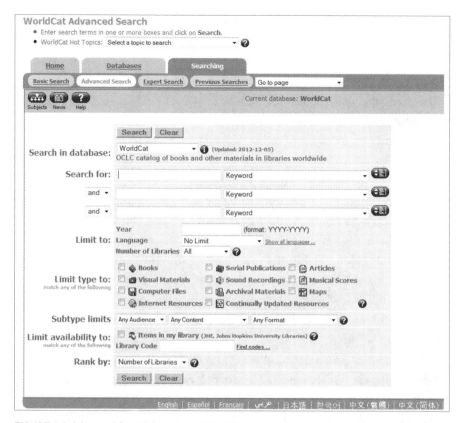

FIGURE 4.4 Advanced Search interface of WorldCat, the library database

does not include all the books on our topic. There could be some important books that are missing in the collection. It would be a disaster if we think we have finally completed a major research project, only to find out later that we have missed a key publication on the subject matter. So, it is very important to search far and wide, at the beginning of our research, for all the relevant sources available. Fortunately, in this digital age a thorough search for all relevant books is not only possible but also fairly easy and painless. One important tool for this purpose is WorldCat.

Most academic libraries subscribe to WorldCat. Created in 1971, WorldCat is a union catalog of 72,000 libraries in 170 countries and territories. It is the world's largest bibliographical database (see Figure 4.4). The user interface of WorldCat is fairly intuitive. We can search by keywords or by author, title, subject, and a variety of categories located in the drop-down menu next to each search box. To get a sense of the scope of WorldCat, we can do a simple comparison between the library catalog and WorldCat. We first search "globalization and China" through Catalyst and get a total of 2,186 hits (including books and other library items), a fairly decent result. However, when doing the same search through WorldCat, we get a whopping total of 11,582 hits, including 5,407 book titles.

Notice that on the advanced search page of WorldCat, we can limit our search to our home library collections only. All we need to do is check the box for "Limit availability to items in my library." We can certainly use World-Cat in place of our own library catalog because our library catalog is most likely already included in WorldCat, as most academic libraries are in North America. Even if we do not check this box, we can still easily spot our own library holdings in WorldCat because they are automatically highlighted in the search results list. In short, WorldCat is an excellent and easy-to-use tool for finding books, not only those in our home library collection but also those beyond our home library collection. It is the most complete catalog of books in the world.

If for some reason we cannot access the library database, there is an alternative way to use WorldCat. In an effort to expose library resources to the largest audience possible, OCLC, the maker of WorldCat, has made the database freely available to the public at the URL www.worldcat.org/. Anyone with Internet access can now utilize this important research tool. The two versions of the database, WorldCat as a library database and WorldCat.org as a free Internet resource, have slightly different interface designs but share the same source data. Using either version will get us essentially the same results, even though their displays may be different.

Using Google Books

Another important, and free, tool for finding books is Google Books. What distinguishes Google Books from WorldCat is that it has an ever-growing collection of fully digitized books in its database. The full-text search capability makes Google Books much more effective in discovering information within the book, something neither the library catalog nor WorldCat can achieve. For example, if we do the same search on "globalization and China" as we did through Catalyst and WorldCat, we get an astronomical 615,000 hits. The number itself may or may not mean much, considering that Google searches tend to generate way too many results, many of which may be only remotely relevant. However, it does show that Google Books can be a very powerful tool for research. In addition to exposure to a large number of resources, Google Books is an important research tool for the following reasons.

Linkage with Library Resources

Google Books is linked to WorldCat, which in turn is linked to the library catalog. For example, one of the books on the result list of "globalization and China" is this one, *Globalization and Changes in China's Governance* (see Figure 4.5).

Notice that on the left-hand menu there is a link called "Find in a Library." Click on the link and it goes straight into the record of the book in World-Cat.org (see Figure 4.6). From the WorldCat record, we can tell right away whether our library owns this book. If we click on the library link, it will take us right into our library catalog. From there, we can find out the call number of the book in our library and retrieve the book from the stacks; or if the library does not own the book, we can easily make an interlibrary loan request from the library website.

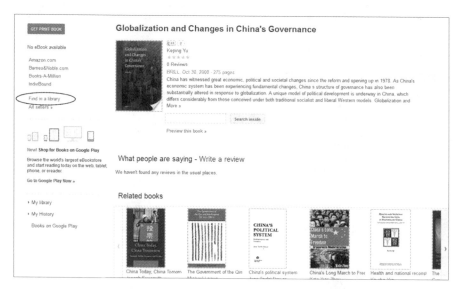

FIGURE 4.5 Sample book discovered through Google Books

FIGURE 4.6 Connecting to WorldCat from Google Books

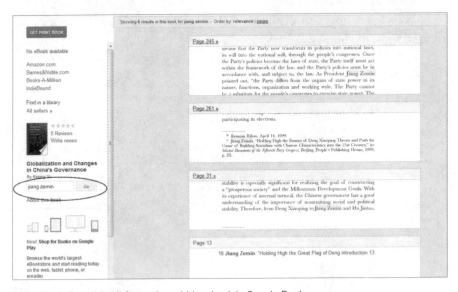

FIGURE 4.7 Searching information within a book in Google Books

Full-Text Search Capability

Thanks to the full-text content in Google Books, we can discover more relevant titles than we could through index databases such as the library catalog and WorldCat. More important, we can uncover information "hidden" in the content of the book by using the "searching within the book" function. For example, in the book *Globalization and Changes in China's Governance* we want to know whether the former Chinese president, Jiang Zemin, is discussed. All we need to do is search "jiang zemin" in the search box on the left-hand menu, and we will see a list of pages with the search term "Jiang Zemin" highlighted (see Figure 4.7).

Finding Chinese-Language Books

To find Chinese-language books, we can use the same tools we have discussed, namely, the library catalog, WorldCat, and Google Books.

Most library catalogs have the option of limiting a search by language. So, in the advanced search page, we can type in a search term and then limit the language to Chinese. The result list we get should mostly consist of Chinese-language sources in the library collection. The accuracy of the result list, however, can vary depending on the library catalog system. Some catalogs may also allow direct input of Chinese characters as search terms. Generally speaking, this method typically generates much more accurate results.

WorldCat works in similar ways. We can find Chinese-language books by typing in search terms in English and limiting our search to Chinese language only. However, compared to most library catalogs, WorldCat has a very robust language searching capability. We can even change the entire search interface into Chinese by clicking on the Chinese-language option on the bottom menu bar (see earlier Figure 4.4).

In terms of Chinese-language content, in 2009 the National Library of China joined the OCLC's WorldCat Resource Sharing Service and uploaded millions of its records into WorldCat (OCLC 2010). As a result, WorldCat boasts an extensive coverage of Chinese-language books.

In Google Books, too, we can choose to search in English and then click on the Advanced Search at the bottom of the page to limit our search to Chinese only. Or we can input Chinese search terms directly and get much better results in terms of Chinese-language sources.

The most powerful tool for finding Chinese-language books, especially for books published since 1949 in mainland China, is neither WorldCat nor Google Books, but a Chinese database called Duxiu (读秀). Since the early stages of digital technology and the Internet, researchers and librarians have dreamed of digitizing everything in the libraries, putting all the content into one gigantic database and making it accessible to anyone, anytime, anywhere. This is what Google is trying to do with its Google Books project. However, up to now, for many reasons, no library database or even Google Books has come even close to this seemingly impossible dream. Duxiu, on the other hand, is China's answer to the challenge. With over three million bibliographical entries and over two million full-text scholarly sources in all subject areas, Duxiu is the largest digital collection of Chinese-language materials in the world, covering essentially all academic publications published in the People's Republic of China since the 1940s.

In particular, Duxiu contains the world's largest full-text collection of Chinese books and has a powerful full-text search capability. To see the power of Duxiu, we can do a simple comparison between Duxiu and WorldCat.

For a keyword search on "全球化", WorldCat yields a list of 6,530 hits, including 4,618 books. In comparison, the same search in Duxiu results in an astounding list of 20,603 books, in addition to 175 reference entries, 185,874 scholarly articles, 18,718 newspaper articles, 4,852 theses and dissertations, 4,315 conference papers, and more. The secret of Duxiu uncovering so many more sources lies in its powerful full-text search capability, plus its enormous knowledge base. For this reason, Duxiu has an unrivalled superiority as a discovery tool for Chinese sources, especially books.

Duxiu, however, primarily works as a content discovery tool. For copyright reasons, it provides limited access to the full-text content. Most books in Duxiu allow a preview of the first 20 pages. In addition to that, Duxiu provides a somewhat indirect way for the user to access the entire book content. Here is how.

Once we identify a book on the result list, we click on the book link. It will take us to the book record page. On this page, we can see a button called "图书馆文献传递," which may sound like the traditional interlibrary loan, but it is not. When we click on the button, a page will pop up asking for the page range of the book that we want as well as our e-mail address. Once we fill in the information and submit the request, the book content we just requested is delivered to our e-mail account almost instantly. The reason why Duxiu can deliver the content so fast is that the database already has the full-text content and the entire process is automated. The only catch is that we can only request up to 50 pages per book per week, but we can request multiple books at a time. Though somewhat cumbersome a process (imagine how frustrating it would be if we needed to get a 500-page book this way), we can at least access those books that would otherwise not be available to us.

Finding E-books

When we search for books in our library catalog, we should be able to find e-books along with print books in the result list. Some library catalogs would give the option of limiting searches to e-books only. In that case, we can easily identify what e-books our library owns and enjoy the convenience of reading the book without a trip to the library.

Alternatively, we could search for e-books directly through e-book databases. There are a number of e-book databases currently on the market. Here we will introduce two major ones: one for English-language books and one for Chinese-language books. Consult the librarian to determine to which e-book databases the library subscribes.

English-Language E-books

The most popular English-language e-book database is probably Ebook Library, or EBL. EBL's popularity among libraries is largely due to its ability to work seamlessly with the library collection development and cataloging systems. For example, its Demand Driven Acquisition feature allows the library to display thousands of e-book titles in the library catalog even before the library has purchased them. As a result, the library user gets exposed to a larger amount of scholarly information when searching the catalog. If the user is interested in one of the titles and clicks on it, it will trigger the mechanism in the library system to loan or purchase the item. On the user's end, it will not indicate whether the library owns the item or not, but the user will get immediate access. This collection development model, often referred to in the library profession as Patron Driven Acquisition (PDA), aims at

FIGURE 4.8 Search results display in EBL

improving cost-effectiveness and utility of library collections by purchasing only the titles that are needed, at the time they are needed.

For researchers, e-book collections such as EBL provide convenient access to books in a way unthinkable prior to the digital age. The e-books can be viewed on most computing devices, from standard desktop/laptop computers to some portable e-reading devices. Figure 4.8 shows the display of the search results of "globalization and China" in the EBL database.

If we are interested in one of the titles in the search results, we can just click on the title (e.g., *Globalization and Labour in China and India: Impacts and Responses*), and it will take us to the book itself, with the table of contents on the left, the text in the center, and a host of functionalities on the menu bars. We can read page by page by clicking on the arrow button, do full-text search within the book, copy and paste the text, have the book read by activating the Reading Aloud feature, or check on the meaning of a word with an embedded dictionary.

Chinese-Language E-books

The most important Chinese e-book collection is called Chinamaxx, produced by Super Star Digital Library, the same company that produces Duxiu.

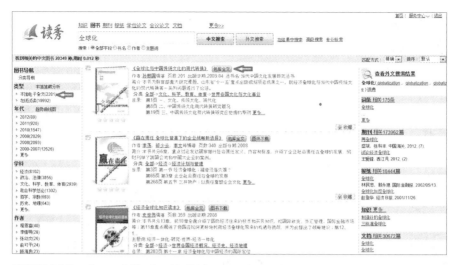

FIGURE 4.9 Result page in Duxiu with Chinamaxx subscription

As a matter of fact, it is essentially the same database as Duxiu. The only difference is that Duxiu primarily serves as a content discovery tool and has limited capability of providing full-text content, mostly because of copyright restrictions. Chinamaxx, even though based on the same source data, includes only the e-book titles to which the database provider has already obtained copyrights. At the present, Chinamaxx includes approximately 800,000 full-text Chinese books, a relatively small number compared to Duxiu's three million titles. Nonetheless, it makes Chinamaxx the largest collection of Chinese books in the world, larger than most of the leading Asian-language collections outside China, and larger than entire library collections in most college libraries in North America.

The libraries have the option to purchase individual titles from Chinamaxx or subscribe to the entire database. Either way, the book records can be uploaded into the library cataloging system, making the books accessible through the library catalog (just like e-books from EBL).

Chinamaxx works seamlessly with Duxiu. As Figure 4.9 illustrates, once the library subscribes to Chinamaxx, a Duxiu search will yield a result list with Chinamaxx full-text titles on the top with the label "包库全文." Also, on the left-hand menu it will indicate how many full-text titles are available in addition to the number of relevant titles.

Finding Theses and Dissertations

Theses and dissertations are unpublished book-length studies by degree candidates. They are excellent sources of scholarly information, especially when we work on cutting-edge topics and there are not yet many books published on those topic areas. Following are two databases for accessing theses and dissertations, one for English and one for Chinese.

ProQuest Dissertations and Theses

ProQuest Dissertations and Theses is the most comprehensive database for dissertations and theses in the English language. It includes millions of searchable citations to dissertation and theses from 1861 to the present day, with over a million full-text dissertations available for download in PDF format. The database offers full text for most of the dissertations added since 1997 and strong full-text coverage for older graduate works as well.

Wanfang Data Theses and Dissertations of China

There are a number of Chinese databases that cover theses and dissertations. Theses and Dissertations of China from Wanfang Data is one of the most popular products. It contains the full-text content of theses and dissertations from China's top universities and research institutions. It covers all disciplines from 1980 to the present.

In addition to the Wanfang product, CNKI and Duxiu also include modules for theses and dissertations. At www.cnki.net/, for example, there is a link on the top menu bar called "博硕." Clicking on the link will take us to the homepage of Theses and Dissertations Full-text Database, which covers theses and dissertations from over 400 higher education institutions in China from 1984 to the present. Similarly, at www.duxiu.com/, there is a link called "学位论文," through which we can search for Chinese theses and dissertations. These resources can be used as an alternative to or supplement the Wanfang product.

Reference

OCLC. 2010. "National Library of China Shares Its Rich Collections with Libraries Worldwide through OCLC's WorldCat Resource Sharing Service." News release, May 27. www.oclc.org/news/releases/2010/201028.htm.

Finding Articles in English

This chapter will show you:

★ How to distinguish between popular and scholarly sources
★ How to find English-language articles
★ Four commonly used general databases
★ Key scholarly journals dealing with China or East Asia

Scholarly books and articles are both important information sources. Books, however, tend to have lengthy publishing delays. In contrast, articles come out much faster and on a more regular basis. Because of their timeliness, journal articles tend to represent the latest, most cutting-edge research in the field. As mentioned previously, books are indexed in library catalogs but articles are not. Articles are indexed (and abstracted) in databases; therefore, we need to use databases to find them. Before we talk about databases, however, we want to make an important distinction between articles published in scholarly sources and those in popular sources. The reason for this distinction is that almost all college-level research requires secondary sources from scholarly publications.

As we know, scholarly research has to be firmly grounded in accurate, objective information—information that comes from authoritative sources, is verifiable, and has been verified. Popular sources like newspapers and magazines that are clearly intended for general audience generally do not meet these criteria. What we said previously about Internet sources like *Wikipedia* also applies to popular sources like newspapers and magazines. They are useful sources of information in many ways, but they are just not the kind of authoritative sources we need to bolster an argument in a research paper. For example, we cannot make a claim in our paper that such and such is true because the local Sunday paper reported it. That is because articles in newspapers and magazines are generally written by staff writers who are not necessarily experts on the topics and issues, and the articles typically do not go through as rigorous a reviewing process as required for scholarly publications. Consequently, articles from popular sources are prone to biases and human error.

In contrast, to publish in a scholarly publication one first has to be well trained in the subject field, often having earned the highest degree ("authoritative") and conducting extensive research before writing a paper. All sources in the paper have to be carefully documented ("verifiable"). After being submitted for publication, the paper will have to go through a rigorous "peer-reviewing" process; that is, other experts in the field (peer reviewers or referees) will scrutinize the paper to ensure that the information in the paper is up-to-date and accurate, the paper itself is original and well researched, and the arguments are well presented, logical, and theoretically sound. The comments and recommendations of peer reviewers will serve as the basis for the editor to make the final decision as to whether the paper will be published, returned for revision, or rejected. As a result of this process, publications in scholarly (peer-reviewed) journals are usually of high quality. They become part of the accumulated body of knowledge that later scholars can use as foundation for further research. That is the reason why we must use scholarly sources when we look for secondary literature for our research projects.

Distinguishing a scholarly article from a popular source is not difficult. Most of the time, if we check the following three areas of the article, we can determine whether it is scholarly:

- *Author*. Most academic publications include information about the author, such as academic credentials, institutional affiliations, and the like—in short, enough information for us to judge whether the author is qualified to write on the topic.
- *Bibliography*. Since scholarly papers are all research based, they typically include a lengthy bibliography, called "Works Cited" or

"References," often in addition to copious footnotes and/or end-notes. This meticulous documentation not only allows the reader to verify the information sources but also serves as a good indication of the extent of research work done in preparation for writing the paper.

- *Publishing source.* Most scholarly journals are published through research centers and institutions (especially university presses), with editors and boards of directors consisting mostly of well-known scholars in the field.

This chapter will cover some of the most popular multidisciplinary databases. These databases all cover a wide range of subjects and disciplines, and they are all very user friendly and easily accessible with mostly full-text contents. We will introduce more specialized databases in later chapters when we talk about resources specific to disciplines in humanities and social sciences. At the end of the chapter, we will list some of the most important academic journals dealing with China or East Asia. A large portion of China Studies scholarship is published in those journals.

There are literally hundreds of databases now available for finding English-language sources. Here, we will just limit our discussion to four of the most popular ones that are relevant to Modern China Studies. Each of these databases has its own unique content and focus. If we use all of them, we should be able to cover the most important literature on any China-related topic. This, however, does not mean that by searching these databases we will have exhausted all the scholarly literature on the topic. For a thorough and complete search, we will have to use more specialized databases. But these general, multidisciplinary databases are usually a good place to start.

JSTOR and Project Muse

JSTOR is probably the most widely used database on any college campus and for good reason. The database was designed to serve as a digital depository for the archives of key journals in humanities and social sciences. With JSTOR, libraries no longer need to have the physical copies of these journals in their buildings, thus freeing up valuable shelving space for newer materials. For researchers, JSTOR provides easy access to high-quality scholarly content with its robust full-text search capability and immediate access to full-text content. JSTOR is also a boon for beginning researchers, because most college research assignments require using scholarly sources that students can safely rely on and JSTOR provides just such sources. The only downside of JSTOR is its time coverage. Because JSTOR serves as a journal archival depository, it typically does not cover the most recent issues. For most journals covered in JSTOR, there exists a "moving wall" of anywhere from one to five years, sometimes even longer.

JSTOR Advanced Search provides multiple search boxes for easy input of search terms (see Figure 5.1). The search boxes can be expanded up to five rows to accommodate complex searches. They also allow for limiting searches to different types of sources, including "Articles," "Reviews," "Miscellaneous," and "Pamphlets." Here is a word of caution: If we are looking specifically for scholarly sources, we should limit our search to articles only. Even though JSTOR only includes high-quality scholarly journals, not everything

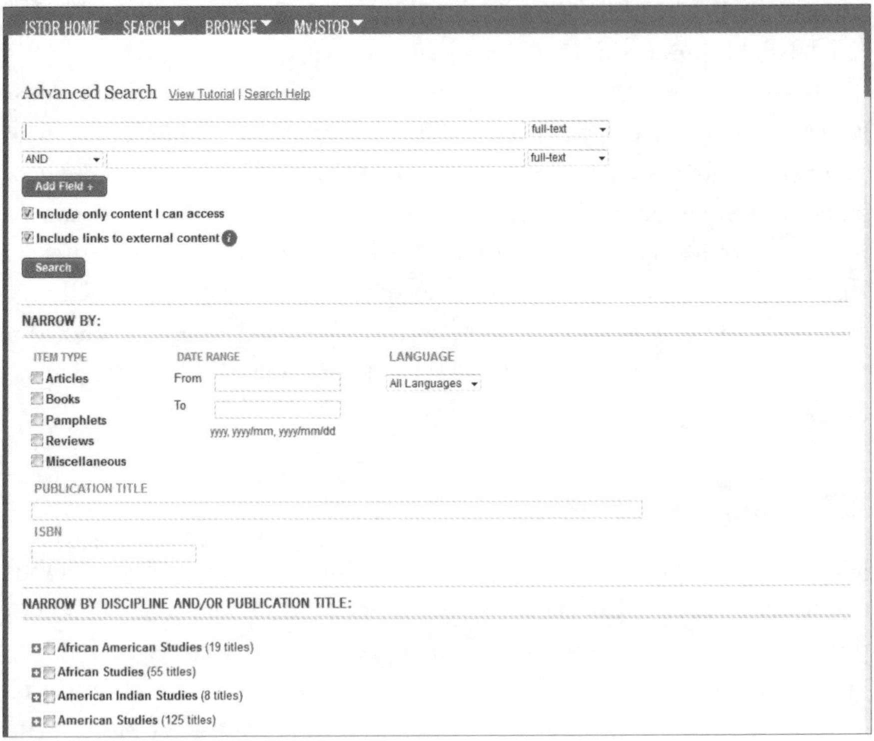

FIGURE 5.1 Advanced Search of JSTOR

published in those journals counts as scholarly, which is usually defined as research based and peer reviewed. For example, editorials, prefaces or brief introductory essays, or book reviews, because they are not peer reviewed, are typically not considered scholarly sources.

As for coverage in Modern China Studies, JSTOR includes 73 journals in Asian Studies. Among them, seven journals deal exclusively with China. Table 5.1 provides a list of the seven journals with their corresponding time coverage in JSTOR.

TABLE 5.1

JStor journal coverage of Modern China Studies

Journal Title	Time Coverage
The China Journal	1995–2012
The Australian Journal of Chinese Affairs	1979–1995
The China Quarterly	1960–2006
Chinese Literature: Essays, Articles, Reviews (CLEAR)	1979–2008
Frontiers of Philosophy in China	2006–2008, 2009–2010
Modern China	1975–2008
T'oung Pao	1890–2006

Because of the time lag ("embargo"), it is a good idea to use Project Muse in conjunction with JSTOR. Like JSTOR, Project Muse also only includes high-quality journals (and books) from reputable academic publishers. Also like JSTOR, it is a full-text database with robust full-text search capability. Currently, Project Muse includes 34 journals in Asian Studies, of which six titles deal exclusively with China topics. See Table 5.2 for the list of the China-related journals and their corresponding time coverage in Project Muse.

As we can see from these tables, the journals covered in Project Muse are mostly different from those in JSTOR. All the journals in the two databases are generally considered highly reputable publications. More important, Project Muse covers mostly recent issues of the journals, whereas JSTOR covers mostly archival issues. This means that when we search both JSTOR and Project Muse, we can cover scholarship both past and present with some of the most important journals in the field.

TABLE 5.2

Project Muse journal coverage of Modern China Studies

Journal Title	Time Coverage
China: An International Journal	2003–present
China Review International	1994–present
Journal of Chinese Overseas	2005–2008
Journal of Song-Yuan Studies	2009–present
Late Imperial China	1965–present
Twentieth-Century China	2007–2010

Academic Search Complete (ASC)

This flagship database from EBSCOhost, a major online content provider in North America, includes more than 9,300 journals and a total of 10,900 publications covering virtually all subject areas in humanities, social sciences, and sciences. With more than 5,300 full-text periodicals, including 4,400 peer-reviewed journals, it is a convenient and solid starting point for research on almost any topic.

Specifically for Chinese Studies, Academic Search Complete (ASC) includes 107 Asia-related periodicals and 54 China-specific titles. For lack of space, we will not list all 54 journals but just a selected few, with their corresponding coverage, in order to demonstrate the scope of the database and variety of its sources (see Table 5.3).

If we compare the list with those of JSTOR and Project Muse, we notice some major differences between ASC and JSTOR/Project Muse: (1) ASC covers a much wider ground, including not only humanities and social sciences but also sciences (such as *China Chemical Reporter*). (2) While JSTOR and Project Muse only cover academic journals, ASC covers popular sources as well (such as *China Today* and *Beijing Review*), in addition to academic sources. (3) All the sources in JSTOR and Project Muse are full text, but ASC is mixed with some full text and some index only.

The point I want to make here is that each database is different in terms of the covered range of subjects, variety of sources, years covered, availability of full text, and so on, as we can see from the previous discussions. Therefore,

TABLE 5.3

Academic Search Complete coverage
of selected titles in Modern China Studies

Title	Type	Index Coverage	Full-Text Coverage
Harvard China Review	Academic	04/01/2004 to 04/01/2005	04/01/2004 to 04/01/2005
China Today	Popular	07/01/1993 to present	08/01/2006 to present
China Quarterly	Academic	06/01/1991 to present	N/A
China Journal	Academic	07/01/2004 to present	07/01/2004 to present
Journal of China Lawyer & Jurist	Academic	03/01/2007 to present	03/01/2007 to present
NAN NU—Men, Women & Gender in Early & Imperial China	Academic	01/01/2000 to present	01/01/2000 to present (with a 12-month delay)
Modern China Studies	Academic	12/01/2009 to present	12/01/2009 to present
China Chemical Reporter	Academic	06/06/2004 to present	06/06/2004 to present
Beijing Review	Popular	07/05/1993 to present	08/10/2006 to present

we cannot depend on one database or a couple of databases alone, hoping to find everything we need for our research. Instead, we should always try different databases, because some databases may work better than others for a particular topic. That, however, does not mean we should just pick random databases. To be a proficient researcher, we need to learn which databases are most relevant to our field of study and what sources they each contain. Based on that knowledge, we should try all the relevant databases to ensure we have covered all the ground.

Many academic libraries today have adopted a "one-stop search" approach, using discovery tools (such as EBSCO Discovery Service, or EDS) that can cross-search many databases at the same time. While this technology definitely has made finding articles easier, especially for beginners, for a variety of reasons such tools would be best used as a starting point rather than the only tool for research (Fagan et al. 2012). For in-depth subject-specific sources, we would still need to learn and use individual databases.

ASC can serve as a good alternative if our local library does not yet have a "search all" discovery tool. Because of the variety of content in ASC, the database provides a sophisticated, yet fairly intuitive search interface that allows the user to easily filter the search results and find what they want (see Figure 5.2). For example, because ASC contains both full-text articles and articles with indexes only, the database provides a check box for full text that would limit the research results to full-text content only. However, I would suggest using this feature with caution. Some of the best sources may only exist as indexes in the database. By choosing full text only we may inadvertently filter out the best sources on our topic. I would not recommend using this feature when we are just starting out with our research or if we are conducting a major research project and aiming at a comprehensive search for all the sources on the topic. In either case, we should leave the full-text box unchecked so that we can first see the full range of sources available on the topic.

The database also provides the option of filtering out unwanted popular sources (e.g., news magazines) and retaining scholarly (peer-reviewed) articles only. All we need to do is check the box for "Scholarly (Peer Reviewed) Journals."

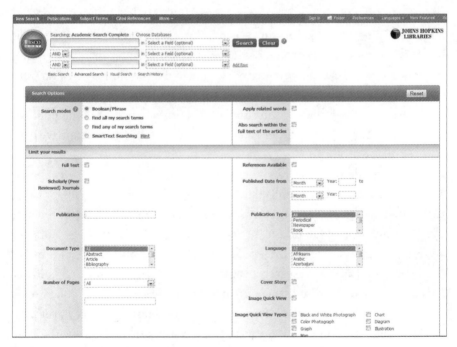

FIGURE 5.2 Interface of Academic Search Complete

Bibliography of Asian Studies Online (BAS)

Unlike the databases discussed previously, the Bibliography of Asian Studies Online (BAS) specializes in Asian Studies (i.e., not a general database) and is an index only, which means we can only get citations of the articles (i.e., title, author, year, source, etc.) but not the articles themselves. Even though it is fairly easy to obtain a copy of an article once we have the citation, either from print or online resources that our library owns or from other libraries via the interlibrary loan service, it is nonetheless less convenient than full-text databases like the ones we discussed previously.

That said, BAS is still a very important tool for finding English-language sources on China. Initially published in print as early as 1941, BAS has been recognized as the standard bibliographical tool in Asian Studies. The online database covers articles and book chapters on all parts of Asia in Western languages from 1971 to the present, including hundreds of thousands of sources gleaned from journals, books, and conference proceedings that may or may not be generally cataloged as Asia related (Association of Asian Studies n.d.). The result is a database that searches a wide range of sources for Asia-related content.

For example, a simple search of "globalization" and "China" (using the country limiter) results in 1,181 articles, 1,072 book chapters, and 106 books (see Figure 5.3). We can easily narrow down the search by clicking on any of the subject categories, type of the materials, region, or publishing source. We can save the results by selecting the hits we are interested in or locate the full text by using the link resolver, the "Find it @ your library" button.

Some users might find BAS less forgiving in terms of search terms. For example, a student wants to find sources on how globalization affects coal mining in Shaanxi province, China's coal mining stronghold. If he types in the search terms "globalization," "coal mining," and "Shaanxi," he will get zero results. That does not mean that there is absolutely nothing on the topic among the sources in BAS; it just means that there is no record of any source in BAS that includes all the search terms. As an index database, BAS only searches the "records" of the sources, not their full-text contents. So, when we use BAS, we have to be mindful of that and try to use as few search terms as possible. If we get rid of "Shaanxi," a very specific geographical term that may not have been included in the citation information of any sources, we will get three results. If we broaden our search by replacing "coal mining" with the more general term "energy," we would get 72 results, many of which may very well include information on coal mining in Shaanxi, or at least are relevant to the research topic.

In short, when we use BAS we have to remember that the database searches not the full text but mostly the citation information of the sources. That means we should use as few search terms as possible and avoid highly specific search terms, so that we can retrieve as much relevant information as possible.

Google Scholar

For library subscription databases, we know exactly what journals are included and how the searches work. For Google Scholar, however, we just don't know. But we do not need to understand what is going on under the hood in order to utilize this free, convenient, and powerful research tool. Assuming most people are familiar with Google's signature search box and know how to do a

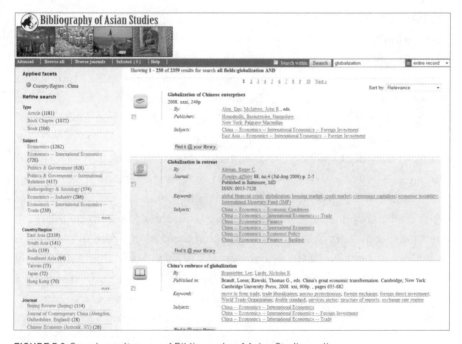

FIGURE 5.3 Search results page of Bibliography of Asian Studies online

general search, we will focus on two advanced features of Google Scholar that could make its use more effective.

We will start with Google Scholar's Advanced Search feature. You can find it by clicking on the small black arrow at the right corner of the search box. Once you click on the arrow, the Advanced Search box will pop up (see Figure 5.4). With the Advanced Search, we can do much more precise searches, and it is possible to set various limits on the search terms. We can search for articles and books by a particular author or search within a particular journal.

Another useful feature of Google Scholar is located in what is called Scholar Settings, which we can access by clicking on the "Settings" link on the upper corner of the Google Scholar homepage. In Scholar Settings, we can choose a different language for display or limit our searches to results in a certain language (e.g., Chinese) (see Figure 5.5). This is also the place where we can activate the link to citation management tools such as RefWorks, Endnotes, and the like (see Figure 5.6).

And finally, we can choose to link Google Scholar search results with our library resources. Most of the libraries will have set up the linkage anyway, at

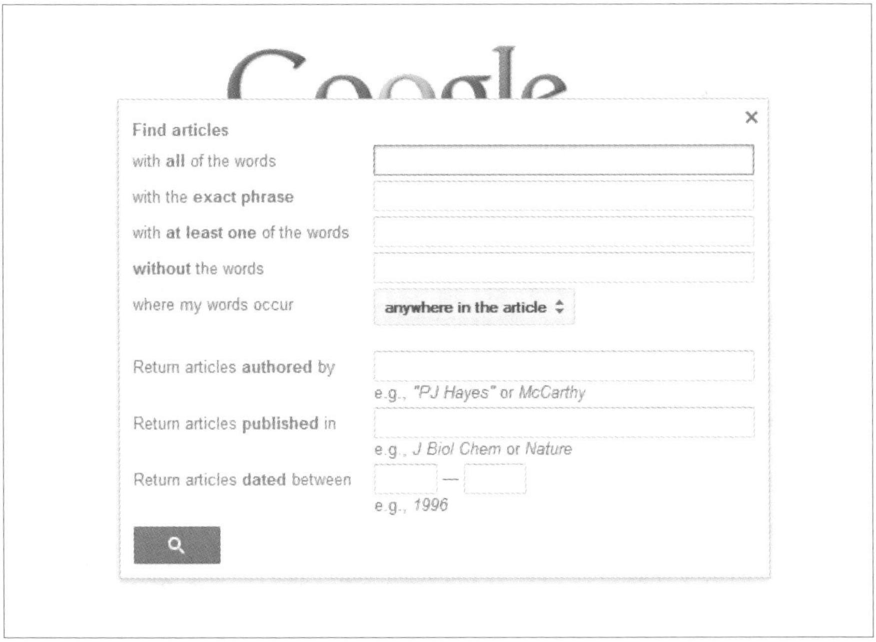

FIGURE 5.4 Advanced Search option of Google Scholar

FIGURE 5.5 Language option in Google Scholar Settings

FIGURE 5.6 Citation option in Google Scholar Settings

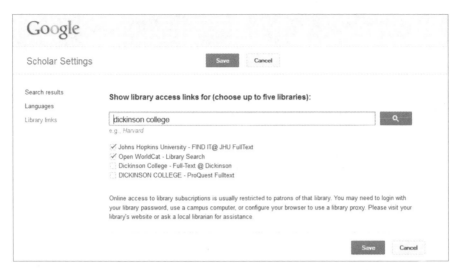

FIGURE 5.7 Setting up library linkage in Google Scholar Settings

least for computers on campus. But if we are using our personal computers off campus, we will have to set up the linkage ourselves, which fortunately is very easy to do. At the Scholar Settings, when we click on Library links we will see a box where we can just type in our school name (e.g., Dickinson College). Then we will see the names of our institution or library pop up on the list. Click on the name and we are done (see Figure 5.7).

Once the settings are set up, when we search Google Scholar all the articles that are available at our home library will either have full text already attached in the result list or be linked to the library Link Resolver (the FindIt button). Also, we can easily save the citations in the citation management tool of our choice, such as RefWorks (see Figure 5.8).

Besides searching for articles through databases, it is also a good idea to browse the latest issues of key journals to get a sense of what is going on in the field. Following is a list of major journals dealing specifically with China or East Asia. The majority of China-related articles come from these journals. These are mostly multidisciplinary journals. We will cover journals specialized in a specific discipline (such as philosophy or business management) in chapters 10 through 13 when we talk about resources specific to individual disciplines.

FIGURE 5.8 Search results page of Google Scholar

- *Journal of Asian Studies.* A leading journal in the field of Asian Studies for over 65 years, this journal publishes high-quality scholarship on Asia, spanning arts, history, literature, the social sciences, and cultural studies.
- *Harvard Journal of Asiatic Studies* (Harvard-Yenching Institute). Publishing since 1936, *HJAS* presents original scholarly research and book reviews in humanities in Asia.
- *Journal of East Asian Studies.* This journal publishes social science research on the entire East Asia region, covering topics such as democratic governance, military security, political culture, economic cooperation, human rights, and environmental concerns.
- *Positions: East Asia Cultures Critique.* This journal examines critically the histories and cultures of East Asia and Asian America. It publishes scholarly articles, commentary, essays, and in-depth book reviews.
- *Journal of Contemporary China.* This journal publishes articles of theoretical and policy research and research notes as well as book reviews. Fields of interest include economics, political science, law, culture, literature, business, history, international relations, sociology and other social sciences, and humanities.

- *Modern Asian Studies.* This journal publishes on a wide range of subjects of Southeast and East Asia with emphasis on the social sciences.
- *Modern China.* This journal publishes scholarship in history and the social sciences on late-imperial, twentieth-century, and present-day China.
- *Twentieth Century China* (formerly *Republican China*). This semi-annual scholarly journal publishes scholarship focusing on the history of China from 1911 to 1949.
- *China: An International Journal* (Singapore). This journal presents diverse international perceptions and frames of reference on contemporary China, including Hong Kong, Macau, and Taiwan.
- *China Information: A Journal on Contemporary China Studies* (Leiden, the Netherlands). This journal publishes scholarly analysis of major developments in contemporary China and overseas Chinese communities in the areas of politics, economics, law, ecology, culture, and society, including literature and the arts.
- *The China Journal* (formerly, *The Australian Journal of China Affairs*, Canberra). This journal publishes scholarly work focusing on topics relating to China, Hong Kong, and Taiwan since 1949, plus studies of the major issues that contribute to understanding Communist Party history and contemporary events.
- *China Perspective* (Hong Kong). This journal provides in-depth analyses of current changes and perspectives in the People's Republic of China, Taiwan, Hong Kong, and Macao.
- *The China Review: An Interdisciplinary Journal on Greater China* (Hong Kong). Published twice a year, this scholarly journal covers various disciplines of study on Greater China and its people, namely, domestic politics and international relations; society, business, and economic development; and modern history, the arts, and cultural studies.
- *American Journal of Chinese Studies.* A multidisciplinary journal published by American Association for Chinese Studies, it publishes scholarly articles primarily in the social sciences, including modern history.

- *The China Quarterly* (SOAS, University of London). *This journal* is the leading scholarly journal in its field, covering all aspects of contemporary China including Taiwan. Its interdisciplinary approach covers a range of subjects that includes anthropology/sociology, literature and the arts, business/economics, geography, history, international affairs, law, and politics.

References

Association of Asian Studies. n.d. "About the Bibliography of Asian Studies Online." Accessed October 8, 2012. www.asian-studies.org/aboutbas.htm.

Fagan, J. C., M. A. Mandernach, C. S. Nelson, Paulo, J. R., and G. Sanders. 2012. "Usability Test for a Discovery Tool in an Academic Library." *Information Technology and Libraries* 31 (1): 83–112.

Finding Articles in Chinese

This chapter will show you:

★ How to find articles from Chinese databases
★ How to find articles translated from Chinese

Scholarly publications from China are increasingly becoming important for scholars outside China for good reasons. First of all, because of their physical proximity to ongoing events, Chinese scholars based in China tend to have better access to information and their work often reflects the latest development. Second, their scholarship is shaped by differences in philosophy, ideology, theoretical approach, or cultural practice in general and represents a different perspective from scholars in the West. And finally, in recent years Chinese scholarship has gradually broken away from the old ideological confinement and isolation of the revolutionary era and enjoyed a greater amount of intellectual independence and freedom and consequently greatly improved quality. Now the question is: where do we look to find and access Chinese sources?

Finding Chinese-Language Articles

The easiest way to find Chinese-language articles is to search Chinese online databases. The good news is that China has seen an explosion of digital scholarly resources in recent years, and many of the products are now available in research libraries in North America. In terms of finding Chinese academic journal articles, two of the most popular databases are China Academic Journals Full-text Online (CAJ), part of China National Knowledge Infrastructure (CNKI) by Beijing-based Tsinghua Tongfang Knowledge Network Technology Company (TTKN), and China Online Journals (COJ) from Wanfang Data. Since these two are comparable products covering essentially the same sources, we will use CAJ as an example to demonstrate how to use Chinese databases.

CNKI is among the largest digitization projects in China, if not the world. It was launched in 1988 by TTKN, an information technology company founded by Tsinghua University with the backing from the Press and Publications Administration of the Chinese government. CNKI includes a series of databases:

- China Academic Journals Full-Text Database
- China Theses Full-Text Database
- China Dissertations Full-Text Database
- China Proceedings Conference Full-Text Database
- China Core Newspapers Full-Text Database
- China Yearbooks Full-Text Database
- China Reference Works Online
- China Statistical Yearbooks Database
- China Government Documents Full-Text Database

As we can see from this impressive list, CNKI practically covers all the major research resources except for monographs, which are covered by Duxiu and Chinamaxx. (See chapter 4 for details.) We have already mentioned one of the databases, China Reference Works Online, in chapter 3 and will talk about some of the other databases in greater detail in later chapters. Here, we will focus on the largest and most popular component in CNKI, China Academic Journals (CAJ).

Most libraries in North America purchase a subscription to CAJ through the only authorized vendor in the United States, East View Information Services, a company based in St. Paul, Minnesota. The version of CAJ offered through East View is actually a mirror site set up to facilitate the North American user's access to the database. It features an English-language search interface, even though the content of the database is in Chinese.

In the East View version, CAJ covers over 7,200 journal titles, representing 96 percent of all core academic journals published in mainland China, mostly from 1994 to the present and updated continuously. A separate database called Century Journals Project (CJP) covers the archival issues of the journals, tracing from 1993 to as far back as 1915. CAJ breaks down into nine modules by subject, including:

- Science-Engineering (A)
- Science-Engineering (B)
- Science-Engineering (C)
- Agriculture (D)
- Medicine/Hygiene (E)
- Literature/History/Philosophy (F)
- Economics/Politics/Law (G)
- Education/Social Science (H)
- Electronics/Information Science (I)

Libraries can choose which modules to buy, a practice that helps bring down the cost and makes the database more affordable.

CAJ features a fairly intuitive search interface and a robust search engine. The article record page includes citation information, links to related articles, and links to downloadable full text (see Figure 6.1).

FIGURE 6.1 Sample record page of an article in China Academic Journals

For those whose home library does not subscribe to the database, the good news is that they can still use CAJ because the database offers free index searches of its bibliographical records. However, if that is the case I would recommend using the CNKI interface directly from China at www.cnki.net/ rather than the mirror site at East View. Even though the Chinese edition being based in China may occasionally be slower, it covers a much wider range of resources and often produces much better results.

Through the CNKI original homepage, we can cross-search all the resources offered by CNKI. Even if we choose to search 期刊 (the equivalent of CAJ) only, we can search the full run of all the journals instead of the limited coverage from 1994 to the present as in CAJ. We will demonstrate the power of CNKI and some very useful resources in later chapters. Suffice it to say here that to access Chinese-language articles, we can use CAJ if our library subscribes to the database; if not, we should try CNKI instead. Even though we will not be able to download articles without a subscription, at least we will be able to do a thorough search of all relevant articles and other sources. Once we have the citations, we should be able to obtain the texts through the library collections or interlibrary loan service, or purchase the needed articles directly from the North American vendor, East View.

Besides CAJ and CNKI, another convenient way to find Chinese articles is via Google Scholar. As we discussed in the previous chapter, we can easily limit search results in Google Scholar to Chinese only. Alternatively, we can use Chinese characters directly as search terms and the result will mostly be in Chinese as well.

Besides its convenience, another reason to use Google Scholar is that it searches CAJ as well as many other Chinese databases (such as 维普 at www. cqvip.com/), thus exposing us to a wider range and greater variety of sources. Also, Google Scholar can be linked to our library resources. Any time we find a source through Google Scholar that is available through our library resources (e.g., CAJ), we can access the full text right away through the result list. In short, Google Scholar is not only good for finding English-language sources but also an excellent tool for finding Chinese-language sources.

Finding Articles Translated from Chinese

For those who are less proficient in the Chinese language, reading a scholarly paper in the original can be a challenge. Fortunately, there are now many American journals that are specialized in publishing translated academic articles from Chinese sources. These resources can be a big help for those who study China but lack adequate language skills. Following is a list of journals that publish translated Chinese scholarly articles with information on where these journals are indexed (see the publishers' websites for more information). To search for articles in one of these journals, just go to the indexing database, type in the journal title as the source, and search within the journal. Alternatively, we can search the contents of these journals in the Advanced Search in Google Scholar (see chapter 5). If the database does not contain full text, we can always try to obtain the articles elsewhere in our library collection or obtain them through interlibrary loan.

- *The Chinese Economy*. *The Chinese Economy* is published by M. E. Sharpe. The chief editor is Hung-Gay Fung of the University of Missouri at St. Louis. As the title suggests, the journal primarily publishes scholarly work on economic issues concerning China and aims to provide expert insight on China's economic development and directions for future research and policy analysis. It features research papers by scholars from around the world as well as selected translations of important articles from Chinese sources. The articles in this journal are indexed and abstracted in Bibliography of Asian Studies Online, Economic Literature (EconLit), International Bibliography of the Social Sciences, International Bibliography of Periodical Literature on the Humanities and Social Sciences (IBZ), PAIS International, ProQuest Database, and Scopus.
- *Chinese Education and Society*. Also published by M. E. Sharpe, with coeditors Stanley Rosen of the University of Southern California and Gerard A. Postiglione of the University of Hong Kong, this journal specializes in analyzing the latest Chinese thinking on educational policy and practice, educational reform and development, pedagogical theory and methods, colleges and universities,

and schools and families, as well as the education for diverse social groups across gender and youth, urban and rural, and mainstream and minorities. It features unabridged translations of the most important articles in the field from Chinese sources, including scholarly journals and collections of articles published in book form. The articles in this journal are indexed and abstracted in Bibliography of Asian Studies Online, Current Contents/Social and Behavioral Sciences, Current Index to Journals in Education, Education Resources Information Center (ERIC) Database, Educational Administration Abstracts, Journal Citation Reports/Social Sciences Edition, Scopus, Social Sciences Citation Index, and Wilson Education Index.

- *Chinese Law and Government.* Another M. E. Sharpe publication, with James Tong of the University of California, Los Angeles, serving as editor, *Chinese Law and Government* brings scholarly analysis to the inner workings of Chinese politics and governance through careful selection, translation, and annotation of primary documents, analytical studies, and other authoritative sources. The materials translated for publication in the journal's thematic issues and series may be laws, regulations, court records, policy directives, and published or unpublished, official or scholarly reports and analyses of critical questions. Insight into the significance of the topic and content of each issue is provided in a substantive introduction by the editor or expert guest editor. The articles in this journal are indexed and abstracted in Bibliography of Asian Studies Online, International Bibliography of Periodical Literature on the Humanities and Social Sciences (IBZ), Journal Citation Report/Social Sciences Edition, Scopus, Social Sciences Citation Index, and Wilson Social Sciences Index.

- *Chinese Sociology and Anthropology.* Published by M. E. Sharpe, *Chinese Sociology and Anthropology* is coedited by Gregory Guldin of Pacific Lutheran University, Tacoma, and Zhou Daming of Zhongshan University, People's Republic of China. The studies featured in this journal focus on the People's Republic of China as well as Hong Kong and Taiwan and are all unabridged translations of research papers or published articles from Chinese sources, including scholarly journals and collections of articles published in book form. It provides access to the most influential Chinese viewpoints on such themes as social stratification, social movements, popular culture, newly emerging subcultures and social mores, marriage patterns and family structure, and ethnic minorities. The articles in this journal are indexed and abstracted in Anthropological Index Online, Bibliography of Asian Studies Online, International Bibliography of the Social Sciences, Journal Citation Reports/Social Sciences Edition, Scopus, Social Sciences Citation Index, and Wilson Social Sciences Index.

- *Chinese Studies in History. Chinese Studies in History* is another journal published by M. E. Sharpe, with Q. Edward Wang of Rowan University as its editor. The journal makes available noteworthy works and important trends of historical study in the Chinese-speaking world to English-language readers. Topical coverage ranges over all periods and subfields of Chinese and East Asian history as well as more general theoretical and historiographical questions of interest to historians of many specialties. Each issue includes a substantive introduction by the editor or specialist guest editor. The articles in this journal are indexed and abstracted in America: History and Life, Arts and Humanities Citation Index, Bibliography of Asian Studies Online, Current Contents/Arts and Humanities, Historical Abstracts, MLA International Bibliography, and Scopus.

- *Contemporary Chinese Thought.* This journal is published by M. E. Sharpe and edited by Carine Defoort of Katholieke Universiteit Leuven. This wide-ranging journal features translations of the most current and influential Chinese writings on all aspects of philosophical endeavor, from theoretical essays on systems to studies of China's cultural and religious development, from interpretations of the Chinese classics to exegeses on Marxist thought. The articles in this journal are indexed and abstracted in Arts and Humanities Citation Index, Bibliography of Asian Studies Online, Current Contents/Arts and Humanities, International Bibliography of Periodical Literature on the Humanities and Social Sciences (IBZ), The Philosopher's Index, and Scopus.

- *Social Sciences in China.* Published by Routledge, *Social Sciences in China* is a peer-reviewed quarterly academic journal comprising articles translated from the prestigious journal published by the Social Science in China Press on behalf of the Chinese Academy of Social Sciences. Every article is selected for quality, fully reviewed, and meticulously translated into English. The journal focuses on recent important developments across the breadth of social sciences and humanities in China. The journal is indexed and abstracted in Bibliography of Asian Studies Online and International Bibliography of the Social Sciences.

Finding Related Articles
for Literature Review

This chapter will show you:

★ How a research paper is structured
★ The importance of a literature review
★ How to find related articles

In the previous chapters, we talked about the basics of academic research, such as finding books and articles from various sources. Obviously, for any research project our goal is not just to find interesting sources but to produce a research paper of our own. Toward that end, finding information is a crucial and necessary step. In this chapter, we will talk about how information finding fits into the big picture of writing a research paper and ways to help speed up the information-finding process and make our research more efficient.

The Structure of a Research Paper

A typical research paper may look very different in different subject fields and disciplines. However, generally speaking most research papers consist of the following components:

1. *Introduction.* The opening paragraph or section introduces the broad issue or problem and then moves toward a specific topic, hypothesis, or thesis statement.

2. *Literature Review.* Following the introduction is a section that traces the history of the topic through the body of published research literature; for example, how the topic originated and has evolved over time and what landmark, seminal works are and how they are related to one another. In short, a literature review is a summary and synthesis of the existing scholarship to date. It sets the stage for introducing the thesis idea, which will be our own contribution to the topic.

3. *Methodology or Theoretical Framework.* Depending on the discipline, for sciences and social sciences we need to describe the methods used to collect data; for humanities, we introduce the theoretic framework or a unique perspective that we will use to examine the issue or problem.

4. *Data or Text.* This is the section where we introduce the primary sources such as data collected (sciences and social sciences) or the text (a primary source such as a work of art or historical document as in humanities) to be analyzed and interpreted.

5. *Analysis or Interpretation.* This is the part of the paper where we dissect the data or text, often with the aid of a specific theory. In doing so, we try to make the case for our thesis idea. Depending on the complexity of the issue or problem, we often have to tackle it from various angles, citing various sources, in order to make a sound and compelling argument.

6. *Conclusion.* The final section summarizes succinctly all the main points in the argument and places the thesis idea in perspective.

Preparing for a Literature Review

A literature review is a crucial part of the research paper. It is important because it is literally the foundation of the paper. It gives our thesis idea an intellectual context. At the same time, it serves as a rationale for our research project and answers the question of why people should care about our project. As mentioned earlier, scholars rarely work in total isolation and start from scratch every time they work on a research project. Rather, they build on each other's work and engage each other in scholarly dialog through published work. In this sense, the literature review section is the place where we acknowledge what other people have said and done before we add our own voice to the conversation and make our own contribution to the existing body of knowledge.

More specifically, as we research in preparation for writing a literature review we should keep the following questions in mind (Hart 1998, 14):

- What are the major issues and debates about the topic?
- What are the origins and definitions of the topic?
- What are the key theories, concepts, and ideas?
- What are the key sources?
- What are the landmarks or seminal scholarly works?
- What are the main questions and problems that have been addressed to date?
- Is there a gap in the existing body of literature or room for a different analysis and interpretation from a different theoretical approach that might shed new light on the topic?

The more we research the topic, the more likely we will be able to identify common themes among scholarly articles. These thematic threads link together the seemingly scattered books and articles that are published in different times and places. Once we are able to identify a thematic thread within a discrete body of scholarly literature and the major scholars and their works that contribute to the continual development of the thematic thread, and see how and where our own work may fit in (the "gap"), we are ready to write our literature review.

Finding Related Articles

The key to preparing for a literature review is to identify a series of articles (and books) linked to a common thematic thread. In order to do this, we will have to read all the sources we have collected. If we have done enough research and read enough papers, some common themes will emerge out of the readings. Besides picking up thematic threads, we should be able to identify key authors and key texts as well, since they are most likely to have been discussed or referred to in different articles. Granted, this can be a time-consuming process, but it is a very important one. As we read through the materials, we are not just finding out what other people have talked about, we are also learning about the topic itself and refining our own thoughts and ideas.

The good news is that there are some databases that can help us speed up the process, particularly in finding related articles and identifying key articles and authors. We will focus on one database, Social Sciences Citation Index Database (SSCI), and use it as an example, while briefly mentioning other databases that have similar functionalities.

Social Sciences Citation Index (SSCI)

SSCI, one of the Web of Science databases, is a multidisciplinary index database with broad coverage of scholarly journal literature and some books in the social sciences. It has great strength as an author and title index and for tracing the use of key books and journals in later scholarly research. The coverage begins with items published in 1956. The major disciplines covered in SSCI include anthropology, history, industrial relations, information science and library science, law, linguistics, philosophy, political science, psychiatry, psychology, public health, social issues, social work, sociology, substance abuse, urban studies, and women's studies.

First, we will talk about how to use SSCI to quickly identify key articles on a topic. SSCI can be used like any other database to find articles on a topic. For example, if we want to do a research project on "cultural revolution in China," we can do a quick keyword search on "cultural revolution" in SSCI, the same way we search any other database. This general search returns over 1,000 results (see Figure 7.1).

At this point, we probably need to narrow down our search, since obviously 1,000 results are way too many. We can easily trim down the result list simply by limiting the search through the categories listed on the left-hand menu or by doing another search within the results to further narrow down our topic. For the sake of demonstration, we will just work with the search as it is for now. What makes SSCI different from other databases is that for each article, SSCI tracks an extra piece of information, namely, the number of times an article is cited ("Times Cited"). While a high citation number does

FIGURE 7.1 Search results of SSCI on "Cultural Revolution"

not necessarily imply high quality of a paper, it can serve as an indication of possible influence of the article among the scholarly community and its importance to the topic.

This is exactly how the database can help us quickly identify key articles on a topic. All we need to do is to sort the result list by times cited, and instantly the articles that have been cited the most times will appear on the top (see Figure 7.2).

Now we just need to browse the articles down the list and see if any article is of particular interest. If we can find one or more relevant articles with high citation numbers, we probably need to check them out, because these articles are likely to have had the most influence on the subject matter.

In addition to identifying key articles, SSCI can help us quickly find articles that are related through "Citing Articles" (other articles that cite the article that we have found particularly interesting) and through "Cited References" (articles cited in this particular article). For example, suppose we decide an article on the result list is of particular interest. It is titled "The impact of cultural revolution on the trends in educational attainment in the People's Republic of China" (Figure 7.3).

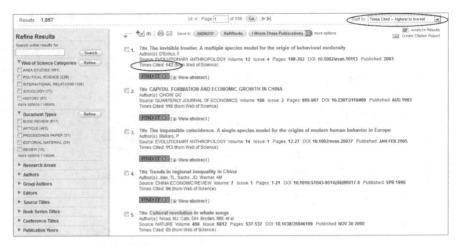

FIGURE 7.2 SSCI search results sorted by "Times Cited"

This article has been cited 45 times. If we click on "45" on the page, SSCI will display a list of all 45 articles that have cited this particular article. Most likely, these articles deal with the same or similar topic and therefore should be relevant to our topic. Since obviously they were published after the article they cite, these articles represent later development on the topic.

Similarly, we can click on "63," the number of references on the same page, and find the list of the articles that are cited by the article we are interested in. Again, many of them probably deal with the same or similar topic and therefore are sources that could also be relevant to our research. Since these articles were published prior to the article, they represent earlier scholarly literature on the topic.

We can keep tracing articles through "Citing Articles" and "Cited References," and very quickly we will have a series of articles linked through citation that represent the evolution of the topic from past to present. This is how we can use SSCI to trace the development of a topic both backward (through "Cited References") and forward (through "Citing Articles") in time and quickly identify related sources.

Another unique feature of SSCI is Analyze Results. We can only see this option on the search results page. Click on the link "Analyze Results" and it will take us to another page where we can analyze the search results by authors, book series titles, conference titles, institutions, publishers, languages, years, and so forth. If we select "Authors," we will get a list of authors ranked by the number

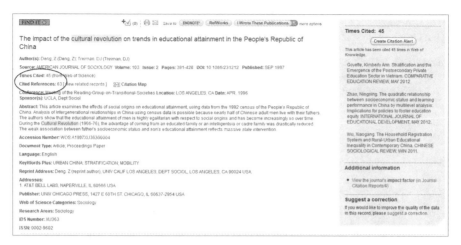

FIGURE 7.3 Sample article record in SSCI

of articles they have published on the topic (limited to the articles included in SSCI) (see Figure 7.4). In the case of our "cultural revolution" search, the first named author on the top of the list is "Schoenhals, M." SSCI has 15 articles published under his name on the topic. If we select this author, we can find the citation information for all 15 articles. In short, SSCI gives us an easy way to find out who has published the most on a given topic and what they have published.

We can also choose to analyze results by other criteria. For example, if we choose to analyze by "Institution," we will get a list of institutions ranked by number of articles published on the topic. This could give us a sense of which institutions have the strongest faculty in this area of research. Suppose a student is applying to graduate schools and wants to know which schools have the strongest programs in his research area. The analyzing-by-institution function can easily provide this information.

Another function of SSCI is to allow us to see the research trend on the topic. Again, on the result list page, next to "Analyze Results," there is a link called "Create Citation Report." Click on this link and we will get two graphics: "Published Items in Each Year" and "Citations in Each Year" (see Figure 7.5). Generally speaking, if the graphics show an upward trend, it implies that this research topic still generates a lot of scholarly interest; otherwise, it might indicate that the topic has become a moot issue and few people are now interested in it. This could help a researcher to decide whether it is worthwhile to pursue a research topic.

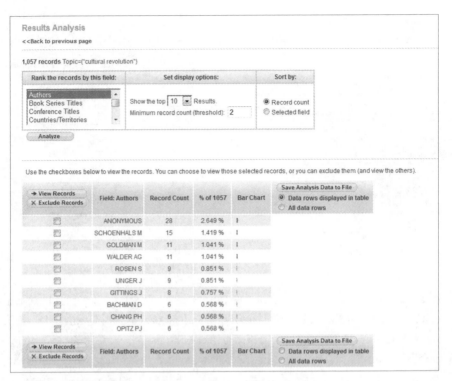

FIGURE 7.4 Sample results analysis by authors in SSCI

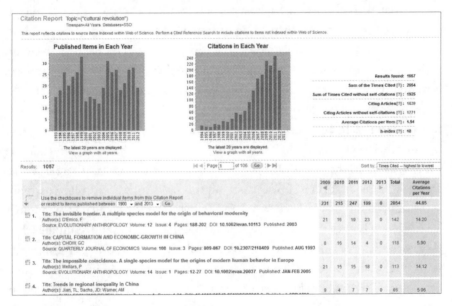

FIGURE 7.5 Sample citation report in SSCI

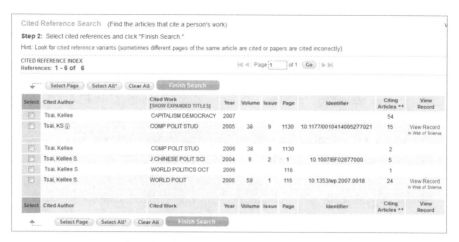

FIGURE 7.6 Example of SSCI cited reference search

Finally, SSCI also makes it easy to connect one scholar's work with the work of other scholars who share similar research interests. There is a tab on the top of the SSCI homepage called "Cited Reference Search." With Cited Reference Search, we can easily find out what articles and books an author has published and their respective citation numbers and what articles or books are citing these published works. For example, suppose we are interested in a work by Dr. Kellee Tsai (a political scientist at Johns Hopkins University), titled *Capitalism without Democracy: The Private Sector in Contemporary China* (Cornell University Press, 2007), and we want to find out how other scholars are reacting to her work. We can do a Cited Reference Search on "tsai, kellee" and retrieve a list of works by Tsai with their corresponding citation numbers (see Figure 7.6).

If we are only interested in her work on capitalism without democracy, we can select the first entry on the result list and finish the search. Then we have a list of articles that has cited this book. They represent more recent development since the publication of Tsai's book and likely contain commentaries on Tsai's work.

Other Citation Databases

SSCI is one of many Web of Science databases. All of the Web of Science databases can perform the same functions as we described for SSCI. Web of Science includes the following databases:

- Science Citation Index Expanded (SCI-EXPANDED)—1899–present
- Social Sciences Citation Index (SSCI)—1956–present
- Arts and Humanities Citation Index (A&HCI)—1975–present
- Conference Proceedings Citation Index–Science (CPCI-S)—1990–present
- Conference Proceedings Citation Index–Social Science and Humanities (CPCI-SSH)—1990–present

Besides Web of Science databases, there are other databases that track citation information and therefore have similar capabilities. The most important one is Scopus (SciVerse Scopus). This database, from Elsevier, the world's leading publisher of scientific journals, is a strong competitor for Web of Science databases. It boasts a broad and strong coverage of peer-reviewed publications from all disciplines in sciences, the social sciences, and arts and humanities. It has all the capabilities that we have described for SSCI. Some people may find the interface design of Scopus even more user friendly. We would recommend using both databases for comprehensive searches, since neither is all inclusive and therefore both are complementary to one another.

Another popular database that tracks citation numbers is Google Scholar. The search results page in Google Scholar displays "Cited By" and "Related Articles." The drawback is that there is no way to sort the results in Google Scholar, and no way to analyze them. Nonetheless, because of its broad coverage and easy accessibility, Google Scholar is still a very convenient tool to discover related sources.

Finally, for Chinese scholarly sources CNKI databases are best designed to track citation information and find related articles. On the record page of each article, the database displays a graphic of an elaborate citation network (see Figure 7.7).

As shown in Figure 7.7, CNKI digs even deeper than SSCI into citation data to track down related articles:

- Like SSCI, CNKI tracks Cited References (参考文献) and Citing Articles (引证文献).
- In addition, from Cited References, CNKI also tracks articles that share the same references (共引文献) on the assumption that

FIGURE 7.7 Sample of CNKI citation network

these articles share the same or similar research background and foundation and therefore are related.

- Similarly, from Citing Articles, CNKI also tracks articles that are cited in the same articles that are citing the article of our interest on the assumption that since these articles are cited at the same time, they are also related.

- CNKI also tracks articles that cite the articles that cite the original article of our interest (二级引证文献), as well as articles that are cited in the articles that are cited in the original article (二级参考文献).

Through a sophisticated system of tracking citation linkage among articles, CNKI creates a web of knowledge for our research project. This is how citation databases like SSCI and CNKI could dramatically accelerate our research process and make our work much more efficient.

Reference

Hart, Chris. 1998. *Doing a Literature Review: Releasing the Social Science Research Imagination.* London: SAGE Publications.

Finding Government Documents

This chapter will show you:

★ General strategies for finding primary sources
★ Tools for finding Chinese government documents

Compared with secondary sources discussed in previous chapters, primary sources may sometimes be harder to find and can present a challenge to researchers. Yet, primary sources are crucial in any scholarly research. Secondary sources can only help us understand the context (what other people have talked about so far) and clarify our thoughts and refine our own ideas (our thesis). Ultimately, we will have to build our argument based on rigorous analysis of primary sources. Without primary sources, our paper would be a mere regurgitation of what other people have said. It would not be an original research paper, but a review of other people's work.

The trouble with finding primary sources is that there is no magic button in any database that we can press to retrieve exactly the primary sources we are looking for. Oftentimes, we will not even know whether the primary sources we are looking for, be they statistical data or historical archives, actually exist. In this section, we will start out with some general strategies on finding primary sources. Then we will discuss ways to find a major type of primary source, government documents. In the next chapter, we will continue the discussion of primary sources, focusing on other types of sources, such as archives, statistical data, news, and images.

General Strategies

As we mentioned earlier, primary sources are firsthand accounts or original sources, including:

- Creative works of art (literature, music, art work, film, etc.)
- Eyewitness accounts or first record of events (a diary, news footage of an event, records of an organization, etc.)
- Data from original research, whether statistical or scientific

There are many different types of primary sources, and what constitutes primary sources may vary from discipline to discipline. Another point I want to make is that even though primary sources are a vital part of any research project in any discipline, this does not mean we have to start our research with primary sources. On the contrary, in most cases we should start a research project with secondary sources—namely, scholarly books and articles—not primary sources. This is especially true for beginners. It would be a waste of time if a beginning researcher tried to find primary sources first before having become thoroughly familiarized with the existing scholarship. That is because a letter from the nineteenth century (a primary source) does not mean anything unless we already have the background knowledge and know how to analyze and interpret it in the larger historical context.

Another reason for starting with secondary sources is that as we read through the secondary literature we can often find useful primary sources mentioned in an article or book. If we can identify a primary source with its citation information (title, author, publisher, year, etc.), we should be able to obtain the material fairly easily if we decide to use the source in our paper. With citation information in hand, we should be able to obtain the material either through our own library collections or from another library through the interlibrary loan service.

Besides finding primary sources through secondary sources, we can also find primary sources directly through the library catalog or WorldCat. Both the library catalog and the WorldCat database use the same Library of Congress classification system, so we can apply the same search strategy to both tools. For example, if we are looking for historical sources on the Chinese Cultural Revolution, we can do a search in WorldCat using the keywords

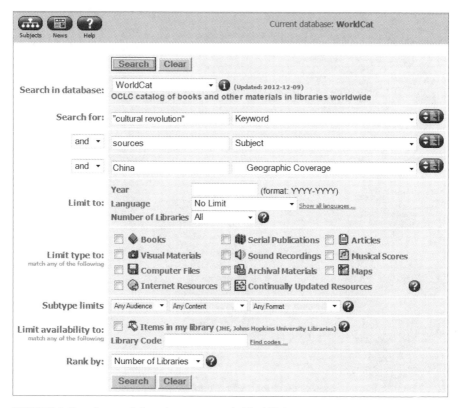

FIGURE 8.1 Sample search for primary sources in WorldCat

"cultural revolution" (as one phrase), plus "sources" as subject and "china" as geographical coverage (see Figure 8.1).

The search yields 730 hits, including 617 books. Judging from the titles (see Figure 8.2), the results are fairly accurate, with all publications containing at least in part primary sources from the Cultural Revolution era.

In most cases, we should be able to find relevant primary sources (especially if they are published in book format) through WorldCat using the search strategy as demonstrated: conduct a search with the topical term as keyword, plus the type of primary source as subject, such as "correspondence," "diaries," "interviews," "sermons," or simply "sources."

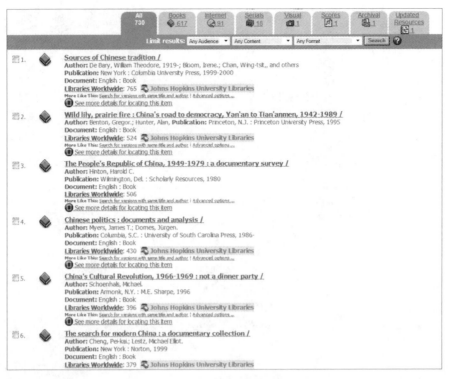

FIGURE 8.2 Search results of primary sources in WorldCat

Finding Government Documents

Government documents are an important source of information for many fields of study, but perhaps even more so in the case of Modern China Studies. As we mentioned in chapter 2, China is a unique country in terms of politics: all the political power is monopolized by one party, the Chinese Communist Party (CCP). The enormous bureaucratic system that the CCP has created since taking over the country in 1949 penetrates all public spheres and controls virtually every aspect of social and cultural life. Even though the CCP's grip on Chinese society has loosened a bit in recent years, the sheer enormity of the Chinese government and its absolute monopolization of power remain mind-boggling. Because of the dominating role of the government in Chinese society, government documents become the key to our understanding of what is going on in China and where it is going in the years ahead.

There is a great variety of government documents coming out of all branches of Chinese government at all levels. Following is a list of the major types:

- *National People's Conference documents.* The National People's Conference (NPC), in theory, is China's parliament and highest organ of state. In practice, the NPC merely rubber-stamps the decisions already made by a handful of senior officials who make up the standing committee of the politburo (BBC News 2009). Its functions are laid down in the Constitution, including amending and supervising the Constitution, enacting and amending laws, and electing or dismissing the PRC president and vice president. The documents that come out of the NPC become national laws and policies.
- *Speeches of national leaders.* A unique feature of Chinese politics is the importance of speeches given by national leaders. They are seen as directives on national policies and almost carry the same weight as national law.
- *Government/Party notices/decisions.* Numerous notices and decisions by the government and the CCP lay out the rules by which to interpret policies and law.
- *Internal documents.* There is a great variety of internal documents that circulate within the government branches but are never openly published. These documents instruct the government branches and agencies on how to carry out policies.
- *Government annual reports (white papers).*

There are many tools that could help us find Chinese government documents. We will discuss four major ones that I have found the most useful: WorldCat, Google, CNKI, and Oriprobe.

WorldCat

WorldCat can be used as a general tool to find and locate published primary sources, including government documents. We should be able to find many Chinese government documents by doing the following search: "China" as geographical coverage, "sources" as subject, plus "politics and government" as subject. This search will retrieve primary sources related to Chinese politics and government, many of which will be documents issued by the Chinese government.

Many of the Chinese government documents (and other types of primary sources as well) are translated into English. If we are particularly looking for English translations, all we need to do is to limit the search above to English only. Similarly, we can also limit our search to Chinese.

For original Chinese-language sources we can also search directly in Chinese, which often produces better results. For example, if we are looking for Chinese Communist Party documents, we can use "中共" (CCP) and "文献" (documents) as keywords, and instantly we will find over 3,000 Chinese documents.

Google

While WorldCat is especially useful for finding historical documents that are published in book format, Google is a great tool for finding up-to-date government documents. For this purpose, we will have to use the Advanced Search option, which unfortunately is not easy to locate.

For example, if we are looking for documents related to human rights from Chinese government agencies, instead of going to each Chinese government agency website, we can first do a general Google search on "人权" (human rights). Not surprisingly, we will retrieve millions of hits. Instead of plowing through all the hits, we can scroll down to the bottom of the page and click on the Advanced Search link. Google Advanced Search provides a number of options to make our search more precise, one of which is to limit our search to a certain site or domain. To target our search to Chinese government sites only, all we need to do is to limit our search to ".gov.cn," which is the domain name for all Chinese government websites (see Figure 8.3).

This search retrieves numerous government documents from various government agencies regarding human rights, including news, policy statements, speeches, and government reports (see Figure 8.4).

China National Knowledge Infrastructure (CNKI)

We discussed CNKI in chapter 6 (finding Chinese articles). Besides academic journal articles, CNKI also includes many other types of research resources.

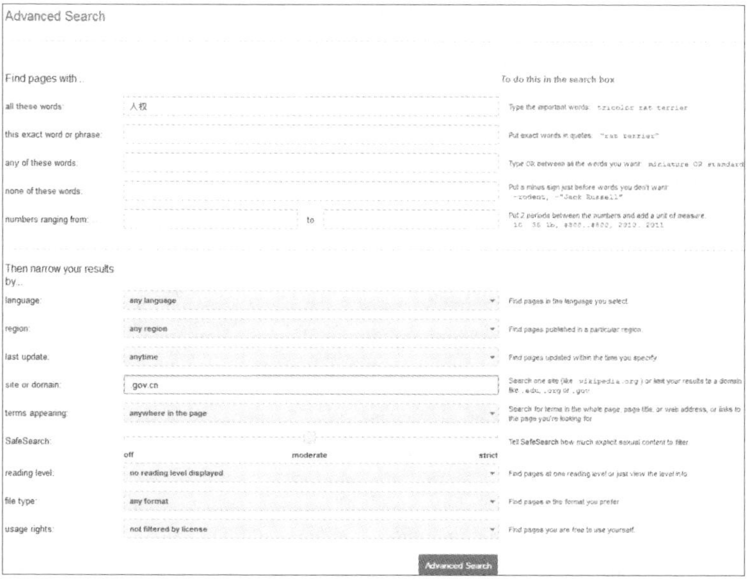

FIGURE 8.3 Search for Chinese government documents through Google Advanced Search

FIGURE 8.4 Sample result of Google Advanced Search for Chinese government documents

One of the subdatabases, called 中国政报公报期刊文献总库 (Database of Chinese Government Documents), contains the most comprehensive collection of Chinese government documents from central to local government departments and agencies.

To get a sense of the scope of the database content, here is a list of selected government documents included in the database (as of October 16, 2012):

- Speeches by key government officials—3,604
- Legislative documents—1,826
- Administrative rules—11,334
- Interpretations of law—148
- Legislative histories—3,097
- Local regulations—3,600
- International treaty—582
- Reports and studies—4,559
- Theoretical studies—2,059
- Statistical data—1,246
- Government white papers—173

For example, if we do a simple search on "人权," the database instantly retrieves over 1,000 results, all from government publications of various levels. We can easily narrow down our search by selecting any of the categories on the left-hand menu or by choosing the "Search within the result" option to further refine our topic. In addition, CNKI also provides "Similar Articles" on the record page, which makes it very easy to track down other related sources. CNKI provides free index searches. For full-text articles, we need to subscribe to the database or obtain the documents through interlibrary loan. We could also contact the North American vendor, East View, for purchasing the needed articles.

Oriprobe Databases

Oriprobe Information Services, a Chinese-language database provider based in Ontario, Canada, sells a number of databases specialized in documents of the Chinese government and Chinese Communist Party. Since we can only access the databases through subscription (no free index search), we will just list the database names here without going into detail:

- *Archives of the Chinese Communist Party.* It includes archives of important historical documents, such as the CCP's Constitutions over the years and Party internal documents; documents from the Communist Party's National Congress since 1921, such as reports, name lists, pictures, news reports and commentaries, audio/video files, and other research materials; publications of legendary leaders, including Mao Zedong, Zhou Enlai, Liu Shaoqi, Zhu De, Ren Bishi, Deng Xiaoping, and Chen Yun; daily activities of current party elites since 1989; historical events in the Party history since 1921; and who's who in the Communist Party over the years.
- *Archives of the Chinese government.* It includes archives and publications of the Chinese central government, its ministries and subsidiaries, such as National Policies (2001–present); Regional Policies (2001–present); Speeches/Publications of Ministerial/Provincial Officers (2004–present); National/Provincial/Ministerial Government Annual Statements (1983–present); Foreign Minister's Spokesperson's Statements and Speeches (1997–present); and the Foreign Minister's Press Conference (2001–present).
- *Database of National People's Congress.* It includes reports, primarily by *People's Daily* and *People's Daily Online,* on the National People's Congress from the first session of the first NPC to the second session of the eleventh NPC.

Reference

BBC News. 2009. "How China Is Ruled." Accessed October 17, 2012. http://news.bbc.co.uk/2/shared/spl/hi/in_depth/china_politics/government/html/1.stm.

Finding Archives, Statistical Data, News, and Images

This chapter will show you:

★ How to find archives

★ How to find statistical data

★ How to find newspapers and periodicals

★ How to find images

Following up on our previous discussion on general strategies of finding primary sources and on finding government documents, in this chapter we will discuss resources and search strategies for finding other types of primary sources, including archives, statistical data, news, and images.

Finding Archives

This section will primarily deal with archives in or from China. We will talk about US and British archives on China in the next chapter, on researching humanities.

A unique feature of archives in China is that they are all under strict government control, in the same way that the Chinese media (newspapers, television, and radio) are controlled by the government. The government can choose to open or publish certain archives while keeping others closed, as they see fit, to ensure that they would not let out any information that might potentially damage the reputation of the Party or undermine its rule.

Despite the censorship, Chinese archives are crucial for studies of modern China. Neil Diamant, a political scientist at Dickinson College, muses on what a difference it would make if scholars could have unfettered access to the archives in China:

> Imagine the scope of data, and new insights about politics, that could be gleaned from a year-long immersion in this and other archives, or if local archives opened their doors to researchers examining other seminal political events in the PRC, such as land reform, the Korean War, the Great Leap Forward, or diplomatic relations with the USSR! These sources would activate tremors in the field; to stay intellectually honest we would have to revise our lectures, textbooks, and "consensus" histories of the period.... We would also have to recalibrate our interpretations of the post-Mao period, particularly if scholars offer "path-dependent" and historically grounded explanations for political and economic phenomena, or alternatively, argue that the present presents a sharp break from the past. (Diamant 2010)

There are two major national archives in mainland China. The First Historical Archives of China (中国第一历史档案馆), located in Beijing, holds the central government archives from the Ming and Qing dynasties. The Second Historical Archives of China (中国第二历史档案馆), located in Nanjing, contains government archives from the Republic Era (1912–1949). Each of these two archives publishes its own journal. The First Historical Archives publishes 历史档案 (*Historical Archives*), and the Second Historical Archives publishes 民国档案 (*Archives of Republic Era*). These journals could be useful for learning about the latest scholarship utilizing archival resources as well as new publications by the two national archives.

In addition to these two major national archives, the Archives of the Ministry of Foreign Affairs (外交部档案馆) specializes in People's Republic of China (PRC) diplomatic archives. It has recently opened parts of its collections from 1949 to 1965 (Archives of the Ministry of Foreign Affairs 2007).

For scholars and advanced students, the best way to research Chinese archives is to go and visit the archives on-site. There is an excellent website called *Dissertation Reviews* where scholars (mostly PhD students working on their dissertations) share their experiences of visiting archives outside the United States, including various sites in China (http://dag.fmprc.gov.cn/chn/dajmkf/).[1]

For beginning researchers, the easiest way to access Chinese archives is through published archival materials. These archival materials can be found through the library catalog or WorldCat. For example, if we are researching topics related to nineteenth-century China and we know that the First Historical Archives of China has the strongest collection of materials from that time period, we can search WorldCat and find out what materials have been published by the national archives. All we need to do is conduct an author search in WorldCat, with "zhongguo di yi li shi dang an guan" as author.

If we have a research topic in mind, say, "opium war," we want to find relevant archival sources on the topic. We can do a keyword search on "opium war," plus "sources" as subject. We should be able to retrieve a list of primary sources on the topic, including archival materials. Or more accurately, if we search "opium war" plus "dang an," we will be able to retrieve a list of mostly Chinese archival publications on the topic. The same strategy can be applied to the library catalog, if we want to find out what Chinese archives or primary sources may be in the library collections.

Finding Statistical Data

For general statistical data on China, there are two major print sources, one in English and the other in Chinese:

- *China Facts and Figures Annual* (*CHIFFA*). Published annually since 1978, *CHIFFA* annually accumulates all basic and statistical information about the PRC in English. Most information is on the national level, and each volume contains all new data.
- 中国统计年鉴 (*China Statistical Yearbook*). Published by the National Bureau of Statistics of China, the *China Statistical Yearbook* includes national and provincial data on social and economic indicators.

In addition to these annual publications, there are also many compiled cumulative statistics published in print:

- 新中国六十年统计资料汇编: 1949–2008 (*China Compendium of Statistics: 1949–2008*)

- 中国工业交通能源50年统计资料汇编, 1949–1999 (*China Compendium of Statistics of Industry, Transportation, and Energy, 1949–1999*)
- 中国妇女统计资料, 1949–1989 (*Statistics on Chinese Women, 1949–1989*)
- 中国性别统计资料, 1990–1995 (*Gender Statistics in China, 1990–1995*)

We can find these published print statistical sources fairly easily through WorldCat. Just do a subject search on "China, statistics," or more precisely, "China, economics, statistics," or "women, China, statistics," "industries, China, statistics," and so on, and we should be able to find relevant statistical publications.

The most convenient way to find statistical data, however, is through online resources. Following are some of the most important databases that include statistical information from China.

China Data Online

Provided by the China Data Center at the University of Michigan, China Data Online is the most commonly used database outside China for current and historical Chinese statistical information. It includes China statistics, economic data, census data, and statistical yearbooks. Recently, it has added a GIS function through an upgrade of China Geo-Explorer.

CNKI/China Social and Economic Development Statistical Database

The statistics database in CNKI includes 650 titles of statistical sources, totaling 3,839 volumes. It is accessible at CNKI's homepage (www.cnki.net/) under "统计数据." The index search is free.

CNKI/China Yearbook Full-text Database

As of 2009, the yearbook database in CNKI consists of 2,000 yearbook titles and over 12,681 volumes. It is the largest, continuously updated yearbook full-text database in China. The database is distributed by East View and can also be accessed directly from CNKI's homepage under "年鉴." Index search is free.

Wanfang Data/Local Gazetteer Database

Besides statistical yearbooks, local gazetteers are another very important source of statistical information and can be useful for scholars from a variety of fields, such as history, sociology, and more. However, because of the large quantity of this type of publication, very few libraries outside China have the resources to build a meaningful collection. With this new product from Wanfang Data, now scholars outside China could have convenient access to these valuable research resources. The database can be accessed at the Wanfang Data homepage (www.wanfangdata.com/).

Finding Newspapers and Periodicals

We will devote this section to discussions on three types of sources: newspapers and periodicals from contemporary China (1949 to the present), those from the Late Qing and Republic Era (late nineteenth century to 1949), and those available in English, including translations of Chinese sources and original English publications in China.

Newspapers and Periodicals after 1949

Under the rule of the Chinese Communist Party (CCP) since 1949, the PRC has earned a sorry reputation of being among the least free countries in the world. According to the *Press Freedom Index*, an annual ranking of countries by Reports Without Borders (RWB, an international nongovernmental organization), based on the organization's assessment of press freedom records of the previous year the PRC ranked 174 out of 179 countries in 2011–2012, with some of the worst press freedom records (RWB 2012b). The PRC is also among a handful of nations labeled by RWB as an "enemy of Internet" (RWB 2012a).

The CCP has always seen the media as instruments for political propaganda. As early as 1942 in a famous speech titled "Talks at the Yenan Forum on Literature and Art," CCP leader Mao Zedong, who later became the first president of the PRC, demanded that all literature and art serve "workers, peasants, and soldiers" and the cause of revolution (Mao 1942). Hijacking the arts and media for political propaganda has since become the CCP's long-standing policy and standard practice. As recently as December 2011, a high-ranking Chinese media official was reported to have said, "The first social responsibility and professional ethic of media staff should be understanding their role clearly and be a good mouthpiece [for the Party]" (Goodman 2011).

On the other hand, even though the majority of Chinese media are run and controlled by the government, these state-run institutions have to compete for market share in the new market economy (which was fully established in the early 1990s). Therefore, they are allowed certain amount of wiggle room for independence and diversity, as long as what they do is well within the parameters set by the government. The rise of the Internet, especially the social media in recent years, has further loosened the government's grip on the media.

In short, when we approach China from the perspective of Chinese media, we have to understand and appreciate the dynamics and complexity of the situation, with strict control and censorship from the government on the one hand and certain levels of diversity and freedom as a result of economic reform and advancement of information technology on the other.

Following is a list of the most important Chinese news resources available in many academic institutions in North America, including two digitized major Chinese newspapers with complete runs and two aggregated databases of Chinese news sources:

- *People's Daily Online* (1946–present). As the official organ of the Chinese government, the *People's Daily* is the single most important newspaper in China. It represents the official voice of the government and covers all areas of China's social, economic, and cultural life. The online version, distributed by Oriprobe Information Services, is a robust database with powerful full-text search capability. The articles can be downloaded and printed. Each article can be viewed either as a text file or PDF image file.
- *PLA Daily* (1956–present). The *People's Liberation Army (PLA) Daily* is the official newspaper of the military of the PRC. The publication was established on January 1, 1956, and acts as the authoritative media of the PLA to release military news and comprehensive military-related information. The database, distributed by East View Information Services, contains the complete run of the newspaper.

- *China Core Newspapers Full-text Database* (2000–present). Part of the CNKI databases, China Core Newspapers Full-text Database includes 500-plus major newspapers from 23 provinces, five regions, and four major cities of mainland China. The database is distributed by East View. Index searching is free at the CNKI website (http://epub.cnki.net/kns/brief/result .aspx?dbPrefix=CCND/).
- *Wise Search* (1979–present). Wise Search claims to be the largest Chinese database of published news sources from Greater China, including all leading Chinese and English newspapers of Hong Kong and other top-tier newspapers, magazines, newswires, TV channels, and radio stations of Greater China. For researchers that need access to information beyond mainland China, this database would be an excellent choice.

Newspapers and Periodicals Prior to 1949

The databases already mentioned mostly cover newspapers from contemporary China (after the founding of the PRC in 1949). If we need to search for news reports prior to 1949, we need to consult different sources. Below are the major resources that cover the newspapers and magazines during the late nineteenth century and early twentieth century.

- *Shen Bao* (申報1872–1949). *Shen Bao* is one of the first modern Chinese newspapers. It is the most influential and longest lasting commercial newspaper of pre-1949 China. It was established by British businessman Ernest Major in 1872. During its 78 years of existence (1872–1949), there were 256,000 issues published. As an important primary source for late imperial and modern China, *Shen Bao* outlasted three reigns of the Qing Dynasty and witnessed many significant historical events, such as the Sino-French War, the Sino-Japanese War, the Boxer Rebellion, two World Wars, and so on. Known for its rich news reporting, commentary, and advertisements, *Shen Bao* played a pivotal role in the formation of public opinion in the late nineteenth century and the

Republic Era. The digitized edition of *Shen Bao* is full-text searchable and displays articles either in a text file or PDF image file.

- *National Index to Chinese Newspapers and Periodicals* (全国报刊索引|1833–present). *National Index to Chinese Newspapers and Periodicals* (NICNP) was launched in 1955. Compiled by the Shanghai Library, it is the earliest comprehensive Chinese newspapers and periodicals search tool issued in China, published in both print and electronic formats. The paper version of NICNP is a monthly publication, consisting of a Philosophy and Social Sciences edition and a Natural Science and Technology edition. The electronic version of NICNP was first created in 1993 and has become a superindex database covering information for more than one and a half centuries, from 1833 to the present. It lists about 18,000 kinds of newspapers and periodicals published in China. The database contains over 30 million entries, with a yearly update of 3.5 million entries. The database is accessible by subscription at www.cnbksy.com/. It is produced and distributed by the Shanghai Library. More recently, the Shanghai Library has also launched the full-text editions of the database. Given the vast amount of information, the database is broken down into a series of datasets:

  > The Late Qing Dynasty Database (1833–1910)
  > The Republic Era Database (1911–1949)
  > The Socialist Era Database (1950–1977)
  > Contemporary China Database (1978–present)

- *Da Cheng Lao Jiu Kan Full-Text Database* (大成老旧刊全文数据库1840–1949). An alternative to the NICNP, Da Cheng collected the full-text articles of over 6,000 journals published between the late nineteenth century and 1949. Even though Da Cheng covers about the same historical period as the first two modules in the full-text edition of the NICNP, the two databases can be used to complement each other rather than one as a replacement for the other. That is because the two databases do not cover exactly the same sources. Even when they do, because of differences in indexing (NICNP seems superior in this regard) the search results can be very different. For subscription information visit www.dachengdata.com/, or contact its vendor at haiwai@ssreader.com.

For researchers who do not have access to these commercial databases, here is a free online resource for magazines published in the Republic Era (1911–1949):

- *Chinese Periodicals of Republic Era* (民国中文期刊). Created by the National Library of China, Chinese Periodicals of Republic Era is a searchable database containing the full-text content of 4,351 periodicals published during the Republic Era. The database is accessible at the National Library of China homepage (www.nlc.gov.cn/) under "特色资源." First-time users will need to register (free) to access this and many other valuable resources at the National Library of China website.

English-Language Newspapers and Periodicals from China

Researchers without Chinese-language proficiency can access Chinese news sources in translation or in English-language news sources from China. For contemporary China, there are three popular databases for this type of source:

- *Foreign Broadcast Information Service (FBIS) Daily Reports* (1960–1996). Formerly published in print, the online edition of this unique resource provides easy access to English-language translations of broadcast transcripts, news agency transmissions, newspapers, periodicals, and government statements from countries around the world, including China.
- *World News Connection* (1996–present). A valuable research tool for anyone who needs to monitor non-US media sources, the World News Connection (WNC) is compiled from thousands of non-US media sources and covers significant socioeconomic, political, scientific, technical, and environmental issues and events around the world. The information is obtained from full-text and summaries of newspaper articles, websites, conference

proceedings, television and radio broadcasts, periodicals, and nonclassified technical reports. New information is entered into WNC hourly every day. Generally, this information is available within 24 to 72 hours from the time of original publication or broadcast.

For Chinese media, WNC covers the following sources: AFP, The Asia Sentinel, Boxun, China Internet Information Center (Zhongguo Wang), China National Radio, China Radio International, Guoji Xianqu Daobao, *The Hong Kong Economic Journal*, *Hong Kong Economic Times*, Hong Kong iMail, Hong Kong Standard, Information Center for Human Rights and Democracy, Jiefangjun Bao, Kanwa Defense Review, Keji Ribao, Liaowang, Ming Pao, Renmin Ribao, RTHK Radio 3, Sichuan Ribao, Sing Tao Jih Pao, Sing Tao Wan Pao, Ta Kung Pao, Wen Wei Po, Xinhua, Xinhua Domestic Service, Xinhua Hong Kong Service, Xinjiang Ribao, Xinmin Wanbao, *Zhongguo Qingnian Bao* (China Youth Daily), Zhongguo Tongxun She, Zhongguo Xinwen She (China News Service).

- *Access World News*. This database from News Bank covers more than 1,200 international newspapers, plus 300 wire services and over 200 broadcast news transcripts. The sources are translated into English when written in other languages. For Chinese media, Access World News includes the following: Beijing Zhongguo Xinwen She, Business Daily Update, *China Daily* (chinadaily.com .cn), Dazhong Ribao, Guangxi Ribao, Jiefangjun Bao, Renmin Gongan Bao, Renmin Ribao, Sichuan Ribao, SinoCast, SinoCast China Financial Watch, SinoCast China IT Watch, ChinaSinoCast Transportation Watch, ChinaXinhua News Agency, Yangcheng Wanbao, Zhongguo Xinwen Zhoukan.

There are many historical English-language newspapers and periodicals from pre-1949 China (King and Clark 1965). Many of these sources exist in print and/or on microfilm. Their catalog records can be found in WorldCat. The following are two major English publications from China that are now available in digital format:

- *The North China Herald Online. North China Herald* is the prime English language source for the history of the foreign presence in China from around 1850 to the 1940s. It was published weekly in Shanghai. As the official journal for British consular notifications and announcements of the Shanghai Municipal Council, it is the point of reference for a range of foreign and Chinese activities. Translations of Chinese official notifications and news were also regularly included. This journal is full-text searchable and is distributed by Brill.
- *The Chinese Recorder* (1867–1941). Republished in digital format by Gale Archives Unbound as *The Chinese Recorder and the Protestant Missionary Community in China, 1867–1941*, this missionary journal is now easily accessible to anyone interested in China of the late nineteenth and early twentieth centuries. During its long run—remarkable for any publication begun in the nineteenth century and especially one published in English in China—*The Chinese Recorder* covered the beginnings of mission schools, the crusade against opium, the Boxer Rebellion, ecumenical missionary conferences, the 1911 Revolution, the growth of the Chinese church, and the rise of communism in China.

Finding Images

This section will only cover images that are of historical value, mostly photographic works. We will discuss art images in the next chapter in the section on art and architecture.

Hundreds of photographic works have been published from different time periods of Chinese history. Most of these works can be found through WorldCat. They are most likely to be cataloged in WorldCat (and the library catalog) as "China—pictorial works." To find these items, all we need to do is search "China" and "pictorial works" as subject terms and limit the search to "not juvenile" (so as not to get children's books), and we will be able to retrieve a great number of photographic works from China. Since this search will retrieve sources from all historical periods, we can make our search more specific by adding "twentieth century" or "nineteenth century."

Following is a sample list of print images in different categories for the purpose of illustrating the wide variety of image sources now available in library collections[2]:

- Social life and culture
    All Under Heaven: The Chinese World, by Eliot Porter and
        Jonathan Porter (Pantheon Books, 1983)
    Tibet, the Sacred Realm: Photographs, 1880–1950, by
        Lobsang Phuntshok Lhalungpa (Aperture, 1983)
    Toward a Truer Life: Photographs of China 1980–1990, by
        Reagan Louie (Aperture, 1991);
    中国故事：当代中国纪实摄影 (*Contemporary Chi-
        nese Documentary Photography*), by Dongping Yuan
        et al. (Helongjiang jiao yu chu ban she, 2001)
    图说中国百年社会生活变迁 (1840–1949) (*Changes
        in Chinese Social Life over 100 Years through Images*),
        by Fulan Zhong (Xueling chu ban she, 2001)
    十九世纪中国市井风情:三百六十行 (*Customs and
        Conditions of Chinese City Streets in 19th Century:
        360 Professions in China*), by Lianchang Guan, Shi-
        jian Huang, and William Sargent (Shanghai gu ji che
        ban she, 1999)
    老照片 (*Old Photos*) (1997), Shandong hua bao chu
        ban she "Lao zhao pian" bian ji bu
- History
    *The Chinese Century: A Photographic History of the Last
        Hundred Years*, by Jonathan D. Spence and Ann-ping
        Chin (Random House, 1996)
    China: Portrait of a Country (Porträt Eines Landes), by
        Heung Shing Liu (Taschen America, 2008)
    China: Fifty Years inside the People's Republic, by Rae Yang
        (Aperture, 1999)
    中国近代史参考图录 (*Images of Modern China*), by
        Yongzhen Du, Zhongguo li shi bo wu guan, and
        Beijing li shi bo wu guan (Shanghai jiao yu chu ban
        she, 1981–)

中国近百年历史图集 (*Images of China over a Century 1840–1978*), by Zhunguo jin bai nian li shi tu ji bian ji wei yuan hui (Xianggang tian di tu shu you xian gong si, 1978)

中华民国历史图片档案 (*Image Archive of History of Republic of China*), by Zhongguo di 2 li shi dang an guan (Tuanjie chu ban she, 2002)

- Revolution and war

  外国人镜头中的八国联军: 辛丑条约百年图志 (*The Eight-Power Allied Forces through Foreigners' Camera: An Illustrated Record of the Protocol of 1901, 1900–1901*), by Zhongguo ren quan fa zhan ji jin hui and Zhongguo di 1 li shi dang an guan (Wai wen chu ban she, 2001)

  中国人民解放军历史资料图集 (*Archival Collection of the History of People's Liberation Army*), by Jun shi zi liao tu ji bian ji zu (Chang cheng chu ban she, 1981–)

  南京大屠杀: 历史照片中的见证 (*The Rape of Nanking: An Undeniable History in Photographs*), by Yong Shi (Hai nan chu ban she, 1999)

  香港日佔時期 (*Hong Kong during Japan Occupation*), by Gao Tianqiang and Zhuomin Tang (Xianggang san lian chu ban she, 1995)

  紀念辛亥革命七十周年 (*In Memory of 70th Anniversary of 1911 Revolution*) (Zhongguo xin wen she, 1981)

- Chinese cities

  Picturing Hong Kong: Photography 1855–1910, by Roberta Wue (George Braziller, 1997)

  实录北京八十年代印象 (*Photographical Impressions of Beijing in the 1980s*), by Jianming Li and Yu Qian (Shanghai wen yi chu ban she, 2004)

  北京街巷图志 (*Images of Beijing Streets*), by Bin Wang and Xiushan Xu (Zuo jia chu ban she, 2004)

- Chinese women

  世界屋脊上的女人(*Tibetan Women*), by Xinhua Wu
  (Shi jie zhi shi chu ban she, 2004)

  从小脚女人到社会半边天 (*From Small Feet Women
  to Half of the Sky*), by Yan Wu (Sichuan ren min chu
  ban she, 2003)

  百年中国女性形象 (*Images of Chinese Women in 100
  Years*), by Huifen Chen (Zhu hai chu ban she, 2002)

  中国云南农村妇女自我写真集 (*Visual Voices, 100
  Photographs of Village China by the Women of Yunnan
  Province*), by Kunyi Wu, Yunnan sheng fu nü lian
  he hui, and Western Consortium for Public Health
  (Yunnan min zhu chu ban she, 1995)

- Late Qing China

  China in Old Photographs, 1860–1910, by Burton F.
  Beers (Dorset Press, 1978)

  Imperial China: Photographs 1850–1912, by Clark Worswick and Jonathan D. Spence (Penwick Publishing,
  1978)

  晚清映像:西方人眼中的近代中国 (*The Image of Old
  China in the Western Perspective*), by Shen Hong
  (Zhongguo she hui ke xue chu ban she, 2005)

  清史图典:清朝通史图录 (*Images of History of Qing
  Dynasty*), by Chengru Zhu (Zi jin cheng chu ban
  she, 2002)

  紫禁城帝后生活, 1644–1911 (*Life of Empress in Forbidden City*), by Zi Meng, Kong Wu, Tianwei Yu, and
  Gu gong bo wu yuan (Zhongguo lu you chu ban she,
  1982)

Finally, what follows is a selected list of free online image archives of historical China:

- *Sidney D. Gamble Photographs* (http://library.duke.edu/digital
  collections/gamble/). A renowned China scholar, Sidney D.
  Gamble (1890–1968) visited China four times from 1908 to

1932, traveling throughout the country to collect data for social-economic surveys and to photograph urban and rural life, public events, architecture, religious statuary, and the countryside. Thanks to Duke University Libraries, a collection of over 5,000 digitized photographs is made publicly available online.

- *Asian and Middle East: AGSL Digital Photo Archive* (http://www4.uwm.edu/libraries/digilib/agsphoto/html/about.cfm). AGSL Digital Photo Archive presents a selection of images from the extensive photographic holdings of the American Geographical Society (AGS) Library. The images were selected from several collections, including the American Geographical Society Library Print Collection, the Harrison Forman Collection, the Robert W. McColl Collection, the Bert Krawczyk Collection, the Edna Schaus Sorensen and Clarence W. Sorensen Collection, and the Helmut de Terra Collection. The American Geographical Society Library Print Collection represents many decades of research and acquisition. The scope of the collection is worldwide. Dating from the mid-nineteenth century to the present, these photographs document a wealth of geographic themes. The images selected for this project include historical photos of Afghanistan, Egypt, Jordan, Korea, Thailand, Nepal, and China.

- *Bucklin China Archive* (www.bucklinchinaarchive.com/index2 .php). Harold Bucklin, an assistant professor of sociology at Brown University, took a series of photographs during his tenure as visiting professor of sociology at Shanghai College in 1923 and 1924. After sitting in a bank vault for 80 years, Bucklin's extraordinary body of photographic work was discovered and has been preserved and printed.

- *East Asia Image Collection* (http://digital.lafayette.edu/collec tions/eastasia/). Courtesy of Lafayette College Libraries, the East Asia Image Collection is an open-access archive of digitized photographs, negatives, postcards, and slides of imperial Japan (1868–1945), its Asian empire (1895–1945), and occupied Japan (1947–1952). Images of Taiwan, Japan, China, Korea, Manchuria, and Indonesia are included. Each record in the East Asia Image Collection has been assigned subject headings, hyperlinked metadata, and to the fullest extent possible historiographical, bibliographical, and technical data.

- *Historical Photos of China* (http://hpc.vcea.net/). A collaboration among scholars at the University of Bristol, the University of Lincoln, the Institut d'Asie Orientale, and TGE-Adonis, this project aims to locate, archive, and disseminate photographs from the substantial holdings of images of modern China held mostly in private hands overseas. The photographs archived in the project come from the collections of Chinese diplomats, foreign businessmen, staff of the administrations in the Chinese treaty ports, missionaries, and officials of the Chinese Maritime Customs Service. They shed light on political events such as the 1925 May Thirtieth incident, working and social life, treaty port architecture, commercial history, the history of dress and fashion, and of course the history of photography in China.

- *Thomas H. Hahn Docu-Images* (http://hahn.zenfolio.com/). The collection of photographs curated by Thomas H. Hahn includes photographic images of China under various themes, such as China Urban Development, Historical Photographs, Images from the Cultural Revolution, as well as images of different peoples, places, and cultures.

- *International Mission Photography Archive* (http://digitallibrary .usc.edu/impa/controller/). The *International Mission Photography Archive* offers historical images from Protestant and Catholic missionary collections in Britain, Norway, Germany, France, Switzerland, and the United States. The photographs, which range in time from the middle of the nineteenth to the middle of the twentieth century, offer a visual record of missionary activities and experiences in Africa, China, Madagascar, India, Papua New Guinea, and the Caribbean.

- *Virtual Shanghai* (www.virtualshanghai.net/). Virtual Shanghai is a research and resource platform on the history of Shanghai from the mid-nineteenth century to today. It incorporates four types of documents: essays, original documents, photographs, and maps. The objective of the project is to write a history of the city through the combined mobilization of these various types of documents.

- *China 1972* (www.wellesley.edu/Polisci/wj/China1972/main .html). China 1972 is a collection of photographs taken by professor William A. Josephy, Wellesley College, during his visit to China in March–April 1972 as a participant in the second delegation of the Committee of Concerned Asian Scholars (CCAS) to the PRC. The photos gave a glimpse of life in China during the Cultural Revolution.
- *The Tibetan Album: British Photography in Central Tibet 1920– 1950* (http://tibet.prm.ox.ac.uk/tibet_collections.html). *The Tibet Album* presents more than 6,000 photographs spanning 30 years of Tibet's history. These extraordinary photographs are a unique record of people long gone and places changed beyond all recognition. They also document the ways that British visitors encountered Tibet and Tibetans.
- *Tibet: From the Collections of American Geographical Society Library* (http://www4.uwm.edu/libraries/digilib/tibet/). This digital collection presents historical maps and images of Tibet from the holdings of the AGS Library. The collection includes a set of early photographs of central Tibet and Lhasa as well as images from Harrison Forman's expeditions to northern Tibet between 1932 and 1937.
- *Visualising China* (http://visualisingchina.net/). Visualising China allows users to explore and enhance more than 8,000 digitized images of photographs of China taken between 1850 and 1950. It provides access to many previously unseen albums, envelopes, and private collections, and also major collections such as Historical Photographs of China, the Sir Robert Hart Collection, and Joseph Needham's Photographs of Wartime China.

---

1. I want to thank Li Tang, the Chinese Studies Librarian at Yale University, for drawing my attention to this website.
2. This list is informed by a section on finding images in the *Chinese Studies Research Guide* by Luo Zhou, Librarian for Chinese Studies at Duke University. Her research guide is accessible at http://library.duke.edu/research/subject/guides/chinese_studies/.

References

Archives of the Ministry of Foreign Affairs, People's Republic of China. 2007. "Dang an jie mi kai fang." Accessed October 17, 2012. http://dag.fmprc.gov.cn/chn/dajmkf/.

Diamant, Neil J. 2010. "Why Archives?" In *Contemporary Chinese Politics: New Sources, Methods, and Field Strategies*, edited by Allen Carlson, Mary E. Gallagher, Kenneth Lieberthal, and Melanie Manion, 33–50. New York: Cambridge University Press.

Goodman, David. 2011. "Journalists Should Be Government Mouthpieces, Chinese Media Leader Says." *New York Times*, December 5. http://thelede.blogs.nytimes.com/2011/12/05/journalists-should-be-government-mouthpieces-chinas-state-tv-president-says/.

King, Frank, and Prescott Clark. 1965. *A Research Guide to China-Coast Newspapers, 1822–1911*. Cambridge, MA: Harvard University Press.

Mao Zedong. 1942. "Talks at the Yenan Forum of Literature and Art." *Selected Works of Mao Zedong*. Revised 2004. www.marxists.org/reference/archive/mao/selected-works/volume-3/mswv3_08.htm.

RWB (Reporters Without Borders). 2012a. "Internet Enemies: China." Accessed October 18. http://en.rsf.org/internet-enemie-china,39741.html.

———. 2012b. "Press Freedom Index 2011–2012." Accessed October 18. http://en.rsf.org/press-freedom-index-2011-2012,1043.html.

Researching Humanities in Art, Film, and Media Studies

This chapter will show you:

★ Core resources for the humanities
★ Specialized databases for art, film, and media studies
★ Primary sources for the disciplines
★ Reference and introductory works for the disciplines

In the previous chapters, we have discussed ways to find different types of research materials. In the following two chapters, we will take a different approach by focusing on resources most relevant to major fields of study in the humanities and social sciences. These specialized resources and tools can help us find materials outside the scope of the general databases we discussed in the previous chapters. For example, JSTOR, a general database, covers 74 journal titles in Asian Studies. In comparison, Bibliography of Asian Studies Online (BAS), a specialized database and major index for the field of Asian Studies, covers thousands of sources from around the world. If we just rely on JSTOR and do not use BAS, we will potentially miss a large body of useful information. That is why we need to learn about and use specialized subject-specific resources.

Core Resources in the Humanities

- *Arts and Humanities Citation Index* (AHCI). AHCI, accessed via Web of Science, provides researchers with quick, powerful access to the bibliographic and citation information they need to find research data, journals, and researchers and to analyze trends and to share their findings, similar to SSCI (see chapter 7). This database includes over 1,395 of the world's leading arts and humanities journals.

- *Humanities Full Text*. This database offers full text for many of the most important academic sources in the humanities. It provides coverage of feature articles, interviews, bibliographies, obituaries, and original works of fiction, drama, poetry and book reviews, as well as reviews of ballets, dance programs, motion pictures, musicals, radio and television programs, plays, operas, and more. Periodical coverage dates as far back as 1910.

- *Humanities International Index*. Humanities International Index is a comprehensive database covering journals, books, and other important reference sources in the humanities. Formerly the American Humanities Index, this database contains bibliographic records from a multitude of US and international journals, books, and reference works. Humanities International Index provides citations and abstracts for articles, essays, and reviews, as well as original creative works such as poems, fiction, photographs, paintings, and illustrations.

- *Bibliography of Asian Studies Online* (BAS). BAS covers all subjects pertaining to Asia published worldwide from 1971 to the present (see chapter 5).

- *China Academic Journals Full-text Database* (CAJ). A primary source of Chinese academic journals, CAJ includes all subject fields in humanities (see chapter 6).

- *Duxiu*. A comprehensive database for Chinese scholarship from a wide variety of sources, Duxiu is especially strong in its digital collection of Chinese books (see chapter 4).

Arts Resources

Search Strategies

- For general sources on Chinese art, search "China, art," "China, art, 20th century," "Avant-garde, China."
- For images of art, search "China, art, catalogs," "China, art, exhibitions."
- Following is a list of selected subject headings on Chinese art and architecture:

  Buddhist art—China
  Buddhist art and symbolism—China
  Folk art—China—Catalogs
  Socialist realism in art—China
  Art—Awards—China
  Folk art—China—Themes, motives
  Decorative arts—China—History
  Socialism and the arts—China
  China painting—Themes, motives
  Painting—China—History
  Architecture—China—History
  Architecture—China—History—20th century
  Architecture, Domestic—China
  Vernacular architecture—China
  Architecture—China—Western influences
  Landscape architecture—China

Core Resources

- *Art Index Retrospective*: 1929–1984. Providing users access with over half a century of art literature, this database includes high-quality indexing of nearly 600 publications, many of which are peer-reviewed, and citations of over 25,000 book reviews. Coverage includes fine, decorative, and commercial arts.
- *Bibliography of History of Art*: 1975–2007. The Bibliography of the History of Art (BHA) indexes important scholarly journals in art, art history, and related fields in the humanities focusing on

visual culture of Europe and the Americas. It includes the complete database of Répertoire de la litterature de l'art (RILA). The coverage spans the years 1975 to 2007.

- *International Bibliography of Art:* 2008–present. Successor to the BHA, the International Bibliography of Art includes detailed abstracts for all new content, in-depth abstracts for scholarly articles, and authority files of controlled terms. Together, they provide detailed, high-quality records to direct researchers to the most important information in the field.
- Key journals:

> *Art Asia Pacific.* Established in 1993, *Art Asia Pacific* (*AAP*) magazine is an English-language periodical covering contemporary art and culture from Asia, the Pacific, and the Middle East. Published six times a year, *AAP* includes features, profiles, essays, and reviews by experts from all over the world.
>
> *Archives of Asian Art* (in print and electronic format). *Archives of Asian Art* is an annual journal specializing in the arts of Asia. Each issue presents articles by leading scholars and a selection of outstanding works of Asian art acquired by North American museums during the previous year.
>
> *Asian Arts* (www.asianart.com/). *Asian Arts* provides a free online forum for Asian art scholars, museums, and commercial galleries. It includes scholarly articles and samplings of Asian arts.
>
> *Chinese Contemporary Art Document/* 中國當代藝術文獻 (in Chinese and English). Published annually by Hunan Mei Shu Chu Ban She, each volume of *Chinese Contemporary Art Document* features the recent works that represent the major achievements and trends in Chinese art.
>
> *Yishu: Journal of Contemporary Chinese Art* (in English): *Yishu* is the first English-language journal to focus on Chinese contemporary art and culture. Each bimonthly issue features scholarly essays on topical

issues, interviews with artists and curators, conference proceedings, and critical commentary on
exhibitions and books.

Primary Sources[1]

- *ARTstor.* This library database consists of searchable digital images
  and associated catalog data, with new image collections added several times a year. ARTstor covers many time periods and cultures,
  including thousands of images from China. The images document
  the fields of architecture, painting, sculpture, photography, decorative arts, design, anthropology, and ethnographic and women's
  studies, as well as many other forms of visual culture. Users can
  search, view, download, and organize images.
- *Innovations of Chinese Painting 1850–1950* (http://huntington
  archive.osu.edu/Exhibitions/5000years/intr/innovintr.html).
  Courtesy of Ohio State University, Columbus, this free web resource includes an essay on the history of Chinese painting from
  1850 to 1950, with digitized images of sample paintings and cal-
  ligraphical works.
- *Tse-Tsung Chow Collection of Chinese Scrolls and Fan Paintings*
  (http://www4.uwm.edu/libraries/digilib/scroll/). Courtesy of
  the University of Wisconsin, this free web resource includes over
  120 calligraphic and painted Chinese scrolls and fans from the
  eighteenth through the twentieth centuries.
- *Art and China's Revolution: Asia Society Exhibit 2008* (http://sites
  .asiasociety.org/chinarevo/). This website includes sample Chinese art works from the Socialist Era (1950s through 1970s) with
  background information.
- *Picturing Power: Posters of the Cultural Revolution 1963–1979*
  (http://huntingtonarchive.osu.edu/exhibitions/picturingpower
  exhibit.html). Picturing Power is a traveling exhibit that originated at Indiana University and makes use of a unique collection
  of posters held at the Centre for the Study of Democracy University of Westminster, London. The online version of the exhibition, including 73 images of posters from different stages of the

Cultural Revolution, represents approximately 10 percent of the total poster collection. It is also published in book format as *Picturing Power in the People's Republic of China,* edited by Harriet Evans et al. (Rowman and Littlefield, 1999).

- *ArtZine: A Chinese Contemporary Art Portal* (www.artzinechina .com/): ArtZine is an online portal to contemporary Chinese art, including information on artists and their sample works as well as art-related news and articles.

- *Asia Art Archive* (www.aaa.org.hk/). Through collecting and making information on the recent history of contemporary art in Asia easily accessible, Asia Art Archive aims to facilitate understanding, research, and writing in the field. The online collection includes scanned images, correspondences, artists' personal documents, and streaming audio and video of performance art, artist talks, lectures, and other art events.

- *Inside Out: New Chinese Art* (http://sites.asiasociety.org/arts/ insideout/index.html). Inside Out has been organized by the Asia Society Galleries and the San Francisco Museum of Modern Art and is curated by Gao Minglu. The exhibition was presented at the Asia Society and P.S.1 Contemporary Art Center from September 15, 1998, through January 3, 1999. This website on the exhibition includes selected images of the artworks, biographies of the artists, and a selected bibliography citing more than 150 articles, books, and catalogs. It is also published as a book, *Inside Out: New Chinese Art,* by Gao Minglu (University of California Press, 1998).

- *New Chinese Art* (www.newchineseart.com/). Including a section of paintings and a section of photography, this free online resource is designed to facilitate viewing and purchasing works from contemporary Chinese artists. It includes images of artworks by different artists but does not provide information on the artists.

- *Hoover Institute Political Poster Database* (http://hoohila.stanford .edu/poster/browse.php). The database includes over 300 images of political posters from China.

- *Online Image Collections at National Digital Library of China* (http://mylib.nlc.gov.cn/web/guest/search/). National Digital Library of China provides access to a series of digitized special collections, including image collections of children's picture books (少儿连环画), Chinese New Year posters (年画撷英), and old photographs (老照片).

- *Contemporary Chinese Art: Primary Documents (MoMA Primary Documents)*, edited by Wu Hung and Peggy Wang (Duke University Press, 2010). This book brings together primary documents regarding the development of Chinese avant-garde art in English translation from 1976 to 2006.
- *China Onward: The Estella Collection: Chinese Contemporary Art, 1996–2006*, by Britta Erickson (Louisiana Museum of Modern Art, 2007). At more than 450 pages with lavish full-spread images, this book features the work of virtually every major contemporary Chinese artist who has contributed to the ongoing Chinese modern art movement since the 1970s.
- *Mahjong: Contemporary Chinese Art from the Sigg Collection*, edited by Bernhard Fibicher and Matthias Frehner (Hatje Cantz, 2005). *Mahjong*, named after the popular and ancient Chinese game of chance, presents more than 200 paintings, drawings, sculptures, photographs, video pieces, and installations from Swiss collector Uli Sigg's collection.
- *The Revolution Continues: New Art from China*, by the Saatchi Gallery (Rizzoli, 2008). This volume presents in stunning images a collection of over 200 contemporary Chinese artworks collected by Charles Saatchi, with accompanying introductory essays to provide historical contexts.
- 中国当代艺术年鉴 (*The Yearbook of Contemporary Art of China*). The yearbook covers news, reviews, and interviews, as well as representative scholarly literature on contemporary Chinese art.

Reference Sources and Introductory Texts

- *The Grove Art Online.* The *Grove Dictionary of Art* is a comprehensive art reference work covering all forms of the visual arts: painting, sculpture, architecture, graphic and decorative arts, and photography from prehistory to the 1990s. Global coverage includes the arts of Asia, Africa, the Americas, the Pacific, and

Europe. It includes an extensive essay on the history of traditional Chinese art.

- *Art Speak China* (www.artspeakchina.org/). This wiki-style online encyclopedia covers biographies of artists and art critics, images of sample works of art, and major art movements from contemporary China.

- *A Century in Crisis: Modernity and Tradition in the Art of Twentieth-Century China,* by Julia F. Andrews and Kuiyi Shen (Guggenheim Museum, 1998). Spanning between 1850 and the end of twentieth century, this book offers the first systematic exploration of modern and contemporary Chinese art. It includes essays by leading scholars that show the ways in which Chinese artists have grappled with modernity, tradition, self-definition, and the adoption and rejection of Western convention, in addition to sumptuous color plates showcasing a dazzling array of achievements from Shanghai School paintings, modern calligraphy, commercial art, 1920s and 1930s woodblock prints, and modern guohua (traditional ink and color paintings) to socialist realist paintings and other contemporary works.

- *Art and Artists of Twentieth-Century China,* by Michael Sullivan (University of California Press, 1996). A comprehensive survey of Chinese art in the twentieth century by a renowned expert in the field.

- *Modern Chinese Artists: A Biographical Dictionary,* by Michael Sullivan (University of California Press, 2006). The first biographical dictionary of its kind in any Western language, this pioneering work provides short, information-packed entries for approximately 1,800 Chinese artists of the twentieth and twenty-first centuries.

- *Hong Kong Art: A Bibliographical Guide,* by David J. Clarke (Hong Kong Art Archive, 2004). The guide lists all the news and reports from the 1800s to 2004 related to Hong Kong art, withholding information of the sources. It is downloadable at www.aaa.org.hk/Collection/Details/12388/.

- *A History of Art in 20th Century China,* by Lu Peng (Edizioni Charta, 2010). A comprehensive and definitive account of the extraordinary development of Chinese art in the last century by its foremost expert, this book in over 1,200 pages of fully illustrated close analysis traces the evolution of modern Chinese art.

Film and Media Studies Resources

Search Strategies

- For feature films, search keywords "feature films China," "feature films Taiwan," or "feature films Hong Kong."
- For documentaries, search keywords "documentary films China," "documentary films Taiwan," or "documentary films Hong Kong."
- For TV drama, search the subject phrase "television plays, Chinese."
- Search the director as author and limit the format to "video" in the advanced search.
- For history and criticism, search "motion pictures, China" or "motion pictures, China, history."
- For popular film reviews, search a newspaper database (such as the *New York Times*) and limit the search to "review."
- For scholarly film reviews, search a scholarly database (such as JSTOR) and limit the search to "review"; for Chinese film reviews, search the China Academic Journals Database (CAJ).
- Following is a list of selected subject headings for Chinese film:
    Motion pictures—China—History
    Motion pictures—China—Reviews
    Motion pictures—China—Hong Kong
    Motion pictures—China—History—20th century
    Motion picture actors and actresses—China—Biography
    Motion picture producers and directors—China—
        Biography
    China—In motion pictures
- Following is a list of selected subject headings for Chinese media:
    Mass media—Social aspects—China
    Mass media—Political aspects—China
    Mass media and culture—China

Core Resources

- *Film and Television Literature Index.* This library database consists of a comprehensive index covering the entire spectrum of television and film writing produced for a broad target audience from film scholars to general viewers. Subject coverage includes film and television theory, preservation and restoration, writing, production, cinematography, technical aspects, and reviews.
- *International Index to Performing Arts* (IIPA). The IIPA is a comprehensive guide to the journal literature on performing arts—drama, theater, dance, film, television, and more—searchable together for the first time in one electronic database.
- *Film Literature Index* (FLI). The FLI annually indexes 150 film and television periodicals from 30 countries cover-to-cover and 200 other periodicals selectively for articles on film and television. The periodicals range from the scholarly to the popular. More than 2,000 subject headings provide detailed analysis of the articles.
- *MLA International Bibliography Online.* MLA International Bibliography offers a detailed bibliography of journal articles, books, and dissertations. Subjects consist of literature, language and linguistics, folklore, literary theory and criticism, and dramatic arts, as well as the historical aspects of printing and publishing.
- *Communication and Mass Media Complete* (CMMC). CMMC incorporates CommSearch (formerly produced by the National Communication Association) and the Mass Media Articles Index (formerly produced by Penn State), along with numerous other journals, to create a valuable research and reference resource for studies in the communication and mass media fields.
- *Communication Studies: A SAGE Full-Text Collection.* This full-text collection includes the full text of 16 journals published by SAGE and participating societies, some going back 23 years, and encompasses over 5,000 articles. It covers such subjects as journalism, public opinion, political communication, mass communication, interpersonal communication, cultural studies/intercultural communication, television/film studies, media studies, business communication, organizational/management communication, written communication, rhetoric, and literacy studies.

- Key journals:[2]

  Cinema Journal. Published by the University of Texas
  Press on behalf of the Society of Cinema and Media
  Studies, the journal publishes essays on a wide
  variety of subjects from diverse methodological
  perspectives. Research articles on Chinese cinema
  are included.

  Film Quarterly. Published since 1958, the journal provides readers analyses of film, the film industry, and
  international cinemas, including in-depth articles,
  reviews, and interviews that examine all aspects
  of film history, film theory, and the impact of film,
  video, and television on culture and society.

  PAJ: A Journal of Performing Arts. Published by the MIT
  Press on behalf of Performing Arts Journal Inc., *PAJ*
  is widely admired for its thoughtful essays and in-
  depth interviews with major international figures in
  the arts. It features artists' writings, critical commentary, interviews and dialogs, roundtable discussions,
  historical documents, book reviews, performance
  texts, and plays.

  Wide Angle. Published by Johns Hopkins University,
  the journal presents scholarship in film studies and
  examines a variety of topics ranging from international cinema to the history and aesthetics of film.
  Each issue concentrates on a single topic and offers
  extensively illustrated articles, interviews with
  prominent filmmakers, and reviews of recent books
  in the field.

  Asian Cinema. Published since 1995 by the Asian Cinema Studies Society (and now published by Intellect as part of the Film Studies journal portfolio),
  the journal presents a variety of scholarly material
  on all forms and aspects of Asian cinema, including
  research articles, interviews, book and film reviews,
  and bibliographies.

Asian Theater Journal. Published by the University of
Hawaii, the journal is dedicated to the performing
arts of Asia, focusing on both traditional and modern theatrical forms. It offers descriptive and analytical articles, original plays and play translations,
book and audiovisual reviews, and reports of current
theatrical activities in Asia.

Journal of Chinese Cinemas. Published by Intellect, the
journal is a major refereed academic publication
devoted to the study of Chinese film, drawing on
the recent worldwide growth of interest in Chinese
cinema.

China Media Research (*CMR*). An official joint publication of the American Chinese Media Research
Association and Communication Studies Institute
of Zhejiang University, this peer-reviewed journal
includes papers directly related to all the fields of
Chinese media research as well as media research
papers from any parts of the world that are useful for
media scholars within China. The journal includes
articles, book reviews, news items, letters, interviews, and other works containing information or
commentaries on relevant matters.

Chinese Journal of Communications. Interdisciplinary in
scope, this peer-reviewed journal covers all Chinese
societies in mainland China, Hong Kong, Taiwan,
Macau, Singapore, and the global Chinese diaspora.
It publishes scholarly works using social scientific
or humanistic approaches on such topics as mass
communication, journalism studies, telecommunications, rhetoric, cultural studies, media effects, new
communication technologies, organizational communication, interpersonal communication, advertising and public relations, political communication,
and communications law and policy, as well as
articles on key issues in the Chinese media industry,

including film, Internet, mobile communication, creative industry, and so on. It also includes a section for review articles.

Primary Sources

- *Asian Studies in Video* (http://alexanderstreet.com/products/asian-studies-video/). Asian Studies in Video is an online streaming video collection of nearly 600 narrative feature films, documentaries, and shorts offered through Alexander Street. It includes many award-winning films. Twenty-four countries across the region are represented, with a strong concentration on China, India, Iran, South Korea, and Southeast Asia.

- *Asia Pacific Films: An Asia Pacific Online Film Library* (www.pacificfilms.com/). Working in concert with notable scholars, critics, and curators, Asia Pacific Films streams culturally and historically significant films from Asia. The subscribed user can have access to high quality videos of films from Asia along with relevant information such as synopsis, film director, and cast, as well as reviews, essays, and interviews.

- *China Independent Documentaries Film Archive* (www.cidfa.com/video/index.php?route=common/home/). An online distributor of Chinese independent documentary films, the site provides previews of selected films produced in the PRC since 1990 with information about the films and filmmakers. Films can be purchased in DVD format with some titles streamed online.

- *Reel China: A Collection of Chinese Documentaries* (www.filmideas.com/?film=reels/). Distributed by Film Ideas: Education Through Visualization, the growing collection of Reel China consists of documentaries by China's independent filmmakers, including *The Final Migration* (2008) by Huang Lingping, *Flavor and Affinity: Behind the Scenes of Canton's Chao Restaurants* (2011) by Wang Feng, *The Graduates* (2008) by Song Gao, and others. The films can be purchased as DVDs or streamed online.

- *dGenerate Films* (http://dgeneratefilms.com/). Established in 2008 by a team of filmmakers, writers, and media innovators, dGenerate Films procures and distributes contemporary independent films from contemporary China. The site provides previews of the films with synopses and information on filmmakers.

- *Chinese Movie Database* (www.dianying.com/). This free online database for Chinese-language movies and TV programs includes three versions: in simplified Chinese, traditional Chinese, and English. It covers production, cast and production crew, reviews, and books that are related to Chinese-language movies made in mainland China, Hong Kong, and Taiwan. Coverage begins in 2006.

- *Hong Kong Movie Database* (http://hkmdb.com/db/index.php). This free online database is a good source for Hong Kong movie news, reviews, and relevant information for individual films.

- *Chinese Taipei Film Archive* (www.ctfa.org.tw/). Supported by the Taiwan government, the archive preserves classic films made by Taiwanese filmmakers and provides relevant information on the history and people of the Taiwan film industry.

- 中国电影研究资料1949–1979 (*Sources for Chinese Film Studies*), by Di Wu (Wen hua yi shu chu ban she, 2006). This three-volume collection includes primary sources on Chinese cinema during the revolutionary era, including information not only on the cinema but also on political culture of the time and its impact on the cinema.

Reference Sources and Introductory Texts

- *Media: Chinese Literature and Culture Resource Center* (http://mclc.osu.edu/rc/filmbib.htm). This free online resource maintains an up-to-date bibliography on Chinese films and filmmakers.

- *Encyclopedia of Chinese Film*, by Yingjin Zhang (Routledge, 1998). This alphabetically organized volume is the first authoritative, scholarly source on directors, genres, themes, and actors from mainland China, Hong Kong, and Taiwan. Including synopses of 300 Chinese films, the entries are heavily cross-referenced and offer, where possible, annotated suggestions for further reading.

- *An Annotated Bibliography of Chinese Film Studies*, by Jim Cheng (Hong Kong University Press, 2004). The bibliography covers a wide range of materials—including monographs, conference proceedings, and theses—that relate to film studies in and about mainland China published between 1920 and 2003.
- *The Chinese Filmography: The 2444 Feature Films Produced by Studios in the People's Republic of China from 1949 through 1995*, by Donald J. Marion (McFarland, 2008). From A to Z, this comprehensive reference work provides filmographic data on 2,444 Chinese features released since the formation of the PRC.
- *Chinese National Cinema*, by Yingjin Zhang (Routledge, 2004). This introduction to Chinese national cinema covers three "Chinas": mainland China, Hong Kong, and Taiwan. Historical and comparative perspectives bring out the parallel developments in these three Chinas, while critical analysis explores thematic and stylistic changes over time.
- *Pop Culture China! Media, Arts, and Lifestyle*, by Kevin Latham (ABC-CLIO, 2007). This book includes overview essays on various aspects of mass media and popular culture in contemporary China, including a general introduction to mass media in China and essays on television, radio, newspapers, magazines, cinema, film, video, the Internet and telecommunications, and topics on lifestyles.

---

1. In compiling this list, the author consulted the "Chinese Studies Guide" by Luo Zhou, librarian for Chinese Studies at Duke University, among other online and print sources.
2. The list only features some of the best film studies journals that have strong international coverage and are specialized in Chinese and Asian cinema. One should also consult some of the general Chinese Studies journals (see chapter 5) for scholarship on Chinese film.

Researching Humanities in Modern Chinese History

This chapter will show you:

★ General search strategies for researching modern Chinese history
★ Core resources for the discipline
★ Selected primary sources for the discipline
★ Selected reference and introductory works for the discipline

The study of modern Chinese history often falls into two subfields: the study of "modern China" (近代中国), namely, Chinese history from the late nineteenth century up to 1949, also referred to as the Late Qing and Republic Era; and the study of "contemporary China"(当代中国), Chinese history from 1949 to the present. In this chapter, we will discuss research strategies and resources for each subfield, particularly primary sources from the corresponding historical periods. We have talked about how to find Chinese archival sources in chapter 9. In this chapter, we will focus on English-language archival sources.

General Search Strategies

- For books on modern Chinese history try the following subject terms:

    China—History—Revolution, 1911–1912

China—History—Republic, 1912–

China—History—May Fourth Movement, 1919

China—History—Warlord period, 1916–1928

China—History—Northern Expedition, 1926–1928

China—History—Civil War, 1945–1949

China—History—1949–

- Or try searching keyword combinations for specific topics, such as "nationalism and China and 20th century."
- For primary sources, add subject terms "sources" (or more specifically "diaries," "interviews," "personal narratives," "archives") or "dang an" or keyword "document."

Core Resources

- *Historical Abstracts.* The Historical Abstracts database covers the history of the world (excluding the United States and Canada) from 1450 to the present, including world history, military history, women's history, history of education, and more. The database indexes more than 1,700 academic historical journals in over 40 languages back to 1955. The most unique feature of the database is that it allows the user to limit a search to a certain historical period. For example, for sources on "Chinese revolution during the 20th century," we can do a keyword search on "China and revolution" and limit the search to the historical period from year "1900 AD" to year "2000 AD."
- *National Index to Chinese Newspapers and Periodicals* (NICNP). The NICNP is the largest Chinese newspaper and periodical online index database created by the Shanghai Library. It covers the period from 1857 to the present, with 15,000,000 items from 15,000 newspapers and periodicals published in mainland China, Hong Kong, and Taiwan (see chapter 9).
- Key journals in modern Chinese history:
    East Asian History (Australia). Published twice a year, this peer-reviewed journal covers any topic of historical significance in East Asia.

Modern China (UCLA). This journal is an indispensable source for scholarship on history from late imperial China to the present.

Twentieth Century China (formerly *Republican China*). This peer-reviewed journal specializes in Chinese history from 1911 to 1949.

Journal of Modern Chinese History (Routledge, in collaboration with the Institute of Modern Chinese History, CASS Beijing). This is an international journal that provides a platform for scholars from China and other parts of the world to exchange ideas on the history of Chinese society, foreign affairs, and gender, as well as regional research and historiography.

The Chinese Historical Review (formerly *Chinese Historians*). A fully refereed and vigorously edited transnational journal of history, the journal publishes original research on the history of China in every period, China's historical relations with the world, the historical experiences of the overseas Chinese, as well as comparative studies of history.

Late Imperial China (formerly *Ch'ing shih wen-t'i*) (Johns Hopkins University). The principal journal for scholars of China's Ming and Qing dynasties, *Late Imperial China* presents scholarly work in political and intellectual history and social, economic, cultural, and gender history as well as historical demography, art history, religious studies, philosophy, and literature.

二十一世纪 (*Twenty-first Century*) (Hong Kong) (in Chinese). An intellectual journal published in Hong Kong, it played a significant role in intellectual debates in mainland China in the 1990s and continues to cover all aspects of modern and contemporary China.

中国史研究动态 (*Trends of Recent Researches on the History of China*) (Beijing) (in Chinese). This Chinese academic journal reviews the latest scholarship in Chinese history from antiquity to the present.[1]

Primary Sources[2]

Contemporary China (1949–Present)

Chinese-Language Sources

- *People's Daily* (1946–). As the official organ of the Chinese government, the *People's Daily* has comprehensive coverage of China's social, economic, and political affairs.
- *PLA Daily* (1956–). As the official newspaper of the People's Liberation Army (PLA), the *PLA Daily* is the authoritative source on Chinese military matters.
- *CNKI—Chinese Core Newspapers Full-Text Database*. The database includes full-text content of more than 1,000 Chinese newspapers published in mainland China since 2000. Free index search at www.cnki.net/ (click on 报纸).
- *CNKI—Chinese Government Documents Full-Text Database*. The database includes Chinese government documents of all levels. Free index search at www.cnki.net/ (click on 政报).
- *Chinese Cultural Revolution Database*. This digital archive contains historical materials related to the Cultural Revolution, including Chinese Communist Party documents, speeches, and writings by party leaders and media commentaries.

English-Language Sources

- *World News Connection* (1996–). WNC is a US government service that offers translated news from around the world, including major media sources from the PRC.
- *Foreign Office Files for China, 1949–1980*. The archives from the British Foreign Office covers a crucial period of Chinese history from the foundation of the People's Republic in 1949 to the death of Zhou Enlai and Mao, the arrest of the Gang of Four, and the end of the Cultural Revolution in 1976. The digitized archive is distributed by Adam Mathew Digital.

- *China and the United States: From Hostility to Engagement, 1960–1998.* Part of the Digital National Security Archive (DNSA), this archive includes over 2,000 digitized documents from various government agencies (such as the State Department, Defense Department, Commerce Department, CIA, Defense Intelligence Agency, etc.) concerning the relationship between the United States and China, with an emphasis on the 1969–1998 time period.
- *Records of the National Council for United States–China Trade 1973–1983.* Part of Gale's Archives Unbound, this digital archive documents the formation of the National Council for United States–China Trade and its role in the development of US-China trade and the council's library holdings relating to China's trade and economy.
- *Tiananmen Square and US-China Relations, 1989–1993.* Part of Gale's Archives Unbound, this digital archive includes documents from the White House Office of Records Management (WHORM) subject file categories and the staff and office files relating to the 1989 Tiananmen Square demonstrations and US-China relations during that time and afterward.
- *US Intelligence and China Collection, Analysis, and Covert Action.* Part of the DNSA, this database is a compilation of digitized declassified documents from various government agencies (such as the CIA, Department of State, US Army, US Embassy in Taiwan, Director of Central Intelligence, etc.) concerning US intelligence activities directed at both the People's Republic of China and Taiwan.
- *The Amerasia Affair, China and Postwar Anti-Communist Fervor* (1945–1973). Part of Gale's Archives Unbound, this digital archive of government sources documents the perceptions of espionage and inner workings of the postwar anticommunist movement in the United States.
- *China Political Reports 1911–1960,* edited by Robert J. Jarman (Cambridge Archives Editions, 2009). This 11-volume set of archives covers the history of the rise of communism in China and its effects over more than half a century.

- *China Political Reports 1961–1970*, edited by Robert J. Jarman (Cambridge Archives Editions, 2003). This three-volume set of archives covers the history of the "Great Leap Forward," "Great Proletarian Cultural Revolution," and huge foreign relations disputes that grew out of the complications of the Cold War.
- *The Kissinger Transcripts: The Top Secret Talks with Beijing and Moscow*, by Henry Kissinger and William Burr (New Press, 1999). This declassified collection includes Kissinger's talks with Mao Zedong, Zhou Enlai, Deng Xiaoping, Leonid Brezhnev, Andrei Gromyko, Richard Nixon, Gerald Ford, George Bush, and others.
- *Tracking the Dragon National Intelligence Estimates on China during the Era of Mao, 1948–1976*, by Robert L. Hutchings (GPO, 2004). This long-classified National Intelligence Estimates on China includes a comprehensive collection of more than 70 National Intelligence Estimates covering the Mao era (1948–1976) in China.
- *The China Reader: The Reform Era*, by Orville Schell and David L. Shambaugh (Vintage Books, 1999). This volume includes some of the most important documents, articles, and statements on China from 1972 to the present, from regulations to control Chinese cyberspace to a Party member's Orwellian justification of the military crackdown in Tiananmen Square.
- *Twentieth Century China: A History in Documents*, by R. Keith Schoppa (Oxford University Press, 2004). The book chronicles the history of twentieth-century China with a wide variety of primary sources, including official reports and public statements, articles, political posters, cartoons, poetry, songs, and advertisements.
- *The Chinese Human Rights Reader: Documents and Commentary, 1900–2000*, by Stephen C. Angle and Marina Svensson (M. E. Sharpe, 2001). Includes translations of 60 selections from China's twentieth-century human rights discourse along with commentary on the context.
- *China Since 1919—Revolution and Reform: A Sourcebook*, by Alan Lawrance (Routledge, 2004). Includes over 150 extracts from political statements, telegrams, speeches, memoirs, letters, and poems that illuminate the historical development of China.

- *Mao Zedong and China's Revolutions: A Brief History with Documents*, by Timothy Cheek (Bedford/St. Martin's, 2002). Includes an introductory essay that traces the history of twentieth-century China and a selection of Mao's writings and writings about Mao and his legacy by both his contemporaries and modern scholars.
- *The Great Famine in China, 1958–1962: A Documentary History*, by Xun Zhou (Yale University Press, 2012). Contains the most crucial primary documents concerning the fate of the Chinese peasantry between 1957 and 1962. It covers everything from collectivization and survival strategies, including cannibalism, to selective killing and mass murder.
- *Sources in Chinese History: Diverse Perspectives from 1644 to the Present*, by David G. Atwill and Yurong Y. Atwill (Pearson/Prentice Hall, 2010). Each chapter examines a key event, personage, or theme with an introductory essay and selection of primary sources.

Modern China (Late Nineteenth Century–1949)

CHINESE-LANGUAGE SOURCES

- *Shen Bao* (1872–1949). The database contains the full-text articles in the most important Chinese newspapers from the Republic Era.
- 民国时期社会调查丛编 (*Social Surveys in Republic Era*) (2004–) (ten titles in the original series) and 民国时期社会调查丛编 (*Social Surveys in Republic Era*, 2nd ed.) （二编） (12 titles in the follow-up series) (2009–), by Wenhai Li et al. (Fujian jiao yu chu ban she). Contains a comprehensive collection of primary sources from early twentieth-century China (the Republic Era).

ENGLISH-LANGUAGE SOURCES

- *North China Herald* (1850–1940s). The most important English-language newspaper published in Shanghai, the *North China Herald* is the prime source for foreign presence in China during the Republic Era.

- *Asia and the West: Diplomacy and Cultural Exchange* (nineteenth century). Part of Nineteenth Century Online, this database includes an archival collection of records of Western (British and American) interaction with a number of Asian countries including China and Japan during the nineteenth century.
- *China: Trade, Politics and Culture, 1793–1980.* This digital collection provides a wide variety of original source material detailing China's interaction with the West from Macartney's first Embassy to China in 1793 through to the Nixon/Heath visits to China in 1972–1974, primarily from the School of Oriental and African Studies and the British Library as well as a few other libraries and archives in the UK and United States.
- *China: Culture and Society.* This digital collection includes pamphlets from the Charles W. Wason Collection on East Asia in the Carl A. Kroch Library of Cornell University. Mostly in English and published between circa 1750 and 1929, these rare pamphlets form part of one of the deepest and most extensive collections of literature on China and the Chinese in the Western world and constitute a rich resource for scholars and teachers in numerous disciplines.
- *Policing the Shanghai International Settlement, 1894–1945.* Part of Gale's Archives Unbound, this digital collection includes archives of the British-run municipal police force based in Shanghai's former International Settlement.
- *Political, Economic, and Military Conditions in China: Reports and Correspondence of the U.S. Military Intelligence Division, 1918– 1941.* Part of Gale's Archives Unbound, this digital collection reproduces the six principal MID files relating exclusively to China for the period 1918 to 1941 (general conditions, political conditions, economic conditions, army, navy, and aeronautics).
- *Political Relations and Conflict between Republican China and Imperial Japan, 1930–1939: Records of the U.S. State Department.* Part of Gale's Archives Unbound, this digital collection includes records on the Japanese occupation of Manchuria beginning with the Mukden incident in 1931, military action at Shanghai in 1932, further Japanese political and economic penetration into China

from 1935 to 1936, and the course of the undeclared war between Japan and China from 1937 to 1939.

- *The Chinese Civil War and U.S.-China Relations: Records of the U.S. State Department's Office of Chinese Affairs, 1945–1955.* Part of Gale's Archives Unbound, this declassified archive by the State Department provides valuable insight into numerous domestic issues in Communist and Nationalist China and US containment policy.
- *The Chronicles of the East India Company Trading to China 1635– 1834*, by Horsea Ballow Morse (Global Oriental, 2007). This five-volume set is a comprehensive survey based on primary sources and covers in detail every aspect of the conditions of trade between the West and China in the crucial 200 years before the start of the Opium Wars and the imposition of unequal treaties.

Reference Sources and Introductory Texts

- *Historical Dictionary of the People's Republic of China*, by Lawrence R. Sullivan (Scarecrow Press, 2007). Contains more than 400 cross-referenced dictionary entries on individual topics spanning China's political, economic, and social system along with short biographies on important figures—from politicians to writers and movie directors—who have shaped Chinese history during the period of Communist rule from 1949 to 2006.
- *Columbia Guide to Modern Chinese History*, by R. Keith Shoppa (Columbia University Press, 2000). A concise beginner's guide to Chinese history since 1780, this book includes historical narratives, an annotated bibliography, and other helpful information such as a chronology, key figures, and more.
- *Modern China: A Guide to a Century of Change*, by Graham Hutchings (Harvard University Press, 2001). A useful reference guide to the people, places, ideas, and events crucial to an understanding of modern China, the book provides over 200 insightful short essays, arranged alphabetically, that cover central figures and events from Sun Yat-sen to Jiang Zemin and the Boxer Rebellion to Tiananmen Square.

- *Search for Modern China*, by Jonathan D. Spence (Norton, 1999); *The Search for Modern China: A Documentary Collection*, by Pei-kai Cheng, Michael Lestz, and Jonathan Spence (Norton, 1999). *Search for Modern China* is a widely acclaimed survey of modern China from the sixteenth century to 1989 by Professor Spence, a renowned American scholar of Chinese history. Many sources in the companion documentary collection were translated into English for the first time.

- *State and Economy in Republican China: A Handbook for Scholars*, by William C. Kirby (Harvard University Asia Center, 2000).

- *Chinese History: A Manual*, by Endymion Wilkinson (Harvard University Asia Center, 2000). Since its initial publication in 1998, the book has become an indispensable guide to researching the civilization and history of China. This revised and enlarged second edition discusses some 4,300 primary, secondary, and reference works.

- *A Research Guide to China-Coast Newspapers, 1822–1911*, by Frank H. H. King (Harvard University Press, 1965). This is an essential guide to newspapers published in late Qing.

---

1. There are many Chinese academic journals for historical studies, such as 历史研究, 中国史研究, 近代史研究, 当代中国史研究, etc. They are all included in the CNKI database. For a complete list of core Chinese journals for historical studies, see the website of the Chinese Academy of Social Sciences at http://ich.cass.cn/Article_Show.asp?ArticleID=328/.

2. The list focuses on digitized archival materials in English. It also includes some major Chinese newspapers and other print archival sources that have wide coverage, thus being potentially useful for different research topics. For a more complete list of print primary sources, search WorldCat with subject terms "China, history, sources." For archival sources in China, see chapter 9 on Chinese archives.

Researching Humanities in Literature, Philosophy, and Religion

This chapter will show you:

★ Core resources for researching modern Chinese literature
★ Core resources for researching Chinese philosophy and religion
★ Selected primary sources for the disciplines
★ Selected reference and introductory works for the disciplines

C hinese philosophy and religion have long been the staples in traditional Sinology. On the other hand, there had been no serious study of modern Chinese literature until 1961, when *History of Modern Chinese Fiction* by C. T. Hsia, professor emeritus of Columbia University, was first published. This classic, pioneering work examined Chinese literary works from the literary revolution of 1917 through the Cultural Revolution of 1966–1976, and introduced major Chinese writers such as Lun Xun and Eileen Zhang to Western academia. Half a century later, the world has seen two Chinese-language writers winning the Nobel Prize in Literature: Gao Xingjian in 2000 and Mo Yan in 2012. The study of modern Chinese literature has not only taken root in Western academia but also thrives on the abundance of research resources available. We will discuss a few major resources as well as research strategies.

Modern Chinese Literature

Search Strategies

- For Chinese literary works, search the author, if known, or search subject terms "China, fiction" or "China, poetry."
- For translated Chinese works, add the subject term "translations."
- For literary history and criticism, search the subject term "Chinese literature, history and criticism."
- Following is a list of selected subject headings on Chinese literature:
    Chinese literature—History and criticism
    Chinese literature—Bibliography
    Comparative literature—Chinese and Western
    Chinese literature—History and criticism—Theory, etc.
    Chinese literature—20th century—History and criticism
    Chinese literature—Periodicals
    Chinese literature—Translations into English
    Buddhist literature, Chinese—History and criticism
    Comparative literature—Chinese and English
    Chinese literature—Philosophy
    Literature—Dictionaries—Chinese
    Folk literature, Chinese—History and criticism
    Chinese literature—20th century—Periodicals
    Chinese literature—Taiwan—History and criticism
    Chinese literature—20th century—History and criticism—Periodicals
    Reportage literature, Chinese—History and criticism
    Comparative literature—Western and Chinese
    Chinese literature—Minority authors—History and criticism
    Chinese prose literature—Women authors
    Chinese literature—Women authors—History and criticism

Core Resources

- MLA International Bibliography. The most important tool for literary research, MLA International Bibliography offers worldwide coverage of journal articles, books, and dissertations on literature and more.
- Literature Criticism Online. This database brings together most of the popular Gale literary criticism series, including Contemporary Literary Criticism, Twentieth-Century Literary Criticism, Nineteenth-Century Literary Criticism, and others. Depending on the library subscription, it can be cross-searched with Dictionary of Literary Biography Complete Online. It covers many of the major modern and contemporary Chinese authors.
- Key journals:

    Modern Chinese Literature and Culture (formerly *Modern Chinese Literature*). *Modern Chinese Literature and Culture* is a peer-reviewed scholarly journal devoted to the culture of modern and contemporary China. The journal publishes on literature of all genres, film and television, popular culture, performance and visual art, print and material culture, and so on.

    Chinese Literature Today (Oklahoma). Publishes high-quality English translations of the best Chinese literature and critical essays.

    Frontiers of Literary Studies in China (edited by Xudong Zhang). This new journal aims to showcase significant, innovative literary scholarship from China and abroad.

    Journal of Modern Literature in Chinese (Hong Kong). A bilingual journal published twice a year by the Centre for Humanities Research, Lingnan University, this journal provides a forum for discussing issues related to any aspect of modern or contemporary literature in Chinese.

Renditions (Hong Kong). This is a leading journal that publishes translations of Chinese literary works from antiquity to the present.

Primary Sources[1]

- *The Columbia Anthology of Modern Chinese Literature,* by Joseph S. M. Lau and Howard Goldblatt (Columbia University Press, 2007). This new edition of an authoritative source of translated Chinese literature provides an up-to-date, complete overview of twentieth-century writings from China, Taiwan, and Hong Kong, with additional samplings of literary works from the twenty-first century.
- *Modern Chinese Stories and Novellas, 1919—1949,* by Joseph S. M. Lau et al. (Columbia University Press, 1981). This anthology brings together some of the short fiction by the most important authors in the history of modern Chinese literature, such as Lu Xun, Mao Dun, Ding Ling, and Shen Congwen.
- *The Lost Boat: Avant-Garde Fiction from China,* by Yiheng Zhao (Wellsweep, 1993); *China's Avant-Garde Fiction: An Anthology,* by Jing Wang (Duke University Press, 1998). These two anthologies collect in translation some of the most innovative literary works produced in the PRC in the late 1980s.
- *Selected Stories by Mo Yan,* Chinese-English Bilingual Edition, translated by Howard Goldblatt (Chinese University of Hong Kong Press, 2011). This book offers a selection of short stories by the 2012 Nobel Literature Award winner, translated by the best translator of Chinese literary works.
- *The Real Story of Ah-Q and Other Tales of China: The Complete Fiction of Lu Xun,* translated by Julia Lovell (Penguin, 2009). These are representative works by Lu Xun, arguably the most important writer of modern China and seen by many as the father of modern Chinese literature.
- *I Love Dollars and Other Stories of China,* by Wen Zhu, translated by Julia Lovell (Columbia University Press, 2007). This collection of stories by contemporary Chinese author Wen Zhu

represents a new generation of Chinese writers growing up in post-revolutionary China and depicts the violence and chaos of China in the middle of fundamental social and cultural changes.

- *Women Writers of Traditional China: An Anthology of Poetry and Criticism*, by Kang-i Sun Chang, Haun Saussy, and Charles Yim-tze Kwong (Stanford University Press, 1999). This anthology of Chinese women's poetry in translation brings together representative selections from the work of some 130 poets from the Han Dynasty to the early twentieth century.

- *Women Writers in Modern China: An Anthology of Women's Literature from the Early Twentieth Century*, by Amy D. Dooling and Kristina M. Torgeson (Columbia University Press, 1998); *Writing Women in Modern China: The Revolution Years, 1936–1976*, by Amy D. Dooling (Columbia University Press, 2004). These two complementary anthologies highlight works by Chinese women writers from the early and middle twentieth century, with critical introductions and biographical information on the writers.

- *Women of Red Plain: An Anthology of Contemporary Chinese Women's Poetry*, by Julia Lin (Penguin, 1992). The anthology includes selections from the works of a wide range and diversity of women poets, from the pioneering Bing Xin and Lin Huiyin, who were writing at the birth of New Poetry in the early 1920s, to the experimental poets from both mainland China and Taiwan in the 1980s and 1990s, who were writing with an increasing feminist consciousness. In total, the anthology collects 245 representative poems of 16 women poets from mainland China and 24 from Taiwan.

- *Modern Chinese Literary Thought: Writings on Literature, 1893–1945*, by Kirk Denton (Stanford University Press, 1996). This collection of translated essays provides an important cultural context for Chinese literature produced at the inception of Chinese modernity.

- *Chinese Writers on Writing*, by Arthur Sze (Trinity University Press, 2010). This collection brings together Chinese writers' reflections on their writings and working under the Chinese political system.

- *May Fourth Women Writers: Memoirs*, by Janet Ng and Janice Wickeri (Chinese University of Hong Kong, 1996). This is a translated collection of memoirs by Chinese women writers from the early twentieth century.

Reference Sources and Introductory Texts

- *Modern Chinese Literature and Culture Resource Center: Literature Resources* (http://mclc.osu.edu/rc/lit.htm). Maintained by Kirk A. Denton at Ohio State University, this free online resource covers bibliographies that comprise published (both print and electronic) materials related to modern Chinese literature. They include (1) translations (mostly in English) organized by author and by thematic collections; (2) general studies (organized by period, theme, and genre); (3) studies of particular authors; (4) important reference works; (5) MCLC biographies of modern Chinese authors; (6) Lu Xun studies; and (7) links to works of Chinese literature in Chinese.

- *Historical Dictionary of Modern Chinese Literature*, by Li-hua Ying (Scarecrow Press, 2010). Includes an introduction, bibliography, and dictionary of key authors and terms.

- 中国现代文学研究网 (www.modernchineseliterature.net/). A project by the Department of Chinese Language and Literature and the Libraries, Chinese University of Hong Kong, in collaboration with major universities in mainland China, this free web resource brings together modern Chinese literary study resources from all over China and provides a research platform for easy access. It indexes a wide range of sources, including journal articles, books, dissertations, in Chinese, English, and Japanese. It also includes a bibliography of modern Chinese writers with biographical information and lists of their works.

- 香港文学资料库 (http://hklitpub.lib.cuhk.edu.hk/index.jsp). This free web resource is developed and maintained by the Chinese University of Hong Kong. It includes biographies of major Hong Kong authors and lists of their works, in addition to interviews, commentaries, criticism, and many other relevant materials.

- *Bibliography of English Translations and Critiques of Contemporary Chinese Fiction, 1945–1992*, by Kam Louie and Louise Edwards

(Taiwan Center for Chinese Studies, 1993). The bibliography covers translations of fiction and literary criticism from mainland China, Taiwan, and Hong Kong.

- *Chinese Drama: An Annotated Bibliography of Commentary, Criticism, and Plays in English Translation*, by Manuel D. Lopez (Scarecrow Press, 1991). This is an annotated bibliography of commentary, criticism, and translated Chinese plays.

Chinese Philosophy and Religion

Search Strategies

- For sources on a Chinese religion, try a subject search on "[name of a religion]" and "China."
- Or try a keyword search on a topic (such as "nationalism"), plus the name of the religion.
- For primary sources, search subject terms "China, religion, sources" or "Chinese philosophy, sources."
- Following is a list of selected subject headings:
    Philosophy—China
    Philosophy—China—History
    Law—China—Philosophy—History
    Education—China—Philosophy—History
    Music—China—Philosophy and aesthetics
    Philosophy, Confucian—China
    Philosophy, Marxist—China
    Philosophy—Dictionaries—Chinese
    Philosophy, Chinese—History
    Philosophy, Chinese—20th century
    China—Religion
    Religion and state—China
    Minorities—China—Religion
    Religion and politics—China
    Freedom of religion—China

Core Resources

- *ATLA Religion Database.* This database is a collection of major religion and theology journals selected by some of the major religion scholars in the United States. The focus of the database is on Christianity but it also covers religions worldwide. The coverage of this database dates back to 1949.
- *The Philosopher's Index.* The world's most current and comprehensive bibliography of scholarly research in philosophy, the index contains more than 485,000 journal articles and book citations drawn from over 1,400 journals, originating from 85 countries in 39 languages. The literature coverage dates back to 1940 and includes print and electronic journals, books, anthologies, contributions to anthologies, and book reviews.
- Key journals:
    - *Dao: A Journal of Comparative Philosophy.* The official publication of Association of Chinese Philosophers in America, it features studies in Chinese philosophy and religion from a comparative perspective.
    - Journal of Chinese Philosophy. Based at the University of Hawaii, the journal publishes the comparative studies of scholars in East and West on Confucianism and Neo-Confucianism, Daoism and Neo-Daoism, Chinese Buddhism, Yijing philosophy, modern and contemporary Chinese philosophy, Chinese philosophy of language, logic and science, Chinese social and political philosophy, and Chinese aesthetics.
    - *Journal of Chinese Religions.* Published by Society for the Study of Chinese Religions, the journal features studies on all aspects of Chinese religions.

Primary Sources

- *Tibetan Buddhist Resource Center* (http://tbrc.org/#home/). A digital library of primary sources of Tibetan Buddhism, this searchable database includes Buddhist scriptures, histories, and biographies and other relevant materials.

- *Digital Archive of Chinese Buddhist Temple Local Gazetteers* (http:// buddhistinformatics.ddbc.edu.tw/fosizhi/). Created by Dharma Drum Buddhist College, Taiwan, and funded by Chung-Hwa Institute of Buddhist Studies, this archive aims to tap into the wealth of information contained in local gazetteers to deepen our understanding of Buddhist history. Currently, 237 gazetteers have been digitized, 13 of which are digitized as full-text archives and marked up with TEI/XML, identifying all person and place names as well as dates.
- *Digital Library and Museum of Buddhist Studies* (http://buddhism .lib.ntu.edu.tw/BDLM/). A project by College of Liberal Arts, National Taiwan University, this website includes a wide variety of research materials for Buddhist Studies, including Buddhist scriptures, bibliographies, journal articles, and more.
- *Buddhist Studies: Electronic Resources* (www.ciolek.com/WWWVL Pages/BuddhPages/EResources.html). This free online resource covers academic research, bibliographies, biographies, directories, Buddhist e-texts (sutra transcripts and translations), poetry, ritual, teachings, and thesis abstracts. The site offers a unique collection of five transcripts of unpublished English-language teachings and sermons by the twentieth-century Zen masters.
- *The Berzin Archives* (www.berzinarchives.com/web/en/index.html). The Berzin Archives is a collection of translations and teachings by Alexander Berzin, primarily on the Mahayana and Vajrayana traditions of Tibetan Buddhism. With coverage on areas of sutra, tantra, Kalachakra, dzogchen, and mahamudra meditation, the archive presents materials from all five Tibetan traditions— Nyingma, Sakya, Kagyu, Gelug, and Bon—as well as comparisons with Theravada Buddhism and Islam. Also featured are Tibetan astrology and medicine, Shambhala, and Buddhist history.
- *Chinese Buddhist Electronic Text Association* (www.cbeta.org/ index.htm). CBETA provides free access to Chinese Buddhist texts electronically, on the Web and through CDs. Currently, its digital collection is based on Taisho Tripikata volumes 1–85 and Shinsan Zokuzokyo volumes 1–90.

- *Chinese Philosophical Etext Archive* (http://sangle.web.wesleyan.edu/etext/). Based at Wesleyan University, this free web resource includes Chinese philosophical texts from pre-Qin to the Republic Era.
- *Chinese Religion: An Anthology of Sources*, by Deborah Sommer (Oxford University Press, 1995). Covers a broad range of primary sources from antiquity to the modern era, from Taoism and Confucianism to Communism.
- *A Sourcebook of Chinese Philosophy*, by Wing-tsit Chan (Princeton University Press, 1962). The first anthology of Chinese philosophy to cover its entire historical development, the sourcebook provides substantial selections from all the great thinkers and schools in every period—ancient, medieval, modern, and contemporary—and includes in their entirety some of the most important classical texts. It deals with the fundamental and technical as well as the more general aspects of Chinese thought.

Reference and Introductory Works

- *Routledge Encyclopedia of Philosophy*. Available both in print and online, the *Routledge Encyclopedia of Philosophy* includes thousands of entries written by scholars on Anglo-American, ethical and political, cross-cultural, interdisciplinary, continental, and contemporary philosophies.
- *Stanford Encyclopedia of Philosophy*. The *Stanford Encyclopedia of Philosophy* is a dynamic reference work and an open access publishing project at Stanford University. The encyclopedia comprises scholarly entries by leading scholars in the field and is growing continually. It covers philosophies worldwide.
- *Routledge Religion Online*. This database includes a full-text searchable collection of encyclopedias, dictionaries, and other texts on world religions. It offers a great starting point for researching on anything from Confucianism to Hinduism and much more. It includes the *Encyclopedia of Buddhism* by Damien Keown et al., the *Encyclopedia of Taoism* by Fabrizio Pregadio, and the *Routledge Curzon Encyclopedia of Confucianism* by Xinzhong Yao.

- *Religious Freedom in China: Policy, Administration, Regulations: A Research Handbook,* by Kim Kwong Chan et al. (SourceNet, 2005). A useful guide to finding legal sources on religions in China, this handbook explains the legal hierarchy of the Chinese system of law, policy, and administration (i.e., the constitution, congress, state council, etc.) in the first section. The second section gives a short historical overview from 1982 to the present. The last section contains hundreds of annotated entries and citations broken down by province.
- *Encyclopedia of Asian Philosophy,* edited by Oliver Leaman (Routledge, 2001). Structured from A to Z, this encyclopedia incorporates cultural and religious contexts and provides a vital guide to the main concepts and thinkers in Asian philosophy.
- *Encyclopedia of Chinese Philosophy,* edited by Antonio S. Cua (Routledge, 2002). This encyclopedia covers the complex and increasingly influential field of Chinese thought from earliest recorded times to the present day, with highlights on the extensive range of concepts, movements, philosophical works, and thinkers populating the field. It includes a thorough survey of the history of Chinese philosophy; entries on all major thinkers from Confucius to Mou Zongsan; essential topics such as aesthetics, moral philosophy, philosophy of government, and philosophy of literature; surveys of Confucianism in all historical periods; trends in contemporary Chinese philosophy; and more.
- *Chinese Religion in Western Languages* (Association of Asian Studies, 1985). This is a comprehensive and classified bibliography of publications in English, French, and German through 1980.
- *Chinese Religion: Publications in Western Languages, 1981 through 1990* (Association of Asian Studies, 1993). This is a supplementary volume to *Chinese Religion in Western Languages.*
- *Chinese Religion: Publications in Western Languages* (Association of Asian Studies, 1999). This is a supplement to *Chinese Religions: Publications in Western Languages, 1981 through 1990.*
- *Christianity in China: A Scholars' Guide to Resources in the Libraries and Archives of the United States,* by Xiaoxin Wu (M. E. Sharpe,

2009). Provides a thorough introduction and guide to the primary and secondary sources produced by and about Christian enterprises and individuals in China that are preserved in hundreds of primary repositories in the United States.

- *Reference Guide to Christian Missionary Societies in China: From the Sixteenth to the Twentieth Century,* by R. G. Tiedemann (M. E. Sharpe, 2009). This comprehensive guide includes nearly 500 entries identifying both Roman Catholic and Protestant missionary-sending agencies and related religious congregations that played a part in the historical interaction of Christianity and Chinese society prior to 1950.

---

1. This is a list of major anthologies of modern Chinese literature in translation and collections of translated literary primary sources that are representative of modern Chinese literature at different historical periods. For a more complete list of translated Chinese literary works, search WorldCat with "China, fiction, translations" or by the author's name plus "translations"; for literary works in Chinese, just search "China, fiction" and limit the language to "Chinese."
2. For more of Mo Yan's works in translation, search "mo yan, translations."

Researching Social Sciences in Anthropology, Sociology, and Education

> **This chapter will show you:**
> ★ Core resources for the social sciences
> ★ Core resources for anthropology, sociology, and education
> ★ Primary sources for the subject fields
> ★ Reference sources and introductory texts for the subject fields

For social scientists, the biggest challenge is to obtain reliable data, which are the foundation of any scientific inqury. Prior to the early 1980s, obtaining reliable data from China was all but impossible, given the hostility between China and the West during the Cold War. Only toward the end of the 1980s, when China opened its doors to the outside world, did the situation start to improve for China researchers in the West. Today, travel to China to do fieldwork is commonplace, and information resources keep growing. This does not mean, however, that obtaining reliable data is no longer a challenge. The improved access to information has led to a fundamental change in China Studies scholarship. In the past, when information was scarce, social scientists had to content themselves with a "macro approach," using whatever data were available to study China and its social and political institutions on a large scale. Now with more refined, detailed information available, it is possible to take a "micro approach" and conduct more nuanced studies of smaller groups and localities. This results in two trends in the use of information among social scientists: the increased reliance on (1) digital resources, because very few libraries outside of China can afford to build an extensive collection of print sources on Chinese localities (such as local gazetteers), and (2) Chinese-language sources, because very little local data are available in English. In this chapter, we will introduce some of the major databases for social sciences as well as major Chinese data sources.

Core Resources for the Social Sciences

- *Social Sciences Citation Index* (SSCI). Social Sciences Citation Index, accessed via Web of Science, provides researchers with quick, powerful access to the bibliographic and citation information they need to find research data, analyze trends, journals, and researchers, and share their findings. It includes essential data from 2,474 of the world's leading social sciences journals across 50 disciplines.
- *Social Sciences Full Text.* Social Sciences Full Text covers English-language periodicals published in the United States or internationally in sociology, anthropology, psychology, geography, economics, political science, and law. Indexes material from 1983 to the present, includes abstracts for material from 1984 to the present, and contains some full text for material from 1994 to present.
- *International Bibliography of the Social Sciences* (IBSS). IBSS includes over two million bibliographic references to journal articles and to books, reviews, and selected chapters dating back to 1951. It is unique in its broad coverage of international material and incorporates over 100 languages and countries.
- *Bibliography of Asian Studies Online* (BAS). BAS covers all subjects pertaining to Asia published worldwide from 1971 to the present. (See chapter 5 for more information.)
- *China Academic Journals Full-text Database* (CAJ). A primary source of Chinese scholarship, CAJ includes all subject fields in the social sciences. (See chapter 6 for more information.)
- *Duxiu.* A comprehensive database for Chinese scholarship from a wide variety of sources, Duxiu is especially strong in its digital collection of Chinese books. (See chapter 4 for more information.)

Anthropology Resources

Search Strategies

- For a general search for books on anthropology in China, try subject terms "ethnology, China" or "China, social life and customs."
- For a specific people or location in China, add the people's name (such as Naxi) or place name (such as Yunnan).
- For ethnographies that are based on firsthand observation of a particular social or cultural or ethnic group, search by the group's name (such as Naxi).
- Following is a list of selected subject headings relevant to Chinese anthropology:

  Anthropology—China
  Ethnology—China
  Ethnology—China—Periodicals
  Ethnology—China—History
  Ethnology—China—Xinjiang Uygur Zizhiqu
  Ethnology—China—Sichuan Sheng
  Ethnology—China—Yunnan Sheng
  Ethnology—China—Manchuria
  Ethnology—China—Guizhou Sheng
  Ethnology—China, Southwest
  Ethnology—China—Tibet Autonomous Region
  China—Social life and customs
  Minorities—China—Social life and customs
  China—Race relations
  Tibet Autonomous Region (China)—Social life and customs

Core Resources

- *Anthropology Plus*. Uniting Harvard University's highly respected Anthropological Literature database and the United Kingdom's Anthropological Index (Royal Anthropological Institute), Anthropology Plus is the world's most comprehensive, focused index of bibliographic materials from the late 1800s to today in the fields of social, cultural, physical, biological, and linguistic anthropology; ethnology, archaeology, folklore, and material culture; and interdisciplinary studies.

- *AnthroSource.* AnthroSource includes the full text of current and legacy content from journals published by the American Anthropological Association. It provides access to more than 100 years of anthropological knowledge.
- *Anthropology Review Database* (ARD). Published online by the University of Buffalo, ARD is a database of signed, refereed reviews covering the entire gamut of anthropological publications, including books, audiovisual materials, software and multimedia, exhibits, tourist sites, conferences, and online resources.
- Key journals:

  Annual Review of Anthropology. This review journal critically reviews the most significant primary research literature and helps us keep up-to-date in our area of research.

  Reviews in Anthropology. This is another journal dedicated to reviewing current research in the field.

  Asian Anthropology (Hong Kong). While editorially based in Hong Kong, *Asian Anthropology* publishes scholarly work from anthropologists and anthropology-related scholars throughout the world with an interest in Asia. It also publishes English translations of the best Chinese anthropological scholarship.

  Chinese Sociology and Anthropology. From M. E. Sharpe, this is an academic journal that publishes unabridged translations of important articles originally published in journals and article collections in book format in the PRC.

Primary Sources[1]

- *Ethnographical Video Online* (I and II). Ethnographic Video Online provides the largest, most comprehensive resource for the study of human culture and behavior—more than 750 hours and 1,000 films at completion. The collection covers every region of the world and features the work of many of the most influential documentary filmmakers of the twentieth century, including interviews, previously unreleased raw footage, field notes, study guides, and more. Currently, it includes 14 videos about China. The recently published second edition (2012) adds another 500 hours of video, including an Asian Pacific Film collection.

- *eHRAF World Cultures.* This online cross-cultural database contains information on all aspects of cultural and social life. Each culture or ethnic group contains a variety of source documents (books, articles, and dissertations) that have been indexed and organized according to HRAF's comprehensive culture and subject classification systems: the Outline of World Cultures and the Outline of Cultural Materials (OCM). These retrieval systems extend search capability well beyond keyword searching, thus allowing for precise culture and subject retrieval even in a foreign language.

- 中国地方志民俗资料汇编 (*Sources of Folk Culture from Chinese Local Gazetteers*), by Shiliang Ding (Shu mu wen xian chu ban she, 1989–). This six-volume print collection includes materials that record folk cultures from thousands of local gazetteers from all parts of China.

- 民国时期社会调查丛编 (*Social Surveys in Republic Era*), by Wenhai Li et al. (Fujian jiao yu chu ban she, 2004–). This 10-volume set includes primary sources from all areas of Chinese society in the early twentieth century (the Republic Era). It includes sources on folk cultures and popular religions.

Reference Sources and Introductory Texts

- *Anthropological Resources: A Guide to Archival, Library, and Museum Collections*, edited by Lee S. Dutton (Routledge, 1999). This work provides access to information on the rich and often little-known legacy of anthropological scholarship preserved in a diversity of archives, libraries, and museums in North America and other parts of the world (mostly Europe).

- *Encyclopedia of Anthropology*, by H. James Birx (SAGE, 2006). The encyclopedia includes a collection of over 1,000 entries that focus on topics in physical/biological anthropology, archaeology, cultural/social anthropology, linguistics, and applied anthropology. Also included are relevant articles on geology, paleontology, biology, evolution, sociology, psychology, philosophy, and theology.
- *Dictionary of Anthropology*, edited by Thomas Barfield (Wiley-Blackwell, 1998). A reference guide to the discipline of social and cultural anthropology, its core consists of substantial analytical articles focusing on key anthropological concepts, theories, and methodologies.
- *Encyclopedia of Social and Cultural Anthropology*, edited by Alan Barnard and Jonathan Spencer (Routledge, 2002). Covers the many important areas of overlap between anthropology and related disciplines. Also covers key terms, ideas, and people. Features over 230 substantial entries on every major idea, individual, and subdiscipline of social and cultural anthropology.
- *Encyclopedia of Modern China*, edited by David Pong (print by Scribners and Sons, 2009; digital by Gale). This four-volume encyclopedia covers all aspects of the history and culture of China since 1800, including the people, politics, economics, religion, philosophy, traditions, art, and literature. The encyclopedia is the work of an international body of 500 prominent scholars who offer accessible, original, and authoritative analysis of almost 1,000 articles. Includes hundreds of color photos, maps, tables, and graphs.
- *An Ethnohistorical Dictionary of China*, by James Olson (Greenwood, 1998). This book provides individual essays on hundreds of Chinese ethnic groups, including ethnic groups living in the Republic of China on Taiwan. It also includes a chronology, bibliography, and a breakdown of the PRC's ethnic political subdivisions.
- *Anthropology in China: Defining the Discipline*, edited by Gregory Eliyu Guldin (M. E. Sharpe, 1991). This book includes a representative collection of essays by Chinese academics working in the field of anthropological sciences and gives a meaningful insight into the work of the Chinese anthropologists.

- *Sociology and Anthropology in Twentieth Century China: Between Universalism and Indigenism*, edited by Arif Dirlik, Guannan Li, and Hsiao-pei Yen (Chinese University Press, 2012). This collection of essays provides a historical perspective on the development of anthropology and sociology since their introduction to Chinese thought and education in the early twentieth century, with an emphasis on the 1930s and 1980s.
- *Ethnic Minorities in Modern China*, edited by Colin Mackerras (Routledge, 2011). This collection of essays deals with a wide range of questions relating to China's ethnic minorities. It details the individual separatist movements and provides the historical background as well as the politics and policy, economic, social, religious, and educational causes to some of the problems facing China today.
- *Culture and Customs of China*, by Richard Gunde (Greenwood, 2002). This book gives a broad introduction to various aspects of Chinese society and culture, including land, people, and history; thought and religion; literature and art; music and dance; food and clothing; architecture and housing; family and gender; and holidays and leisure activities.

Sociology Resources

Search Strategies

- Following is a list of subject headings related to Chinese sociology:
    China—Sociology
    China—Social conditions
    Social security—China
    Technology—Social aspects—China
    Women—China—Social conditions
    China—Social life and customs
    Shanghai (China)—Social conditions
    Social change—China
    Social classes—China
    Social surveys—China

Education—Social aspects—China
China—Social policy
Science—Social aspects—China
Social service—China
Social security—Law and legislation—China
Social structure—China
Social psychology—China
Minorities—China—Social conditions
Minorities—China—Social life and customs

Core Resources

- *SocINDEX with Full Text* (1895–present). Indexes and abstracts over 2,500 journals, conference papers, and relevant books and dissertations in sociology and related fields. Includes some popular literature and additional full text for many (but not all) citations. Provides deep historical coverage for major journals (e.g., *American Journal of Sociology* is indexed back to 1895).
- *Sociological Abstracts* (1952–present). Indexes and abstracts the international literature in sociology and related fields. Covers almost 2,000 journals, plus relevant dissertation listings, abstracts of conference papers, and selected books. This is a smaller, more academic database with more foreign-language materials than SocINDEX.
- *PsycINFO* (1807–present). Covers the professional and academic literature in psychology and related disciplines. Coverage is worldwide and includes references and abstracts to over 1,300 journals in over 20 languages, and to English-language books and book chapters.
- *ERIC* (1966–present). Indexes published and unpublished sources on all aspects of education and educational research. ERIC also indexes library and information science. Incorporates ERIC Digests, full-text short reports on topics of current interest in education.

- Key journals:

  Annual Review of Sociology. Covers areas of current interest in sociology.

  Contemporary Sociology. Formerly the book review section of *American Sociological Review, Contemporary Sociology* publishes reviews and critical discussions of recent works in sociology and in related disciplines that merit the attention of sociologists.

  American Journal of Sociology. Presents work on the theory, methods, practice, and history of sociology. Also publishes articles on the application of perspectives from other social sciences: psychology, anthropology, statistics, economics, education, history, and political science.

  American Sociological Review. The flagship journal of the American Sociological Association publishes works of interest to the discipline in general, new theoretical developments, results of research that advance understanding of fundamental social processes, and important methodological innovations. All areas of sociology are represented.

  The British Journal of Sociology. Publishes articles, review articles, and extensive numbers of book reviews in all areas of sociology.

  Chinese Sociological Review. From M. E. Sharpe, this peer-reviewed journal publishes high-quality original works from sociologists and other social scientists in mainland China, Hong Kong, Taiwan, and abroad.

Primary Sources

- *China Data Online.* This database covers economic statistics of China arranged by regions and categories. It includes monthly and yearly reports on China's macroeconomic development, statistical data of China's population and economy at the county and city levels, and financial indicators of more than 568 industrial branches. It also includes statistical yearbooks, industrial and marketing surveys, and an atlas of China. Recently, it has added a GIS function in its China Geo-Explorer.

- *China Yearbook Full-text Database* (1912–). Part of China National Knowledge Infrastructure (CNKI), this database is the largest and continuously updated database of China's yearbooks. It collects various types of yearbooks, including national, regional, industry, and enterprise yearbooks. By the end of 2009, there were about 2,000 titles, 12,681 volumes of yearbooks, and 12 million entries in all in the database. Index search is free.

- *China Local Gazetteers Full-text Database* (1949–). One of Wan-fang Data products, this database currently contains over 20,000 volumes of Chinese gazetteer books, covering 31 provinces and autonomous regions. The database provides detailed geographic and historical records of provinces, prefectures, cities, and smaller district administration units.

- *China Dimensions* (http://sedac.ciesin.columbia.edu/data/collection /cddc/). From the Center for International Earth Science Information Network (CIESIN), Columbia University, this free online resource contains a variety of socioeconomic data, mostly from the 1990s, including GIS databases that cover the administrative regions of China presented at a scale of 1:1,000,000. These databases may be integrated with agricultural, land use, environmental, and socioeconomic data to track China's economic growth, population increases, and environmental change.

- 人地系统主题数据库 (*Thematic Database for Human-Earth System*) (www.data.ac.cn/zrzy/g22.asp). This Chinese-language online resource from the Chinese Academy of Sciences contains a wide range of data on China's social and natural resources and datasets on energy resources, land resources, and population and labor, and more.

- 中国社会统计年鉴 (*China Social Statistical Yearbook*). Includes annual statistical reports from all social sectors in China.

- 新中国六十年统计资料汇编, 1949–2008 (*China Compendium of Statistics*). In both Chinese and English, it covers statistics of

China from 1949 to 2008. (See chapter 9 for more on statistical sources.)

Reference Sources and Introductory Texts

- *Blackwell Encyclopedia of Sociology Online.* Continuously updated, this online encyclopedia provides up-to-date information on sociology. It includes coverage of various topics on China.
- *The International Encyclopedia of the Social and Behavioral Sciences,* edited by Neil J. Smelser and Paul B. Baltes (Elsevier, 2001). In print and online, it covers a comprehensive list of subjects in social sciences and includes chapters on East Asia and China.
- *International Encyclopedia of Marriage and Family,* edited by James J. Ponzetti (Macmillan Reference USA, 2003). In print and online, it includes articles specific to countries and to religious traditions, examining the history of family life within these cultures and discussing how families have been affected by political and social change. China-related topics are covered.
- *An Introduction to Chinese Sociology,* by Xiaogang Wu (Routledge, 2013). This book includes a history of Chinese sociology since its reestablishment in 1979, links it to the broad historical contexts of China's economic transitions, and provides an introduction to Chinese sociological thinking, including the main theories and theoretical debates, empirical findings in selected areas, and some key ongoing projects and research issues. It also includes some statistical information about schools and research institutes, sociology journals and publication themes, research grants, number of students enrolled and job placement, and so on.

Education Resources

Search Strategies

- For relevant sources on education in China, try the following subject terms:
    Education, higher—China—History

Minorities—Education—China
Communist education—China
Education—China
Education—China—History—To 1912
Education and state—China
Education—China—History—1949–1976
Physical education and training—China
Education, Higher—China
Adult education—China
Military education—China
Education—China—Philosophy—History
Higher education and state—China
Education—Parent participation—China
Education—China—History—20th century
Education—China—Hong Kong
Education—Awards—China
Education—China—Periodicals
Education, Rural—China
Education, Secondary—China
Education and state—China—History—20th century
Education—Economic aspects—China
Education—Social aspects—China
Education—China—History
Education—China—History—1912–1949
Education—China—History—1976–
Education—China—History—To 1912—Sources
Vocational education—China
Education—China—Japanese influences
Education—China—Tibet Autonomous Region
Education, preschool—China
Education—China—Philosophy
Education, higher—China—History—20th century
Education, elementary—China
Moral education—China
Education and state—China—History

Core Resources

- *ERIC* (Education Resource Information Center). ERIC provides full text of more than 2,200 digests, along with references for additional information and citations and abstracts from over 1,000 educational and education-related journals. Full-text ERIC reports are available online from 1993 to the present.
- *Education Full Text.* This full-text source of education scholarship provides coverage for a wide range of topics, including adult education, continuing education, literacy standards, multicultural/ethnic education, secondary education, teaching methods, and much more.
- *PsycINFO.* This database covers all literature on psychology, including literature in related fields such as education.
- Key journals:

    Review of Research in Education. Provides an annual overview and descriptive analysis of selected topics in education of relevant research literature through critical and synthesizing essays.

    Review of Educational Research. Publishes critical, integrative reviews of research literature bearing on education, including conceptualizations, interpretations, and syntheses of literature and scholarly work in a field broadly relevant to education and educational research.

    Chinese Education and Society. From M. E. Sharpe, publishes unabridged translations of the more important Chinese studies in education and society from Chinese journals, newspapers, and collections of articles published in book form.

Primary Sources

- *The China Educational Development Yearbook* (Brill). A translation of the *Blue Book of Education* (教育蓝皮书), published by the Chinese Academy of Social Sciences, this critical annual report has comprehensive coverage on major issues and challenges facing Chinese education.

- 中国教育年鉴 (*Education Yearbook of China*). This annual yearbook is the official yearbook compiled by the Ministry of Education of the PRC, covering government documents related to education and statistics.
- 中国教育统计年鉴 (*Educational Statistical Yearbook of China*). This bilingual yearbook covers statistical data from all areas of Chinese education.
- 中华人民共和国重要教育文献, 1998–2002 (*Major Education Documents of China*), edited by Dongchang He (Hai nan chu ban she, 2003). Offers a collection of major education-related government documents from 1998 to 2002.
- 中华人民共和国教育史 (*History of Education of China*), by Dongchang He et al. (Hai nan chu ban she, 2007). This two-volume title covers the history of Chinese education from 1949 to 2004. The first volume covers 1949 to 1976; the second covers 1976 to 2004.

Reference Sources and Introductory Texts

- *Asian Higher Education: An International Handbook and Reference Guide*, by Grace Mak and Gerard Postiqlione (Greenwood, 1997). Covers higher education in 20 representative Asian countries. Each entry is written by an expert contributor and provides background information, a discussion of current issues, and an examination of future trends. Entries cite current literature and research, and the volume concludes with an extensive bibliography.
- *China Education System and Policy Handbook* (International Business Publications, USA). Covers government policies and regulations related to education. It is updated annually.
- *Education in China Since 1976*, by Xiufang Wang (McFarland, 2003). This work examines the education system in post-Mao China from 1976 to the present. It explores how the Chinese government sees the development of its educational practices within the nation's broader social, economic, political, and cultural

contexts; how it identifies new issues that emerge in the process of what might be called educational globalization; how it translates these issues into specific educational policies, activities, and goals; how the education reforms fit China's social and political realities and objectives; how the new policies affect foreign-student affairs and Chinese students studying abroad; the ways in which the government promotes international educational cooperation and exchange; the opportunities for Western institutions to introduce programs in China; and current trends and their effect on the internationalization of education.

- *Education Reform in China: Changing Concepts, Contexts and Practices*, edited by Janette Ryan (Routledge, 2011). This work outlines the systematic transformation that has occurred in school curriculum goals, structure and content, teaching and learning approaches, and assessment and administrative structures, including the increasing devolvement of control from the center to provincial, district, and school levels.

---

1. The list includes some of the major sources related to Chinese anthropology. For more sources, search WorldCat using the subject terms suggested. For Chinese sources, search WorldCat or Duxiu using search terms such as "民俗" or "社会调查" or names of the Chinese minorities of interest.

Researching Social Sciences
in Economics and Business

This chapter will show you:

★ Search strategies and core resources for economics and business
★ Primary sources for the subject fields
★ Reference sources and introductory texts for the subject fields

The biggest story of China since the early 1990s has been its spectacular economic success. Not surprisingly, there has been an abundance of information resources in this area. We will discuss in the following pages some of the major resources for economic and business research. Few libraries would have all the resources listed below. Be sure to talk to the librarian about what resources are available in your local library.

Search Strategies

- For sources on the Chinese economy and economic history, search the following subject terms:
    Economics—China
    Environmental economics—China
    Marxian economics—China
    Economics—China—History
    Consumption (Economics)—China

Economics—China—History—20th century

Globalization—Economic aspects—China

China, Northwest—Economic conditions

China—Foreign economic relations—United States

China—Economic policy—1976–2000—Periodicals

Economic development—Environmental
    aspects—China

China—Economic policy—1949–1976

Information technology—Economic aspects—China

Minorities—China—Economic conditions

Economic forecasting—China

Economic zoning—China

Sino-Japanese War, 1937–1945—Economic
    aspects—China

China—Economic conditions—1976–2000—Regional
    disparities

Economic development—China

Economic conversion—China

Technological innovations—Economic aspects—China

Economic development projects—China

- For sources of economic statistics, search the following subject
  terms:

China—Commerce—Statistics

China—Economic conditions—Statistics

China—Industries—Statistics

China—Population—Statistics

China—Statistics

Cities and towns—China—Statistics

Consumption (Economics)—China—Statistics

Cost and standard of living—China—Statistics—
    Periodicals

Economic forecasting—China—Statistics

Employee fringe benefits—China—Statistics

Guangdong sheng (China)—Statistics

Marketing—China—Statistics

Price—China—Statistics

Securities—China—Statistics
Shanghai (China)—Statistics
Stock exchanges—China—Statistics
Tourism—Statistics—China
Wages—China—Statistics
China—Economic conditions—2000—Statistics
China—Statistics—Periodicals
Economic indicators—China
Economic indicators—China—Periodicals
Social indicators—China

- For sources on finance and investment, search the following subject terms:

  Accounting—China
  Accounting standards—China
  Banks and banking—China
  Banks and banking, foreign—China
  Business enterprises, foreign—Taxation—China
  Capital market—China
  Finance—China
  Foreign exchange—China
  Foreign exchange rates—China
  Income tax—China
  Interest rates—China
  Monetary policy—China
  Mortgage loans—China
  Securities—China
  Stock exchanges—China
  Stocks—China
  Tax administration and procedure—China
  Tax evasion—China
  Taxation—China

- For sources on international business, search the following subject terms:

  China—Foreign economic relations
  Exports—China
  Free ports and zones—China

Foreign trade regulation—China
Imports—China
International business enterprises—China
Investments, foreign—China
Joint ventures—China
Technology transfer—China
World trade organization—China

- For company information, search the following subject terms:
    Business enterprises—China—Directories
    Business enterprises—Rankings
    Businessmen China—Biography
    Corporations—China—Directories
    Corporations—China—Finance
    Corporations—China—Rankings
    Corporations—Rankings
    Corporations—Ratings of—China
    Corporations—Valuation—China
    Credit ratings—China
    Government business enterprises—China
    Stock exchanges—China
    Stocks—China
    Success in business—China—Case studies

- For sources on management, search the following subject terms:
    Industrial management—China
    Industrial relations—China
    Labor—China
    Labor market—China
    Management—China
    Personnel management—China
    Wages—China
    Working class—China

- For business-related laws and legislation, search the following subject terms:
    Accounting—Law and legislation—China
    Arbitration and award—China
    Banking law—China

Business law—China
Commercial law China
Investment, foreign—Law and legislation—China
Joint ventures—law and legislation—China
License agreements—China
Taxation—Law and legislation—China
Technology transfer—Law and legislation—China

Core Resources

- *Economic Literature* (EconLit). The most important source of references to economic literature, EconLit contains more than 1.1 million records from 1886 to the present. It covers virtually every area related to economics worldwide.
- *ABI/INFORM Complete.* ABI/INFORM includes worldwide business periodicals and covers business and economic conditions, management techniques, theory, and practice of business, advertising, marketing, economics, human resources, finance, taxation, and more.
- *Business Source Complete.* This database provides coverage of the most important scholarly business journals back to 1886, including all business subject fields, such as marketing, management, MIS, POM, accounting, finance, and economics. Additional full-text, nonjournal content includes financial data, books, monographs, major reference works, book digests, conference proceedings, case studies, investment research reports, industry reports, market research reports, country reports, company profiles, SWOT analyses, and more.
- *Asian Business and Reference.* This database focuses on business and financial news from the eastern hemisphere. It covers Asian business and financial information from key international publications.
- Key periodicals in Chinese economics:
    - *China Economic Journal.* The official journal of the China Center for Economic Research (CCER) at Peking University, it is published by Routledge Journals, an

imprint of Taylor and Francis Group. The journal aims to introduce readers to the examination and analysis of the latest developments in the Chinese economy and government economic policies.

China Economic Review. The official journal of Chinese Economists Society, *China Economic Review* publishes original research works on the economy of China and its relation to the world economy.

China and World Economy. A peer-reviewed journal that provides a unique Chinese perspective on international issues in economics that are related to China, the journal provides an objective, impartial, analytical, and up-to-date account of the problems faced and progress made by China in its interaction with the world economy.

China Economic Quarterly. Published by Dragonomics Research and Advisory, *China Economic Quarterly* provides a source of analysis and understanding of the Chinese economy for business leaders, diplomats, academics, and other China-watchers. Each issue contains a concise yet comprehensive analysis of the latest economic data, an in-depth research article on a major topic, and several short articles on sectors, trends, companies, and people.

China Economic Policy Review. Published by World Scientific starting in 2012, this new international journal publishes high-quality scientific papers related to the economies of Greater China (the mainland, Taiwan, Hong Kong, and Macao) and their relations with other economies.

- Key periodicals in business:

Wall Street Journal. This daily newspaper has a special focus on business and economic news worldwide.

Harvard Business Review. This is a research-based magazine focusing primarily on management.

The Financial Times (Hong Kong). This weekly paper
provides current business, financial, investment,
market, and company ratings information in Asia.
Far East Economic Review (Hong Kong). This weekly
publication is a world-renowned source on Asian
current affairs, business, finance, economics, and
government policy.
The China Business Review. The official magazine of the
US-China Business Council, the journal is the leading authority on China trade and investment.
Journal of Chinese Economic and Business Studies. This
peer-reviewed journal publishes current and relevant
findings from cutting-edge research in Chinese economic, business, and related issues.
China Agricultural Economic Review. This international
journal publishes high-quality academic research
work by scholars from China and globally and provides in-depth analysis of China's agricultural reform
and practice.
China Finance Review International. This international
journal publishes research work by scholars from
China and outside on financial and economic issues
in China.
Chinese Management Studies. This international journal
publishes work by Chinese scholars as well as work
of international researchers on Chinese management
processes, philosophy, and practices.
Journal of Chinese Economic and Foreign Trade Studies.
This international journal publishes both qualitative and quantitative research in all areas of Chinese
business and foreign trade, technical economics,
business environment, and business strategy.
Journal of Chinese Entrepreneurship. Taking an interdisciplinary approach, this journal focuses on the changing contours of Chinese entrepreneurship research

and training and acquaints readers with the latest trends and directions of explorations in the theory and practice of entrepreneurship in China.

Primary Sources[1]

Country Overviews and Statistics

- *EIU.COM Country Report.* Includes up-to-date reporting, analysis, and forecasts of the economic, business, and political environment of China and 180 other countries.
- *CountryData.com.* A database by Political Risk Services Group (PRS), it covers risk ratings and economic data from International Country Risk Guide, as well as forecasts, economic, political, geographic, and social data from PRS for more than 150 countries.
- *China Data Online.* A database by China Data Center at the University of Michigan, it includes economic statistics of China arranged by regions and categories. Includes monthly and yearly reports on China's macroeconomic development, statistical databases about China's population and economy at the county and city levels, and financial indicators of more than 568 industrial branches. Also includes statistical yearbooks, census data, industrial and marketing surveys, and an atlas of China.
- *CEIC Data.* CEIC Data covers macroeconomic, industrial, and financial time series for China and other countries. Data include national accounts, production, government and public finance, demographics, inflation, foreign trade, balance of payments, banking statistics, investment, transport and telecommunication, energy, and financial markets.
- *ISI Emerging Markets.* Arranged by country, this resource includes country profiles; macroeconomic statistics, forecasts, and analysis; reports on financial markets, companies, and industries; exchange rates; analyst reports; and business news.
- *Roubini Global Economics.* Roubini Global Economics (formerly RGE Monitor), founded by New York University economist Nouriel Roubini, provides detailed coverage and timely updates

on international macroeconomic, financial and banking, geostra-
tegic, and geopolitical topics, including original research and analysis of the world's most important economies, emerging markets,
frontier markets, and asset classes. Contents are sourced from
news, research, analysis, blogs, important speeches, and data.

- *World Development Indicators* (World Bank) (http://databank
  .worldbank.org/). Statistics for over 200 countries and 18 country groups include social, economic, financial, and more. Data can
  be scaled, ranged against a particular year, viewed by percentage
  change, and charted.

- *Asian Development Outlook* (Asian Development Bank). An
  annual publication that provides economic reports on developing
  member countries of the Asian Development Bank, this publication also analyzes current economic performance and prospects
  for developing member countries as well as reviews and assessments of important policy issues.

- *Asian Economic Outlook* (Wefa Group). This annual quarterly
  publication covers Australia, China, Hong Kong, India, Indonesia, Japan, Malaysia, New Zealand, Pakistan, the Philippines,
  Singapore, South Korea, Taiwan, and Thailand. Each country covered includes short-term and long-term economic forecasts and
  analysis, economic policy, latest developments, and monthly and
  annual economic indicator tables.

Economic Indicators[2]

- *China InfoBank.* This database provides statistical data selected
  from national and provincial statistical yearbooks, the *China Economic Statistics Bulletin*, the *People's Bank of China Quarterly Bulletin*, and other sources.

- 中国经济社会发展统计数据库 (www.cnki.net/). Part of
  CNKI, this statistical database includes 833 titles of statistical
  yearbooks (as of October 2012). Index search is free.

- *National Bureau of Statistics of China* (www.stats.gov.cn/english/
  statisticaldata/). The official Chinese government website provides

monthly, quarterly, and yearly statistics for over 40 different areas, including national accounts, consumer confidence, retail price, and lots more.

- *People's Bank of China.* This government-owned bank publishes monthly banking and financial statistics, including gold and foreign exchange reserves, money supply, indices of entrepreneur's confidence and business condition, Treasury bonds traded in stock exchanges, and so on. The bank has an English interface at www.pbc.gov.cn/publish/english/963/index.html.

- 中国对外经济统计年鉴 (*China Foreign Economic Statistical Yearbook*). A major resource for statistics on foreign trade, it includes balance of payments, foreign trade, foreign investment, collaboration, and tourism.

- 中国经济景气月报 / 国家统计局 (*China Monthly Economic Indicators*). Published by the National Bureau of Statistics of China, it presents monthly reports on all national economic indicators.

- 中国贸易外经统计年鉴 (*China Trade and External Economic Statistical Yearbook*). This comprehensive resource covers current and some historical statistics on domestic and international trade.

- 中国国民经济和社会发展统计资料汇编 (*The Collection of Statistics on China Economy and Social Development*). This is an annual publication of compiled statistical data from all parts of the PRC.

- *World Development Indicators* (http://databank.worldbank.org/ddp/home.do?Step=2&id=4/). Statistics for over 200 countries and 18 country groups include social, economic, financial, and more. Data can be scaled, ranged against a particular year, viewed by percentage change, and charted.

Industry and Market Research

- *MarketResearch.com.* Current and archived market research reports by ICON, Kalorama, and Packaged Facts are provided by MarketResearch.com for consumer goods, health care, biotechnology, pharmaceuticals, and other industries. Market Looks issued upon publication; some other reports have 12-month delays before availability.

- *MarketLine Advantage.* This database provides company, industry, country, and financial data for every major marketplace in the world. It includes company SWOTs, company overviews, industry profiles, case studies, financial deals, country analysis, news, and a statistics database covering 215 countries and 46 political and geographic regions.
- *Passport GMID* (Euromonitor). Passport GMID offers comprehensive coverage of international consumer markets, consumer lifestyles in other countries, economic statistics, demographic forecasting, US industries, and more.
- *CEIC.* Search sectors for industry overviews (see the database description listed previously in this chapter).
- *ISI Emerging Markets.* Search by country and then select an industry (see the database description previously listed in this chapter).
- *EIU Country Report.* Country Report includes data on industries under Data Tool (see the database description previously listed in this chapter).
- *Standard and Poors NetAdvantage.* NetAdvantage is Standard and Poor's one-stop resource for company and industry information. Contents include company directories, stock reports, mutual fund information, news, rankings, executive biographies, customized search templates, and in-depth company and industry analyses. Its Global Industry Surveys includes industry reports for broad regions of Asia, Europe, and Latin America.

Company and Investment Research

China Securities Market and Accounting Research (CSMAR). CSMAR (GTA Data Online) provides access to the following 24 datasets:

Stock market data:

- China Stock Market Trading Database
- China Securities Market Indices Research Database

- China Special Treatment and Particular Transfer Share Research Database
- China Stock Market Volume Trade Database
- China Securities Market Block Trade Database
- China Stock Trading Suspension and Resumption Research Database
- China Stock Market Equity Division Reform Research Database
- China Stock Market Initial Public Offering Research Database
- China Cash and Stock Dividends Research Database
- China Seasoned New Issue and Rights Offering Research Database

Corporate data:

- China Stock Market Financial Statement Research Database
- China Listed Firms Corporate Governance Research Database
- China Stock Market Analyst Forecasts Database
- China Listed Firms Bank Loans Research Database
- China Listed Firms Shareholders Research Database
- China Listed Firms Merger and Acquisition, Asset Restructuring Research Database
- China Stock-Market-Related Party Transaction Research Database
- CSRCs Enforcement Actions Research Database
- China Listed Firms State-owned Shares Auction and Transfer Research Database
- China Listed Non-state-owned Enterprise Database

- China Annual, Interim and Quarterly...
  Reports Announcement Dates Research
  Database
- China Bond Market Database
- China Stock Market Financial Database—
  Audit Opinion
- China Bank Research Database—Finance

- *ChinaScope Financial.* ChinaScope is a financial data and analytics platform for global investment professionals and researchers seeking critical quantitative and qualitative information on China. It covers extensive data on Chinese public and private companies, 90,000+ industry metrics covering over 40 sectors, over 100,000 economic time series and timely, translated local news.

- *Mergent Online.* Mergent Online (formerly FIS Online) is a database of corporate information covering over 22,000 US and foreign public companies. Information available for each company includes the following: (1) complete corporate history including acquisitions and changes in ownership structure; (2) lists of subsidiaries, property holdings, and key personnel; (3) up to 25 years of annual and quarterly financial data, including balance sheets, income statements, cash flow statements, and financial coverage of SEC filings; (4) extensive information about the corporation's current long-term debt; and (5) links to recent news reports. Data output can be customized and exported as comma-delimited files (readable by Excel and other software). Advanced search capabilities include searching by executive's name, auditor, country code, NAICS or SIC industry code, and selected financial characteristics and ratios.

- *Bloomberg Financial Services.* Bloomberg provides in-depth company profiles, real-time financial data, industry and market news, US and international economic indicators, and quotes and technical analysis on US and international securities.

- *Hoovers Academic.* Hoovers Academic provides information on over 17 million worldwide companies. Company profiles include corporate history, executives, products/operations data, financials, and news. Searches can be filtered by geographical regions.

- *Thomson ONE.* Thomson ONE brings together company information from a variety of sources that are produced by Thomson Reuters. This includes company financials and filings, mergers and acquisition data, and analyst reports. The following types of information are available: company overviews, company news and price charts, corporate governance (takeover defense), corporate financial fundamentals, estimates (and earnings surprises), debt overview, company deals, share ownership information, company research (formerly Investext), company financial filings, officers, and directors. Searches can be filtered by countries.

Reference Sources and Introductory Texts

- *Handbooks in Economics* (ScienceDirect). The *Handbooks in Economics* series is a reference source that covers various branches of the discipline. Titles include *Handbook of Agricultural Economics, Handbook of Econometrics, Handbook of Economic Forecasting, Handbook of Economic Growth,* and more. Each individual handbook covers material from current journal articles and recent research developments.
- *The Chinese Economy: Reform and Development,* by Cai Fang, Justin Yifu Lin, and Cao Yong (McGraw-Hill Education Singapore, 2009). This book provides a historical review of Chinese economic reform and establishment of market economy.
- *Hoover's Handbook of World Business* (Reference Press). This handbook covers valuable information on 250 of the world's most influential companies outside the United States. Contents include rankings of global businesses, rankings and analysis of industry, the world financial sector, services, trading partners, and world stock markets. The handbook also provides company profiles and indexes of profiles by industry, corporate headquarters location, brands, and companies.
- *Dow Jones Guide to the Global Stock Market* (Dow Jones). This publication includes world stock market information and indexes on 29 countries. In addition, 120 industry groups are compiled

into nine sectors. Also included is an industry index, market sector code definitions, and industry group codes and definitions.

- *The Oxford Handbook of Business and Government,* by David Coen, Wyn Grant, and Graham Wilson (Oxford University Press, 2012). This book introduces an interdisciplinary study of business and government and examines how business interacts with government in different parts of the world, including the United States, the EU, China, Japan, and South America.
- *Chinese Business: Landscapes and Strategies,* by Hong Liu (Routledge, 2008). This book provides a comprehensive, practical guide to business in China, featuring both theoretical/academic and practical perspectives.
- *Handbook of Contemporary Marketing in China: Theories and Practices,* by Chenglu Wang (Nova Science, 2011). This book provides reviews of various current marketing research areas in China. It is a useful and comprehensive resource for researchers and practitioners who are interested in contemporary China's markets, marketing research, and marketing practices.
- *Handbook of Chinese Organizational Behavior: Integrating Theory, Research, and Practice,* by Xu Huang and Michael Harris Bond (Edward Elgar, 2012). This handbook explores limitations and challenges arising from attempts to develop indigenous theories and constructs applicable to Chinese social reality. Areas examined include emotional intelligence, creativity and motivation, leadership, team conflicts, trust, power, and business ethics.
- *China's Financial Markets: An Insider's Guide to How the Markets Work,* edited by Salih Neftci and Michelle Yuan Menager-Xu (Academic Press, 2006). Provides a detailed description of the Chinese banking system; money, equity, futures, FX, and bond markets; the insurance sector; mortgage market and mortgage instruments; and regulators.
- *China Business Guide 2012* (China Economic Review Press, Hong Kong). This compact guidebook, updated annually, provides a wide range of facts, figures, overviews, foreign investment reports, expert analysis, maps and data, and other information that is

deemed helpful for those planning to do business in China, travel to China, or set up permanently in China.

- *Chinese Commercial Law: A Practical Guide,* by Maarten Roos (Aspen Publishers, 2010). Drawing on the author's legal work experience in China, the book provides practical guidance to help foreign companies in China devise a corporate strategy and tackle issues relating to common aspects of doing business with Chinese counterparts, investing in a Chinese enterprise, and engaging in business operations there.

---

1. There are a great number of digital and print primary sources for economic and business research, especially in terms of business/economy-related reports and data. The list here represents some of the most important sources.
2. Search the library catalog or WorldCat with subject terms "economic indicators, China" or "social indicators, China" for published sources.

CHAPTER 15

Researching Social Sciences in Law, Politics, and Women's and Gender Studies

> This chapter will show you:
>
> ★ Core resources for researching Chinese law, politics, and women's and gender studies
> ★ Primary sources for the disciplines
> ★ Reference sources and introductory texts for the disciplines

To understand contemporary China, one has to understand China's political (and legal) system. Politics penetrates and affects every aspect of Chinese life. For example, one of the key research questions in Chinese Women's Studies is the complex relationship between women and the Communist state. On the one hand, under Communist rule women are supposed to enjoy full equality with men; on the other hand, do women really feel equal when the government imposes upon them a set of behavior standards (e.g., during the Maoist Era women worked like men and even dressed like men)? Not only does Chinese politics provide a fertile ground for intellection cross-pollination (examining women's issues through the lens of politics), it also demands a higher degree of critical thinking. As we discuss the following research resources, especially those sources from China, we will have to ask ourselves how much of this information is affected by politics.

Law Resources[1]

Search Strategies

- For a general search on Chinese law, search the subject term "law, China."
- For primary sources on the history of Chinese law, search "law, China, history, sources."
- For cases, search a specific law plus "cases," such as "criminal law, China, cases."
- Following is a selected list of subject headings for Chinese law materials:

  Law—China—Philosophy—History
  Administrative law—China—History—Sources
  Criminal law—China—Cases
  Stock exchanges—Law and legislation—China
  Investments, foreign—Law and legislation—China
  Finance—Law and legislation—China
  Government ownership—Law and legislation—China
  Insurance law—China
  Law—China—Congresses
  Environmental law—China
  Government business enterprises—Law and
      legislation—China
  International business enterprises—Law and
      legislation—China
  Constitutional law—China
  Criminal law—China—History—Sources
  Law—China—Bibliography
  Commercial law—China
  Technology transfer—Law and legislation—China
  Law—China—Philosophy
  Civil law—China—History
  Joint ventures—Law and legislation—China
  Law—China—Dictionaries—Chinese
  Civil law—China
  Corporation law—China

Law reform—China
Law—China—Popular works
Business enterprises—Law and legislation—China
Administrative law—China—Cases
Law reports, digests, etc.—China
Practice of law—China
Rural industries—Law and legislation—China
Commercial law—China—Cases
Rule of law—China
Law—China—Cases
Law—China—History—20th century
Law—China—Periodicals
Law—China—Sources
Law—China—History—Sources

Core Resources

- *Campus Research: Law* (formerly Westlaw). Contains all the Hong Kong SAR judgments from all its court levels that were originally published by Sweet and Maxwell Asia. The earliest reports date as far back as 1905, and a full-text version of the 2002 edition of the *Hong Kong Civil Procedure* (The White Book Service) is also available. Several law journals on the laws of the PRC and Hong Kong that were published by Sweet and Maxwell Asia and in popular newspapers such as the *South China Morning Post* are also included in the database.
- *Lexis/Nexis*. The Lexis/Nexis Online Service has resumed its coverage of the laws of the PRC and Hong Kong SAR, as well as the updating service for the same. For Hong Kong case law, important decisions from all court levels in Hong Kong since 1946 are included in its database. Reports are updated regularly, and new case reports are usually available on Lexis/Nexis one or two weeks after the decisions are released. It also comprises the laws of the PRC, including statutes, administrative regulations, important judicial interpretations, and local laws and regulations, covering over 60 subjects of law in total.

- *Current Law Index* (Information Access Company, 1980–, monthly updating). An extensive index to articles that have appeared in more than 850 journals from the United States, Canada, Great Britain, New Zealand, and Australia, *Current Law Index* covers law reviews, bar association journals, and legal newspapers, as well as selected legal articles from newspapers. All the legal articles about China are listed under the main entry of China and then indexed under different subject terms in its subject indexes. The electronic version of *Current Law Index* is also available in CD-ROM (*InfoTrac–LegalTrac Database*) and on Westlaw and Lexis (*Legal Resource Index*).
- *Index to Legal Periodicals* (H. W. Wilson, 1908–, monthly updating, except September). H. W. Wilson's *Index to Legal Periodicals* provides an index to articles from more than 500 legal journals, yearbooks, institutes, bar association organizations, university publications, law reviews, and government publications. The indexed items originate from the United States, Puerto Rico, Great Britain, Ireland, Canada, Australia, and New Zealand. Unlike *Current Law Index*, *Index to Legal Periodicals* does not have geographic terms in the main subject entries. Therefore, to search for legal articles about China in *Index to Legal Periodicals*, we have to look for the subject of interest and then look for the geographic term, such as "China."
- *Index to Foreign Legal Periodicals* (University of California Press, 1960–, quarterly updating). This index covers six Chinese legal periodicals that are published in Chinese vernacular. They are *Zhongguo guo ji fa nian kan* (Chinese Yearbook of International Law), *Fa xue ping lun* (Legal Science Review), *Fa xue yan jiu* (Studies in Law), *Xian dai fa xue* (Modern Law Science), *Zhongguo fa xue* (Chinese Legal Science), and *Zhongguo she hui zhu yi jian she* (Chinese Socialism Construction). *Index to Foreign Legal Periodicals* has a subject index and geographical index for convenient research access.

- Key journals:

  China Law and Practice (Hong Kong). Published in
      English by China Law and Practice Ltd. since 1987,
      the journal collates, translates, and comments on
      Chinese laws to help businesses and government
      organizations keep abreast of legal developments in
      China and how they might affect the way they do
      business in China.

  China Law (Hong Kong). This journal, in both Chinese
      and English, focuses on information about new
      Chinese legislative, judicial, and legal service, as well
      as and law research to help foreign lawyers and busi-
      nessmen who are doing business with China.

  China Law Quarterly (Hong Kong). This quarterly
      publication summarizes recent legal developments
      in China.

  China Law Reporter (American Bar Association, Sec-
      tion of International Law, 1980–). This is a quarterly
      scholarly journal about Chinese law and China's
      legal system.

  Journal of Chinese Law (Center for Chinese Legal Stud-
      ies, Columbia University School of Law, 1987–).
      This semiannual journal publishes scholarly research
      articles related to the law of China (including main-
      land China and Taiwan).

  Chinese Law and Government (M. E. Sharpe). This publi-
      cation translates articles relating to Chinese law and
      government issues from Chinese publications.

  China Law Briefing (FT Law and Tax Asia Pacific, 1995–).
      This Hong Kong monthly periodical provides briefs
      of new Chinese laws and regulations.

  Law Yearbook of China (*China Law Society*). This yearbook
      in Chinese collects the information about legislation,
      administrative regulations, judicial interpretation, and
      the development of the law of the PRC.

Primary Resources[2]

- *ChinaLawInfo.com* (in Chinese) and *LawInfoChina.com* (in English). This is the most comprehensive database for English translation of Chinese laws and cases. It is a fee-based Chinese legal website. However, in addition to free index searching, the site offers many free resources, including English translations of Chinese laws and regulations, full text of the Chinese government's white papers, the tables of contents of the gazettes of the NPC, the State Council, the Supreme Court, and the Ministry of Foreign Trade and Economic Cooperation, and an index to four major Chinese legal periodicals.

- *China Law Knowledge Database* (CLKD) (in Chinese). Part of China National Knowledge Infrastructure (CNKI), this database includes full text of laws and regulations, law-related scholarly articles, theses and dissertations, and cases. Coverage is from 1979 to the present and index search is free.

- *Policies and Laws of China* (PLOC) (in Chinese). This database from Wanfang Data covers state laws and regulations, provincial and regional laws and regulations, policies from state ministries, administrative policies, international treaties and conventions, and judicial cases and interpretation from 1949 to the present.

- 人民日报 (*People's Daily*), 1945–. This is the official Chinese-language newspaper of the Chinese government and contains reports on legislation and legal developments. New laws are usually first released in full text in this newspaper. The newspaper with its archive is available in digital format.

- *South China Morning Post*. This is an English-language Hong Kong–based newspaper that reports a considerable amount of news on the legal disputes from the PRC and Hong Kong. This newspaper is included in LexisNexis Academic, Access World News, and ProQuest.

- 新中国法制研究史料通鉴 (*Compendium of Historical Documents of the Study of Law of China*), by Peitian Zhang (Zhongguo zheng fad a xue chu ban she, 2003). This 11-volume set chronicles the development of Chinese legal system since 1949.

- 中国百年民法典汇编 (*A Centennial Compendium of Civil Law of China*), by Lixin Yang (Zhongguo fa zhi chu ban she, 2011). This book collects different versions of Chinese civil law since it was first drafted in the Qing Dynasty (nineteenth century).

Reference Sources and Introductory Texts

- *Dictionary of Chinese Law and Government, Chinese-English*, by Philip R. Bilancia (Stanford University Press, 1981). A classic title, this dictionary provides translations of over 25,000 Chinese political and legal terms used from 1939 to 1977.
- *Chinese Commercial Law: A Practical Guide*, by Maarten Roos (Aspen Publishers, 2010). Drawing on the author's legal work experience in China, the book provides practical guidance to help foreign companies in China devise a corporate strategy and tackle issues relating to common aspects of doing business with Chinese counterparts, investing in a Chinese enterprise, and engaging in business operations there.
- *Bird in a Cage: Legal Reform in China after Mao*, by Stanley B. Lubman (Stanford University Press, 1999). This book traces the development of Chinese law from the pre-Communist era to Mao's totalitarian rule and legal reforms in contemporary China.
- *The Politics of Lawmaking in Post-Mao China: Institutions, Processes, and Democratic Prospects*, by Murray S. Tanner (Oxford University Press, 1999). This book examines how China's political and legal structures are changing from within through the changing relationship between the National People's Congress and the Communist Party hierarchy.
- *China's Long March toward Rule of Law*, by R. P. Peerenboom (Cambridge University Press, 2002). This book provides an introduction to China's legal reform toward a version of rule of law.
- *The Changing Chinese Legal System, 1978–Present: Centralization of Power and Rationalization of the Legal System*, by Bin Liang (Routledge, 2008). This book examines the changes in the Chinese legal system since 1978, especially crime and punishment functions of the legal system.

- *China Law Reference Service* (Asia Law and Practice, circa 1996–). Based in Hong Kong, it covers Chinese laws from December 1986 to the present. Some laws and regulations are fully bilingual. Some are digested, with the digest in English and the original Chinese title noted.
- *China Law Deskbook: A Legal Guide to Foreign Invested Enterprises*, by James M. Zimmerman (American Bar Association, 2010). The 2010 edition of the *Deskbook* is organized in 24 chapters covering key topic areas such as court system and litigation, contract law, financial regulation, taxation, tender and government procurement, consumer protection, customs and trade, labor and employment, M&A, liquidation and bankruptcy, securities, property rights and land use, environment, and dispute resolution.
- "A Complete Research Guide to the Laws of People's Republic of China (PRC)" (www.llrx.com/features/prc.htm), by Joan Liu and Wei Luo. This free online resource provides an excellent introduction to laws in China and related resources.

Political Science Resources

Search Strategies

- For sources on Chinese politics and government, try "China, politics and government."
- For sources on Chinese economic conditions, try "China, economic conditions."
- For sources on Chinese social conditions, try "China, social conditions."
- Following is a list of selected subject headings for Chinese politics:
      China—Politics and government—1949–
      China—Politics and government—20th century
      Religion and politics—China
      China—Politics and government—1976–2002—Congresses
      Tibet Autonomous Region (China)—Politics and government—1951–
      Rural development—Government policy—China
      Government ownership—Law and legislation—China

Government business enterprises—Law and legislation—
    China
Government business enterprises—China
Government correspondence—China
Minorities—Government policy—China
Local government—China—History
Government property—China—Management
Representative government and representation—China
Food supply—Government policy—China
Municipal government—China
Birth control—Government policy—China

Core Resources

- *Worldwide Political Science Abstracts.* Supplies up-to-date research within the political science discipline and its complementary fields, including international relations, law, and public administration/policy, and covers over 1,000 journals drawn from the international serials literature.
- *International Political Science Abstracts.* Provides current indexing and abstracting of the world's leading journals in political science.
- *PAIS* (Public Affairs Information Service) International, 1972–. Provides access to periodical articles, books, hearings, reports, gray literature, government publications, Internet resources, and other publications. Many of the citations include abstracts and full-text links.
- *CIAO* (Columbia International Affairs Online). Provides searchable access to the full text of working papers and conference proceedings from 45 leading research centers in the field of international policy and scholarship. CIAO also provides abstracts from key foreign policy journals.
- *Historical Abstracts,* 1969–. Covers world history from 1450 to the present.
- *PolicyFile* (formerly Policy Research Online File), 1990–. Provides access to major think tanks, research organizations, and university

research programs. Contains information on a complete range of policy issues, both domestic and international.

- Key journals:
  - *The Annual Review of Political Science.* In publication since 1998, the journal covers significant developments in the field of political science, including political theory and philosophy, international relations, political economy, political behavior, American and comparative politics, public administration and policy, and methodology. It helps keep track of current research in the field.
  - *China Review International* (University of Hawaii Press). This quarterly journal publishes English-language reviews of recently published books and monographs from China, Taiwan, Hong Kong, Japan, the United States, and elsewhere to help scholars keep abreast of cutting-edge research in Chinese Studies.
  - *Modern China* (SAGE). A key journal in Chinese Studies, this journal publishes high-quality scholarship in history and the social sciences on China from late Qing to contemporary periods.
  - *The China Journal* (Australian National University). Another major journal in Chinese Studies, it publishes well-informed and insightful commentary from scholars in China and elsewhere on contemporary China.

Primary Sources

- *China Documents Annual, 1989–. China Documents Annual* reports annually on the developments in China through the use of primary source documents. It covers vital decrees, speeches, laws, and other primary sources.
- *China Facts and Figures Annual, 1978–.* Accumulates annually all basic and statistical information about the PRC.

- *Access World News* (International Edition). Includes full-text information and perspectives from over 700 international sources.
- *Foreign Broadcast Information Service (FBIS) Daily Reports*. Includes translation of daily broadcasts, government statements, and select news stories from non-English sources from 1974 to 1996.
- *World News Connection*. Includes a daily compendium of transcripts of overseas media translated into English. The coverage is from 1995 to the present.
- 人民日报 (*People's Daily*, 1945–). The official organ of the Chinese government, the newspaper and archive are available both in print and electronically.
- 中国重要报纸全文数据库 (*China Core Newspapers Full-text Database*). Includes the full text of nearly 1,000 Chinese newspaper titles published in mainland China since 2000. Distributed by East View Information Services.
- 中国政府资料库 (*Archives of Chinese Government*). Includes the archives and publications of the Chinese central government, its ministries and subsidiaries, and regional authorities. Distributed by Oriprobe Information Services.
- 中国人民政治协商会议资料库 (*Database of the Chinese People's Political Consultative Conference*). A collection of archives and documents of the CPPCC since its first meeting. Format includes texts, graphics, and videos. Distributed by Oriprobe Information Services.
- 中国共产党数据库 (*Database of the Communist Party of China*). Includes archives and publications of the Communist Party since its establishment in 1921. Distributed by Oriprobe Information Services.
- 全国人民代表大会资料库 (*Database of the National People's Congress*). Includes a collection of reports, primarily by *People's Daily* and *People's Daily Online,* on the National People's Congress (NPC) from the first session of the first NPC to the third session of the tenth NPC. Distributed by Oriprobe Information Services.

- *Chinese Cultural Revolution Database* (Chinese University of Hong Kong Press). The database is the most comprehensive source of primary sources on the Chinese Cultural Revolution. It contains more than 10,000 Central Party documents, Communist Party leaders' speeches, official newspaper articles from the early 1960s to the late 1970s, selections of some of the key Red Guard texts, and more. The database is updated annually.
- *Tiananmen Square and US-China Relations, 1989–1993* (Gale Archives Unbound). The digitized collection offers unique primary source documents relating to the demonstrations and their aftermath: public mail, memoranda, reports, cables, meeting notes, news clippings, and much more.
- *Mao Zedong and China's Revolutions: A Brief History with Documents* (Bedford/St. Martin's, 2002). Includes an introductory essay to Mao Zedong and Chinese revolutions, with a selection of Mao's writings and other historical documents.
- *Foreign Relations of the United States, 1964–1968, Volume XXX China,* edited by Harriet Dashiell Schwar (US Government Printing Office) (www.state.gov/www/about_state/history/vol_xxx/). This site is part of the US Department of State website and contains declassified archival material on the diplomatic relations between the United States and China between 1964 and 1968. The material is presented in the Department of State's Foreign Policy and Diplomacy of the United States documentary series. The documents in this volume are drawn from the files of the Department of State and the bureau, office, and other lot files of the relevant departmental units. The volume also includes records from the Department of Defense and the Central Intelligence Agency.
- *Tracking the Dragon: National Intelligence Estimates on China during the Era of Mao, 1948–1976,* edited by Robert L. Hutchings (US Government Printing Office, 2004). This recently declassified collection represents the most authoritative China intelligence assessments of the US government in that period, constituting a unique historical record of a momentous era in China's modern history. The collection spans the pivotal period from the final

stages of the Chinese civil war and the consolidation of the Communist regime through the upheavals of the Great Leap Forward and Cultural Revolution.

Reference Sources and Introductory Texts

- *Dictionary of the Politics of People's Republic of China*, edited by Colin Mackerras, Donald H. McMillen, and Andrew Watson (Routledge, 1998). Covers all aspects of Chinese politics, including major political processes and events, key issues in domestic policy, China's evolving foreign policy environment, key political personalities, major political institutions and groupings, and important aspects of the legal system.
- *Political Leaders of Modern China: A Biographical Dictionary*, by Edwin Leung (Greenwood, 2002). Covers political leaders during the Imperial, Republican, and Communist periods.
- *Politics in China: An Introduction*, edited by William Joseph (Oxford University Press, 2010). Written by an international team of highly regarded China scholars, each chapter of the book offers an accessible overview of a key topic in Chinese politics. Topics include politics in the countryside and the cities, the environment, public health, population policy, and more.
- *Politics of Modern China*, edited by Yongnian Zheng, Yiyi Lu, and Lynn T. White III (Routledge, 2009). This four-volume title includes a collection of the best classic and cutting-edge scholarship. Volume I examines policymaking and policy implementation and includes analyses of elite politics, central–local relations, government reform, and bureaucratic behavior. Volume II explores political economy, including issues such as property rights, the management of foreign investment, reform of state-owned enterprises, and financial reform. Volume III brings together the best political analysis of social problems such as unemployment, the rural–urban income gap, the inadequate provision of social welfare, the exploitation of migrant workers, and new public health challenges. The final volume of the collection focuses on

democratization and is organized around themes such as political reform, the development of civil society, political participation, and political culture.

- *Politics and Government in China*, by Guoli Liu (ABC-CLIO, 2011). This book provides an introduction to the Chinese government and politics, with analyses of China's political history, its key leaders and leadership transitions, and its political party, state institutions, and party policies. Moving beyond a strict definition of politics, the book also explores the China's economic development, social policy, law and order, and foreign relations.

- *Handbook of China's International Relations*, by Shaun Beslin (Routledge, 2010). Covers China's relations with United States and other parts of the world and their economic impacts.

- *Political Developments in Contemporary China*, by Ian Jefferies (Taylor and Francis, 2010). Provides a comprehensive and detailed overview of contemporary political developments in China. Key topics covered include China's international relations with its neighbors and wider international community, demographic developments, Taiwan, Macao, Hong Kong, Tibet, Uighurs, human rights, health issues (including bird flu), food contamination and defective goods, and a chronology of political developments, congresses, and Central Committee sessions since May 2006, and more.

- *China: A Guide to Economic and Political Developments*, by Ian Jefferies (Routledge, 2006). The book traces economic and political developments in China from the early 1990s to 2006.

- *The Cultural Revolution: A Bibliography, 1966–1996*, compiled by Yongyi Sung and Dajin Sun, edited by Eugene W. Wu (Harvard-Yenching Library, Harvard University, 1998). A detailed bibliography on studies in the history of Chinese Cultural Revolution.

Women's and Gender Studies

Search Strategies

- For primary sources on Chinese women, search "women, China, sources."

- For general sources on Chinese women, try the following subject terms:
  - Women—China—Anecdotes
  - Women—China—Fiction
  - Women—China—History—20th century
  - Women—China—Social conditions
  - Women's rights—China
  - Women—Employment—China
  - Women—China—Conduct of life
  - Women—China—Biography
  - Women—Legal status, laws, etc.—China
  - Women and literature—China

Core Resources

- *GenderWatch*. A full-text collection of international journals, magazines, newsletters, regional publications, special reports, and conference proceedings devoted to women's and gender issues. The database provides information on subjects such as family, childbirth, birth control, day care, domestic abuse, work and the workplace, sexual harassment, aging, aging parents, body image, eating disorders, and social and societal roles. It also includes content on the impact of gender and gender roles on areas including the arts, popular culture and media, business and work, crime and criminology, education, research and scholarship, family, health care and medicine, politics, policy and legislation, pornography, religion, sexuality and sexology, sports, and leisure. It contains archival material dating back to the mid-1970s; additional archival material continues to be added.
- *Contemporary Women's Issues* (CWI). A multidisciplinary full-text database, CWI brings together relevant content from mainstream periodicals, gray literature, and the alternative press—with a focus on the critical issues and events that influence women's lives in more than 190 countries.
- *Women's Resources International*. This database consists of nine contributing databases covering women's studies, women's issues,

and gender-focused scholarship from throughout the world, including Women Studies Abstracts (1984–), New Books on Women and Feminism (1987–), Women of Color and Southern Women (1975–1988) and annual supplements (1989–), WAVE: Women's Audiovisuals in English: A Guide to Nonprint Resources in Women's Studies, and other databases and print publications.

- *Women and Gender in Chinese Studies Review* (www.wagnet.ox.ac .uk/wagrev/main/missionstatement.html). An online scholarly review journal launched by the Women and Gender in Chinese Studies Network (WAGNet), it publishes reviews of recent publications in the field of Chinese women and gender studies. Access is free.
- Key periodicals:[3]

   Feminist Review (1979–). British publication featuring theme issues on a variety of topics, often with an international focus. Includes book reviews.

   Feminist Theory (2000–). *Feminist Theory* is an international interdisciplinary journal launched in April 2000 to provide a forum for critical analysis and constructive debate within feminism.

   Gender and Society (1987–). Official publication of Sociologists for Women in Society. Presents the latest research and theory on the social and structural implications of gender and includes articles, research reports, and book reviews.

   Journal of Women's History (1989–). Devoted exclusively to the international field of women's history, this journal recognizes the multiple perspectives captured by the term "feminisms" and focuses on work on women that is sensitive to the particular historical constructions of gender that shape and are shaped by women's experience.

   NWSA Journal (1988–). *NWSA Journal*, an official publication of the National Women's Studies Association, publishes interdisciplinary, multicultural feminist scholarship linking feminist theory with teaching and activism.

Signs: A Journal of Women in Culture and Society (1975). Examines theories and methodologies from a variety of disciplines and provides important links between feminist theory and the realities of women's lives.

Social Politics: International Studies in Gender, State, and Society (1994–). Looks at politics and culture from the perspective of gender and addresses changes in family, state, market, and civil society; interdisciplinary and multicultural in scope.

Women's Studies: An Interdisciplinary Journal (1972–). Publishes feature articles about women in anthropology, art, economics, history, literature, sociology, and the sciences. Also includes book and film reviews and some poetry and fiction.

Women's Studies International Forum (1978–). Publishes feature articles on feminist research of multidisciplinary and international topics and includes a Feminist Forum section of forthcoming conferences, calls for papers, websites, and new books.

Primary Sources

- *Women in Republican China: A Sourcebook,* edited by Hua Lan and Vanessa Fong (M. E. Sharpe, 1999). The book contains a collection of original essays by leaders during the May Fourth Movement that discuss and debate across a broad range of theoretical and practical issues revolving around "the woman question."
- *Chinese Women: A Thousand Pieces of Gold,* edited by Barbara Sue White (Oxford University Press, 2003). This anthology brings together scores of extracts by Chinese women and about Chinese women, ranging in time from the eighteenth century to the modern day.
- *Sexual Behavior in Modern China: Report on the Nationwide Survey of 20,000 Men and Women,* by Dalin Liu, Man Lun Ng, Li

Ping Zhou, and Erwin J. Haeberle (Continuum, 1997). Contains a report on a nationwide survey on sexual behavior of men and women in China.

- 中国近代妇女运动历史资料, 1840–1918 (*Historical Documents of Women's Movements in Modern China*), by Huiqi Xu, Jucai Liu, Yuzhen Xu, Zhonghua quan guo fu nu lian he hui, Fu nu yun dong li shi yan jiu shi (Zhongguo fu nu chu ban she, 1991). Zhonghua quan guo fu nu lian he hui, Fu nu yun dong li shi yan jiu shi (China National Women's Association, History of Women's Movements Research Center) published a series of titles of archival sources on Chinese women from the late nineteenth century up to the 1980s. These titles contain primary sources on various aspects of women's social and political conditions during the historical period. The selection of materials, however, was generally influenced by the Communist ideologies, which makes the series useful only to a certain extent.

- 中国妇女运动历史资料: *1921–1927* (*Historical Documents of Women's Movements in China: 1921–1927*), by Zhonghua quan guo fu nu lian he hui, Fu nu yun dong li shi yan jiu shi (Ren min chu ban she, 1986).

- 中国妇女运动历史资料: *1927–1937* (*Historical Documents of Women's Movements in China: 1927–1937*), by Zhonghua quan guo fu nu lian he hui, Fu nu yun dong li shi yan jiu shi (Zhongguo fu nu chu ban she, 1991).

- 中国妇女运动历史资料: *1937–1945* (*Historical Documents of Women's Movements in China: 1937–1945*), by Zhonghua quan guo fu nu lian he hui, Fu nu yun dong li shi yan jiu shi (Zhongguo fu nu chu ban she, 1991).

- 中国妇女运动历史资料: *1945.10–1949.9* (*Historical Documents of Women's Movements in China: 1945.10–1949.9*), by Zhonghua quan guo fu nu lian he hui, Fu nu yun dong li shi yan jiu shi (Zhongguo fu nu chu ban she, 1991).

- 中国妇女运动文献资料汇编 (1918–1983) (*Collection of Historical Documents of Women's Movements in China: 1918–1983*), by Zhongguo fu nu guan li gan bu xue yuan (Zhongguo fu nu chu ban she, 1988).

- 中国妇女运动历史资料.民国政府卷 (1912–1949) (*Historical Documents of Women's Movements in China, Republic Era: 1912–1949*), by Yang Xiao, Zhonghua fu nu lian he hui, Fu nu yan jiu suo, Zhongguo di er li shi dang an guan (Zhonguo fu nu chu ban she, 2011).

Reference Sources and Introductory Texts

- *Routledge International Encyclopedia of Women: Global Women's Issues and Knowledge,* edited by Cheris Kramarae and Dale Spender (Routledge, 2000). This four-volume set provides comprehensive coverage of women's issues worldwide, from violence and sexuality to feminist theory. It includes entries on women in China.
- *Guide to Women's Studies in China*, edited by Gail Hershatter et al. (University of California, Berkeley, 1998). Includes introductory essays on women's studies in mainland China, Hong Kong, and Taiwan and bibliographic guides to relevant resources.
- *Women of China: Economic and Social Transformation*, edited by Jackie West et al. (Macmillan, 1999). This collection presents original research on a range of key topics, including women and politics, gender and migration, the effect of new employment relations in industry and agriculture, women's roles in the household and attitudes to the one-child family, and the development of women's studies.
- *Women in China from Earliest Times to the Present: A Bibliography of Studies in Western Languages*, by Robin D. S. Yates (Brill, 2009). This reference work is an alphabetical listing, with an extensive index of more than 2,500 citations of books, chapters in books, and articles, and 100-plus dissertations in all social science and humanities disciplines relating to women in China from earliest times to today.
- 中华妇女文献纵览 (Women's Studies in China: A selected bibliography and resource guide from the ancient time to the present), by Wenyi Qi (Peking University Press, 1995). This Chinese-language book covers all areas of women's life in China, including

work, history, organization and movement, ethics, law, economics, literature, and culture.

---

1. Given the vast amount of law literature, we will limit our discussion here to mostly English-language sources, with the exception of some major Chinese electronic resources.
2. For this section, the author has consulted a number of Chinese law research guides, particularly "Laws of the People's Republic of China" (http://law.wustl.edu/library/pages.aspx?id=7083/), by Wei Luo of Washington University School of Law, and "Finding Chinese Law on the Internet" (www.nyulawglobal.org/globalex/china.htm), by Joan Liu of New York University School of Law Library.
3. The information here comes from the ACRL Women and Gender Studies Section, American Library Association, at www.libr.org/wgss/projects/journallist .html#gensoc/.

APPENDIX A

Guide to Buying Chinese Books and Films

There are many vendors dealing with Chinese-language materials both inside and outside China. Following is a list of vendors that many academic libraries in North America have been working with. This list, however, does not imply endorsement of any of the vendors represented here.

Buying Chinese Books in North America

China Classics, Inc.

10566 Giffin Way, San Diego, CA 92126
Contact: Wei Wang
Tel: 858-536-9224; 858-229-9677 (cell)
Fax: 858-536-9223
E-mail: chinaclassics@yahoo.com

China Classics supplies academic libraries in North America with Chinese-language research materials such as books and DVDs and more. Contact Mr. Wei Wang for catalogs. Mr. Wei Wang attends the annual conference of Association of Asian Studies every year and has a booth in the exhibition.

星辉国际图书进出口公司 Starmark International

Headquartered in Long Island, NY
Contact: Peter Wang
Tel: 516-470-1598
E-mail: peterw@thestarmark.com
Website: www.thestarmark.com/

The company serves public, school, and college libraries and organizations with Chinese books and media products as well as customized processing services and collection development programs.

Buying Books from Mainland China

北京珍本国际贸易有限公司 (Beijing Chinese Book Trading Co.)
北京市海淀区苏州街18号院 长远天地大厦4306; 100080
Contact: Zhang Guifang 张桂芳
Tel: 86-10-5128-9389; 139-0123-5443 (cell)
Fax: 86-10-8260-9070
E-mail: zhenbenbook@hotmail.com; Shudian@263.net
Website: www.bookchinese.com/

This company specializes in exporting Chinese cultural products, ranging from books and media products to electronic resources. It provides customized collection development services. Its representative attends the annual conference of Association of Asian Studies every year and has a booth in the exhibition.

中国国际贸易图书总公司 (China International Book Trading Corporation)
北京车公庄西路35号 北京邮政信箱399号; 100044;
35, Chegongzhuang Xilu, PO Box 399, Beijing 100044, China
Contact: Wang Tong 汪彤
Tel: 86-10-6841-3971; 6843-3158; 139-1025-8095 (cell)
Fax: 86-10-6841-4694; 86-10-6841-2023
E-mail: tsg@mail.cibtc.com.cn
Website: www.cibtc.com.cn/gtweb/homeindex.do/

This company serves academic libraries with a range of cultural products from China, including books, DVDs, and electronic services. It provides customized collection development services. Its representatives attend the annual conference of the Association of Asian Studies every year and have a booth in the exhibition.

Buying Books from Hong Kong

星光圖書公司 (Hsing Kuang Book Co.)
香港鴨脷洲漁安苑碧安閣2404室
GPO Box 13562, Hong Kong
Contact: 黃賢明
Tel: 852-2874-1922
Fax: 852-2874-2045
E-mail: hsingbkc@netvigator.com

Chiao Liu Publication Trading Co. Ltd.

PO Box 50324S, Sai Ying Pun Post Office, Hong Kong
Tel: 852-3007-5050
Fax: 852-2858-6379
E-mail: chiaoliu@chiaoliu.com.hk

Buying Books from Taiwan

樂學書局 LEXIS
臺北市金山南路二段138號10號樓之一
Contact: Xinxin Huang黃新新
Tel: 02-2321-9033
Fax: 02-2356-8068
E-mail: lexis@ms6.hinet.net

Buying Chinese Books and Films Online

Dangdang (www.dangdang.com/)

Dangdang is an online store similar to Amazon.com. It started as an online bookstore and has now expanded its service into all categories. It has a robust search engine and good collection of books and other materials appropriate for academic research. It accepts major credit cards such as Visa, MasterCard, and American Express.

Amazon.cn (www.amazon.cn/)

The China branch of Amazon.com, it deals with a wide range of products including books and DVDs. The advantage of Amazon.cn is the familiar brand and interface. It accepts all major credit cards.

ChinaBookShop.net: Center for China Publications (www.chinabookshop.net/)

ChinaBookShop.net is owned by Sunrill Information Limited, a Hong Kong–registered company with headquarters in Hong Kong, server in the United States, and customer service and delivery center in Shenzhen, China. It is a specialty online bookstore that offers the most comprehensive sources for up-to-date statistical data, customs tariffs, market research reports, directories, yellow pages, regulations and laws, and business reference books. The default payment option is PayPal credit card payment.

YesAsia.com (www.yesasia.com/us/en/home.html)

Established in 1998, YesAsia.com has become a leading online store that specializes in films from East Asia (China, Korea, and Japan). Its English interface is very user-friendly and easy to navigate. The store accepts major US credit cards.

APPENDIX B

Guide to Buying Chinese E-resources

This appendix mostly covers the electronic products discussed in the previous chapters. They represent the most important e-resources for Modern China Studies that are currently available on the market.

Vendors in North America

East View Information Services, Inc.

10601 Wayzata Boulevard
Minneapolis, MN 55305 USA
Contact: Robert E. Lee (director) at robert.lee@eastview.com; Tammy Byrne Ziegler (federal sales and account manager) at Tammy.Byrne@eastview.com
Tel.: 1-952-252-1201
Fax: 1-952-252-1202
North America toll-free: 800-477-1005
Website: http://eastview.com/

Major Chinese Products

- China National Knowledge Infrastructure (CNKI) databases. CNKI databases represent the most comprehensive resources from mainland China, encompassing a wide range of research materials. Following is a list of CNKI databases available at East View:

  China Academic Journals (CAJ). Covers the majority of academic journals from mainland China from 1994 to the present.

  Century Journals Project. Includes the archives of CAJ journals dating as far back as 1906.

  China Doctoral/Master Dissertations Full-text Database. Includes theses and dissertations from over 300 higher education institutions in mainland China.

China Conference Proceedings. Includes over 1,500 titles of major conference proceedings.

China Legal Knowledge Database. Includes primary and secondary documents on all legal topics.

China Core Newspaper Database. Covers nearly 1,000 national and local newspapers from 2000 to the present.

China Yearbooks Full-Text Database. Includes over 1,500 titles of yearbooks.

China Reference Works Online. Includes over 1,500 titles of reference works (dictionaries and encyclopedias).

China Statistical Yearbooks Database. Includes 450 titles of statistical yearbooks.

- *PLA Daily (Jiefangjun Bao).* This database contains the full run of the *People's Liberation Army (PLA) Daily*, the official newspaper of the military of the PRC.
- *Green Apple Products.* East View also carries products by Green Apple, one of the major database producers in China, including the following:

  Shen Bao. Contains the complete run of the most important newspaper of the Republic Era from 1872 to 1949.

  People's Daily (Renmin Ribao). Covers the complete run of the most important newspaper in China, *Renmin Ribao* (*People's Daily*), the official organ of the Communist Party of China from 1946 to the present.

  Guangming Ribao. Includes the complete run of *Guangming Ribao*, another major newspaper in China, from 1949 to the present.

- *Apabi Products and Services.* Apabi is known as a preeminent source of e-books from China, currently with nearly half a million full-text electronic book titles. In addition to e-books, Apabi also produces databases of newspapers and art images. Following is a list of products and services that Apabi offers through East View:

  Apabi Chinese Fine Arts Database. Includes over 35,000 artwork images from leading museums in China.

  Apabi E-Books Database. Includes nearly half a million titles from 500 publishers in China. Most titles are recent publications, although some holdings date back to 1949.

  E-Book Approval Plan. Offers a free service to help libraries develop Chinese e-book collections.

  Apabi Newspapers Database. Covers 80 percent of all Chinese newspapers, many of which go back to the first issues.

- 北大法律信息网 *ChinaLawInfo/LawInfoChina*. ChinaLawInfo is an up-to-date, authoritative, and comprehensive database of Chinese laws and regulations in Chinese. It allows access to laws and regulations, judicial cases, tax treaties, the World Trade Organization and China, gazettes, and journals online with ease. The English version, LawInfoChina.com, contains authoritative translations of important legal content relevant to English speakers interested in Chinese law. East View provides subscriptions to both Chinese and English versions of the legal database.
- *E-books and e-serial publications.* East View also offers individual subscriptions to tens of thousands of e-books and e-serial publications (such as yearbooks) from China.

Oriprobe Information Services

3238 Curry Avenue, N9E 2T5, Windsor, Canada
Suite 1-19, Hua Tong Plaza B Tower, Beijing 100044, China
Contact: Danny F. Liu 刘定飞
Tel: 1-519-973-1556, 1-519-977-9050, 86-10-8801-8034
Fax: 1-614-451-0162, 86-10-8801-8285
E-mail: dliu@oriprobe.com; dliu@wanfangdata.com.cn; info@oriprobe.com
Website: www.oriprobe.com/index.html

MAJOR PRODUCTS

- *People's Daily (Renmin Ribao).* Covers the entire run of the paper from 1946 to the present.
- *Archives of the Communist Party of China.* Includes important documents through the history of CPC since its founding in 1921.
- *The Database of the National People's Congress* (NPC). Includes a complete collection of all documents issued by the NPC.
- *The Database of the Chinese People's Political Consultative Conference* (CPPCC). Includes a complete collection of CPPCC documents.
- *The Database of the Chinese Government.* Covers all the policies and documents from the central government, its ministries, and local authorities.
- *Global Times* (1993–present). This is another major newspaper run by the Chinese government, mostly covering international issues and foreign affairs.

China Data Center, University of Michigan

China Data Center, 330 Packard Road, Ann Arbor, MI 48106-1248
Contact: Shuming Bao (director) at sbao@umich.edu

Tel: 734-647-9610
Fax: 734-763-0335
E-mail: chinadata@umich.edu
Website: http://chinadatacenter.org/

MAJOR PRODUCT

- *China Data Online.* This online database on economic statistics of China includes statistics yearbooks at provincial and national levels. It also includes GIS function through its China Geo-Explorer.

Vendors in Mainland China

清华同方知网(北京)技术有限公司

北京华业大厦1区1308室 清华大学84-48信箱100084
Contact: Changsheng An 安昌盛
Tel: 86-10-6279-1819
Fax: 86-10-6279-1944
E-mail: beijing@cnki.net
Website: www.cnki.net/

MAJOR PRODUCTS

- *China National Knowledge Infrastructure (CNKI) databases.* Include all the CNKI products provided through the mirror site managed by East View, the US vendor (see previous listing in this appendix). All products are available at the Chinese website: www.cnki.net/.

北京超星信息技术有限公司

北京市海淀区上帝三街9号嘉华大厦C座710室;100085 Room 4306, Changyuan tiandi Building 18, Suzhou Street, Haidian District, Beijing 100080, China
Contact: Aizhen Zhang 张爱珍
Tel: 86-10-6296-2266 ext. 3061; 86-10-8161-3792 (cell)
Fax: 86-10-6296-1053
E-mail: haiwai@ssreader.com
Website: www.chaoxing.com/

MAJOR PRODUCTS

- *Duxiu* (www.duxiu.com/). Duxiu is a powerful content discovery search engine that searches the full text of over three million books, theses and dissertations, journal articles, newspapers, and reference sources from China. Subscription is required to access the database.

- *Chinamaxx* (http://chinamaxx.net/). Chinamaxx is an online digital library of over 700,000 full-text Chinese books. Subscription is required.
- 大成老旧刊全文数据库 (http://dachengdata.com/). This digital full-text collection offers over 13,000 periodicals from the Republic Era (1911–1949). It is produced by Dacheng Shu ju you xian gong si (Dacheng Data, Inc.) and promoted through Super Star Digital Library to the overseas market.

万方数据Wanfang Data Co. Inc.

北京市海淀区复兴路15号（邮编:100038）

15 Fuxing Road, Suite 243, Haidian District, Beijing 100038, China

Contact: Jason Dai at jason@wanfangdata.com or daijc2002@hotmail.com

Tel: 86-10-5888-2628

Direct: 1-416-900-8266

E-mail: overseas@wanfangdata.com

MAJOR PRODUCTS

- *China Local Gazetteers* (CLG). CLG is a collection of Chinese local gazetteers published after 1949 that cover all regions of China; http://c.g.wanfangdata.com.cn/LocalChronicle.aspx (Chinese); www.wanfangdata.com/gazetteers/intr.asp (Introduction in English).
- *China Online Journals* (COJ). COJ includes about 7,400 journal titles published in China (as of August 2012) that cover a high percentage of core journals; http://c.g.wanfangdata.com.cn/Periodical.aspx (Chinese); www.wanfangdata.com/COJ/intr.asp (English).
- *Dissertations of China* (DOC). DOC is a comprehensive collection of Chinese dissertations and theses from Chinese research institutions since 1980; http://c.g.wanfangdata.com.cn/Thesis.aspx (Chinese); www.wanfangdata.com/DOC/intr.asp (English).
- *Academic Conferences in China* (ACIC). Includes academic papers in Chinese or English from national and international conferences held in China since 1985; http://c.g.wanfangdata.com.cn/Conference.aspx (Chinese); www.wanfangdata.com/acic/intr.asp (English).
- *Policies and Laws of China* (PLOC). PLOC is a comprehensive collection of full-text Chinese legislation, jurisdictions, cases, official announcements, and treaties published since 1949; http://c.g.wanfangdata.com.cn/Claw.aspx (Chinese); www.wanfangdata.com/ploc/intr.asp (English).

上海图书馆全国报刊索引编辑部

Editorial Department
National Index to Chinese Newspapers and Periodicals
Shanghai Library
1555 Huaihai Zhonglu, Shanghai 200031, China
Sales tel: 86-21-6445-3506 (Mon.–Fri. 9:00–17:00 Beijing Time)
Fax: 86-21-6445-1208
E-mail: bksy3@libnet.sh.cn
Website: www.cnbksy.com/ShanghaiLibrary/en/main.html

MAJOR PRODUCTS

- *National Index to Chinese Newspapers and Periodicals* (NICNP). The flagship product from Shanghai Library is an index database covering newspapers and periodicals from 1833 to the present. It indexes about 18,000 newspapers and periodicals published in China. The database contains over 30 million entries, with a yearly update of 3.5 million entries.
- *The Late Qing Dynasty Full-text Database* (1833–1910). Launched in 2009, it includes full-text images of newspapers and periodicals published in the late Qing Dynasty from 1833 to 1910.
- *The Republic Era Full-text Database* (1911–1949). This database is an ongoing project of digitizing over 18,000 titles of periodicals published during the Republic Era.
- *The Socialist Era Full-Text Database* (1950–1977). This ongoing project covers the three decades following the founding of the PRC.
- *The Contemporary China Full-Text Database* (1978–present). This ongoing project covers contemporary China.

China INFOBANK 中国资讯行有限公司

Soshoo 搜数 (part of China Infobank)
北京精讯云顿有限公司
北京东城区安德里北街21号八一综合楼南2楼
No. 21, Andeli North Street, Dongcheng District, Beijing 100120, China
Tel.: 86-10-8413 4405/06/08/09
Fax: 86-10-8413-1720
E-mail: service@soshoo.com
China Infobank website: www.infobank.cn/irisweb/infobank.htm
Soshoo website: www.soshoo.com/index.do/

MAJOR PRODUCTS

- *China Infobank.* The collection of 14 databases provides access to real-time business news, China general news articles and magazines, information and statistics on government, reports, and statistics of various industries and regions in China.
- *Soshoo Database.* The flagship product from China Infobank, the database offers yearly and monthly statistical data on the social and economic situation of China. The information sourced from national and provincial statistical yearbooks, industrial yearbooks, the People's Bank of China Quarterly Statistical Bulletin, China's customs statistics, and so on, since the 1990s with some dating back to 1949. Data can be downloaded into an Excel sheet.

INDEX

f denotes figures; *t* denotes tables

A

ABI/INFORM Complete, 161
Academic Search Complete (ASC), 44–46
Access World News, 94, 183
accessibility of information, effect of, 5–6
ACRL (Association of College and Research
  Libraries), 13
advanced search functions
    in Catalyst, 26–27*f*
    in Google, 80, 81*f*
    in Google Scholar, 49
    in JSTOR, 42
    in WorldCat, 29*f,* 30, 33
AGSL Digital Photo Archive, 99
All Under Heaven: The Chinese World (Porter), 96
Amazon.cn, 195
*The Amerasia Affair, China and Postwar Anti-
  Communist Fervor,* 123
American Geographical Society Library, 99, 101
American Journal of Chinese Studies, 53
American Journal of Sociology, 149
American Nervousness (Beard), 2
American Sociological Review, 149
Andrews, Julia F., 110
Angle, Stephen C., 124
*An Annotated Bibliography of Chinese Film
  Studies* (Cheng), 117
annual reports, locating, 79, 153, 182
Annual Review of Anthropology, 144
Annual Review of Political Science, 182
Annual Review of Sociology, 149
Annual Reviews, 23
Anthropological Resources (Dutton), 145
anthropology sources, 143–147
Anthropology in China (Guldin), 146
Anthropology Plus, 143–144

Anthropology Review Database (ARD), 144
AnthroSource, 144
Apabi Products and Services, 198
*Archival Collection of the History of People's
  Liberation Army,* 97
archives, locating, 85–87
Archives of Asian Art, 106
Archives of the Chinese Communist Party, 83, 199
Archives of the Chinese Government, 83, 183
Archives of the Ministry of Foreign Affairs, 86
art
    core resources on, 104, 105–107
    primary sources on, 107–109
    reference sources on, 109–111
    subject headings for, 105
Art and Artists of Twentieth-Century China
  (Sullivan), 110
Art and China's Revolution: Asia Society
  Exhibit 2008, 107
Art Asia Pacific, 106
Art Index Retrospective, 105
Art Speak China, 110
articles
    Chinese-language, 55–58
    databases for locating, 41–51, 66–73
    for literature reviews, 65–73
    major journals of, 51–54, 59–62
    scholarly *vs.* popular, 39–41
    translated from Chinese, 58–62
    See also journals
Arts and Humanities Citation Index (AHCI),
  104
ARTstor, 107
ArtZine, 108
Asia and the West: Diplomacy and Cultural
  Exchange database, 126
Asia Art Archive, 108
Asia Pacific Films, 115

Asian Anthropology, 144
Asian Arts, 106
Asian Business and Reference database, 161
Asian Cinema, 113
Asian Development Outlook, 165
Asian Economic Outlook, 165
Asian Higher Education (Mak and Postiqlione),
   154
Asian studies, major journals of, 51–54
Asian Studies in Video, 115
Asian Theater Journal, 114
ATLA Religion Database, 136
Atwill, David G., 125
Atwill, Yurong Y., 125
authoritative sources, 13, 39–40
authors, qualifications of, 12–13, 40

B
Baltes, Paul B., 151
Barfield, Thomas, 146
Barnard, Alan, 146
Beard, George, 2
Beers, Burton F., 98
Beijing, xvi, xvii, xxv, 97
Beijing Chinese Book Trading Co., 194
Berzin Archives, 137
Beslin, Shaun, 186
biases, in sources, 1–3, 40
bibliographies, overview of, 40–41
Bibliography of Asian Studies Online (BAS),
   47–48, 59, 103, 104, 142
Bibliography of English Translations (Louie and
   Edwards), 134
Bibliography of the History of Art (BHA),
   105–106
Bilancia, Philip R., 179
Bird in a Cage: Legal Reform in China
   (Lubman), 179
Birx, H. James, 146
Blackwell Encyclopedia of Sociology Online, 151
Bloomberg Financial Services, 169
Bond, Michael Harris, 171
book reviews, 23, 52, 149
books
   buying guide for, 193–196
   Chinese-language books, 33–35
   e-books, 35–37
   from Google Books, 30–33
   from local libraries, 25–28

   from WorldCat, 29–32f, 33–34, 140n1
British Journal of Sociology, 149
Bucklin, Harold, 99
Bucklin China Archive, 99
Buddhism, xvii, 136–137
Burr, William, 124
business resources. *See* economics and
   business
Business Source Complete, 161

C
CAJ. *See* China Academic Journals (CAJ)
Campus Research: Law, 175
Capitalism without Democracy (Tsai), 71
catalogs, library, 18–19, 25–28, 30–31, 33, 35,
   76
Catalyst, 18, 26–27f, 30
CCP. *See* Chinese Communist Party (CCP)
CEIC Data, 164, 167
censorship, 14, 85–86, 89–90
A Centennial Compendium of Civil Law of China
   (Yang), 179
A Century in Crisis (Andrews and Shen), 110
Chan, Kim Kwong, 138
Chan, Wing-tsit, 138
Chang, Kang-i Sun, 133
Changes in Chinese Social Life (Zhong), 96
The Changing Chinese Legal System (Liang), 179
Cheek, Timothy, 125
Chen, Huifen, 98
Cheng, Jim, 117
Cheng, Peikai, 128
Chiao Liu Publication Trading Co. Ltd., 195
children, policy regarding, xxv, 14, 191
Chin, Ann-ping, 96
China, traditional, xix–xxii
   See also People's Republic of China
China 1972 collection, 101
*China: A Guide to Economic and Political
   Developments* (Jefferies), 186
China Academic Journals (CAJ), 23, 56–58, 104,
   111, 142, 197
China Agricultural Economic Review, 163
China: An International Journal, 44t, 53
*China and the United States: From Hostility to
   Engagement,* 123
China and World Economy, 162
China Business Guide 2012, 171
The China Business Review, 163

China Classics, Inc., 193
China Compendium of Statistics, 87–88, 150
China Core Newspapers Full-text Database, 91, 122, 183, 198
China: Culture and Society, 126
China Data Center, 199–200
China Data Online, 88, 149, 164, 200
China Dimensions, 150
China Documents Annual, 182
China Economic Journal, 161
China Economic Policy Review, 162
China Economic Quarterly, 162
China Economic Review, 162
China Education System and Policy Handbook, 154
China Educational Development Yearbook, 153–154
China Facts and Figures Annual, 87, 182
China: Fifty Years inside the People's Republic (Yang), 96
China Finance Review International, 163
China Foreign Economic Statistical Yearbook, 166
China in Old Photographs (Beers), 98
China Independent Documentaries Film Archive, 115
China InfoBank, 165, 202–203
China Information, 53
China International Book Trading Corporation, 194
The China Journal, 43t, 45t, 53, 182
China Law and Practice, 177
China Law Briefing, 177
China Law Deskbook (Zimmerman), 180
China Law journal, 177
China Law Knowledge Database (CLKD), 178
China Law Quarterly, 177
China Law Reference Service, 180
China Law Reporter, 177
China Local Gazetteers Full-text Database, 89, 150, 201
China Media Research (CMR), 114
China Monthly Economic Indicators, 166
China National Knowledge Infrastructure (CNKI)
    for articles, 58, 72–73
    for government documents, 80–82, 122
    overview of, 22, 56
    for statistics, 88
    for theses and dissertations, 38, 178

vendors for, 197, 200
China Online Journals (COJ), 56, 201
China Onward: The Estella Collection (Erickson), 109
China Perspective, 53
China Political Reports (Jarman), 123–124
China: Portrait of a Country (Liu), 96
The China Quarterly, 6–7, 43t, 45t, 54
The China Reader: The Reform Era (Schell and Shambaugh), 124
The China Recorder, 95
The China Review: An Interdisciplinary Journal, 53
China Review International, 182
China Securities Market and Accounting Research (CSMAR), 167
China Since 1919 (Lawrance), 124
China Social and Economic Development Statistical Database, 88
China Social Statistical Yearbook, 150
China Statistical Yearbook, 87, 198
China Studies, traditional, 1–4
    See also Modern China Studies
China: Trade, Politics and Culture, 126
China Trade and External Economic Statistical Yearbook, 166
China Yearbook Full-text Database, 88, 150, 198
ChinaBookShop.net, 195
ChinaLawInfo.com, 178
Chinamaxx, 36–37, 201
China's Avant-Garde Fiction (Wang), 132
China's Financial Markets (Neftci and Menager-Xu), 171
China's Long March toward Rule of Law (Peerenboom), 179
ChinaScope Financial, 169
Chinese Academy of Social Sciences, 128n1, 153
Chinese Buddhist Electronic Text Association, 137
Chinese Business: Landscapes and Strategies (Liu), 171
The Chinese Century: A Photographic History, 96
Chinese Characteristics (Smith), 2
Chinese characters, searching with, 33, 58
The Chinese Civil War and U.S.-China Relations, 127
Chinese Commercial Law (Roos), 172, 179
Chinese Communist Party (CCP)
    history of, xxiii–xxvi
    political power of, 13–15, 78, 89–90

Chinese Communist Party (cont.)
  reference works on, 53, 83, 122, 183–184
Chinese Contemporary Art Document, 106
Chinese Cultural Revolution Database, 122, 183
Chinese Drama: An Annotated Bibliography
  (Lopez), 135
The Chinese Economy journal, 59
The Chinese Economy: Reform and Development
  (Fang, Lin and Yong), 170
Chinese Education and Society, 59–60, 153
*The Chinese Filmography: The 2,444 Feature
  Films* (Marion), 117
The Chinese Historical Review, 121
The Chinese Human Rights Reader (Angle and
  Svensson), 124
Chinese Journal of Communications, 114
Chinese Law and Government, 60, 177
Chinese Literature Today, 131
Chinese Management Studies, 163
Chinese Movie Database, 116
Chinese National Cinema (Zhang), 117
Chinese Periodicals of Republic Era, 93
Chinese Philosophical Etext Archive, 138
Chinese Religion: An Anthology (Sommer), 138
Chinese Religion in Western Languages, 139
*Chinese Religion: Publications in Western
  Languages,* 139
Chinese Sociological Review, 149
Chinese Sociology and Anthropology, 60–61, 144
Chinese Studies in History, 61
Chinese Taipai Film Archive, 116
Chinese Women: A Thousand Pieces of Gold
  (White), 189
Chinese Writers on Writing (Sze), 133
Chinese-language sources
  articles, 55–58
  books, 33–35
  e-books, 36–37
  locating, 21–22
Christianity, xvii, 136, 139–140
Christianity in China (Wu), 139–140
The Chronicles of the East India Company
  (Morse), 127
CIAO (Columbia International Affairs Online),
  181
Cinema Journal, 113
citations
  locating for literature review, 66–68,
  69–71f, 72–73

management tools for, 49– 51, 52f
cities, images of, 97
Clarke, David J., 110
CNKI. *See* China National Knowledge
  Infrastructure (CNKI)
Coen, David, 171
*Collection of Statistics on China Economy and
  Social Development,* 166
*The Columbia Anthology of Modern Chinese
  Literature* (Lau and Goldblatt), 132
Columbia Guide to Modern Chinese History
  (Schoppa), 127
Columbia International Affairs Online (CIAO),
  181
Communication and Mass Media Complete
  (CMMC), 112
Communication Studies Full-Text Collection,
  112
Communist Party. *See* Chinese Communist
  Party (CCP)
company information, 160, 167–170
*Compendium of Historical Documents of Study of
  Law of China* (Zhang), 178
"A Complete Research Guide to the Laws of
  People's Republic of China" (Liu and Luo),
  180
Confucianism, xix, 136, 138, 139
Contemporary China Database, 92, 202
Contemporary Chinese Art: Primary Documents,
  109
*Contemporary Chinese Documentary
  Photography* (Yuan), 96
Contemporary Chinese Thought, 61
Contemporary Sociology, 149
Contemporary Women's Issues (CWI), 187
corporate information, 160, 167–170
CountryData.com, 164
critical thinking, 13, 14, 173
Cua, Antonio S., 138
The Cultural Revolution (Sung, Sun and Wu),
  186
Culture and Customs of China (Gunde), 147
Current Law Index, 176
Customs and Conditions of Chinese City Streets,
  96

D
Da Cheng Lao Jiu Kan Full-Text Database, 92
Dangdang, 195

Dao: A Journal of Comparative Philosophy, 136
Database of National People's Congress, 83, 183, 199
Database of the Chinese People's Political Consultative Conference, 183
Database of the Communist Party of China, 183
databases
    for government documents, 79–83
    index *vs.* full-text, 26, 33, 47
    for literature reviews, 66–73
    multidisciplinary *vs.* specialized, 41
    overview of, 19–21
    See also specific databases
Defoort, Carine, 61
demography, xvi–xvii
Deng Xiaoping, xxv, 5, 83, 124
Denton, Kirk, 133, 134
dGenerate Films, 115–116
Diamant, Neil, 86
dictionaries, as starting point, 10
Dictionary of Anthropology (Barfield), 146
Dictionary of Chinese Law and Government (Bilancia), 179
Dictionary of the Politics of People's Republic of China, 185
Digital Archive of Chinese Buddhist Temple Local Gazetteers, 137
digital environment, research in, 12–13, 34, 36
Digital Library and Museum of Buddhist Studies, 137
Digital National Security Archive (DNSA), 123
digital resources, reliance on, 142
Ding, Shiliang, 145
Dirlik, Arif, 147
Dissertation Reviews, 86
dissertations and theses
    government influence on, 15
    locating, 38, 201
Dooling, Amy D., 133
Dow Jones Guide to the Global Stock Market, 170
Du, Yongzhen, 96
Dutton, Lee S., 145
Duxiu, 34–35, 37*f*, 38, 104, 142, 200

E

East Asian History, 120
East Asian Image Collection, 99–100
East View Information Services Inc., 197–199

Ebook Library (EBL), 35–36
e-books, 35–37
EconLit, 161
economics and business
    core resources on, 161–164
    primary sources on, 164–170
    reference sources on, 59, 128, 170–172
    subject headings for, 157–161
economy
    growth of, xi, xxv, 7, 170
    as market economy, xxv–xxvi, 90, 170
    statistics on, xvii–xviii
education
    sources on, 153–155
    subject headings for, 151–152
Education Full Text, 153
Education in China Since 1976 (Wang), 154
Education Reform in China (Ryan), 155
Education Statistical Yearbook of China, 154
Education Yearbook of China, 154
Edwards, Louise, 134
effective research, 9–13
eHRAF World Cultures database, 145
The Eight-Power Allied Forces through Foreigners' Camera, 97
EIU Country Report, 164, 167
electronic resources
    buying guide for, 197–203
    use of, 19–21
Encyclopedia Britannica Online, 12–13, 20
Encyclopedia of Anthropology (Birx), 146
Encyclopedia of Asian Philosophy (Leaman), 139
Encyclopedia of Chinese Film (Zhang), 116
Encyclopedia of Chinese Philosophy (Cua), 139
Encyclopedia of Modern China (Pong), 146
Encyclopedia of Social and Cultural Anthropology, 146
encyclopedias, as starting point, 10
endnotes, 25, 41
ERIC (Education Resource Information Center), 148, 153
Erickson, Britta, 109
ethnic groups, xvii, 143, 146
Ethnic Minorities in Modern China (Mackerras), 147
Ethnographic Video Online, 144
An Ethnohistorical Dictionary of China (Olson), 146
exchange students, 7, 155

F

Fairbank, John, 4
Fang, Cai, 170
Far East Economic Review, 163
Feminist Review, 188
Feminist Theory, 188
Fibicher, Bernhard, 109
fiction. *See* literature
film
    core resources on, 112–115
    primary sources on, 115–116
    reference sources on, 116–117
    subject headings for, 111
Film and Television Literature Index, 112
Film Literature Index (FLI), 112
Film Quarterly, 113
finance resources. *See* economics and business
The Financial Times, 163
First Historical Archives of China, 86–87
Fong, Vanessa, 189
footnotes, 25, 41
Foreign Broadcast Information Service (FBIS) Daily Reports, 183
Foreign Office Files for China, 1949–1980, 122
Foreign Relations of the United States (Schwar), 184
Foreign Service Information Service (FBIS) Daily Reports, 93, 183
Forman, Harrison, 101
Frehner, Matthias, 109
From Small Feet Women to Half of the Sky (Wu), 98
Frontiers of Literary Studies in China, 131
full-text databases, *vs.* index, 26, 33, 47
funding
    of China Studies, 5
    of research in China, 14–15
Fung, Hung-Gay, 59

G

Gale Virtual Reference Library (GVRL), 20–21
Gale's Archives Unbound, 95, 123, 126–127
Gamble, Sidney D., 98–99
gazetteers, 89, 137, 145, 150, 201
GDP statistics, xvii–xviii
Gender and Society journal, 188
gender studies. *See* women
GenderWatch, 187
geography, xvi

Globalization and Changes in China's Governance, 31–33
Goldblatt, Howard, 132
Google
    advanced search function in, 80, 81*f*
    overreliance on, 12
Google Books, 30–34
Google Scholar, 48–52*f*, 58, 72
government
    facts and figures on, xvi
    political power of, 13–15, 78, 85–86, 89–90
    See also politics
government documents
    from CNKI, 80–82, 122
    types of, 79
    from WorldCat, 76–78*f*, 79–80
Grant, Wyn, 171
Graves, Mortimer, 4
The Great Famine in China (Zhou), 125
Great Leap Forward, xxiv, 124, 185
Great Proletarian Cultural Revolution, xxiv, 124
Green Apple Products, 198
Grove Dictionary of Art, 109
Guan, Lianchang, 96
Guide to Women's Studies in China (Hershatter), 191
Guldin, Gregory, 60, 146
Gunde, Richard, 147
Guomindang (Kuomintang), xxii, xxiii–xxiv

H

Haeberle, Erwin J., 190
Hahn, Thomas H., 100
Han Dynasty, xix
Handbook of China's International Relations (Beslin), 186
Handbook of Chinese Organizational Behavior (Huang and Bond), 171
Handbook of Contemporary Marketing in China (Wang), 171
Handbooks in Economics series, 170
Harding, Harry, 6
Harvard Business Review, 162
Harvard Journal of Asiatic Studies, 52
Harvard Modern China Studies program, 4
He, Dongchang, 154
Hershatter, Gail, 191

Higher Education of China (He), 154

Historical Abstracts database, 120, 181

Historical Dictionary of Modern Chinese Literature, 134

Historical Dictionary of the People's Republic of China (Sullivan), 127

Historical Documents of Women's Movements in China, 190

Historical Documents of Women's Movements in Modern China, 190

Historical Photos of China, 100

history
 core resources on, 120–122
 images of, 96–97
 primary sources on, 122–127
 reference sources on, 127–128
 subject headings, 119–120

A History of Art in 20th Century China (Peng), 110–111

History of Modern Chinese Fiction (Hsia), 129

Hong, Shen, 98

Hong Kong, 94, 97, 110, 116, 175, 177, 194–195

Hong Kong Art (Clarke), 110

Hong Kong during Japan Occupation (Tianqiang and Tang), 97

Hong Kong Movie Database, 116

Hoover Institute Political Poster Database, 108

Hoovers Academic, 169

Hoover's Handbook of World Business, 170

Hsia, C. T., 129

Hsing Kuang Book Co., 194

Hu Jintao, xxv, xxvi, 14

Huang, Shijian, 96

Huang, Xu, 171

humanities, core resources for, 104
 See also specific subjects

Humanities Full Text Database, 104

Humanities International Index, 104

Hung, Wu, 109

Hutchings, Graham, 127

Hutchings, Robert L., 124

I

I Love Dollars and Other Stories of China (Zhu), 132

Image Archive of History of Republic of China, 97

The Image of Old China in the Western Perspective (Hong), 98

images
 of art, 107–109, 198
 photographic, 95–101

Images of Beijing Streets (Wang and Xu), 97

Images of China over a Century 1840–1978, 97

Images of Chinese Women in 100 Years (Chen), 98

Images of History of Qing Dynasty (Zhu), 98

Images of Modern China (Du), 96

Imperial China: Photographs 1850–1912 (Worswick and Spence), 98

imperialism, of Japan, 2–3

In Memory of 70th Anniversary of 1911 Revolution, 97

index databases, *vs.* full-text, 26, 33, 47

Index to Foreign Legal Periodicals, 176

Index to Legal Periodicals, 176

information literacy, definition of, 13

Innovations of Chinese Painting, 107

Inside Out: New Chinese Art (Minglu), 108

internal documents, locating, 79

International Bibliography of Art, 106

International Bibliography of the Social Sciences (IBSS), 142

International Encyclopedia of Marriage and Family, 151

International Encyclopedia of the Social and Behavioral Sciences, 151

International Index to Performing Arts (IIPA), 112

International Mission Photography Archive, 100

International Political Science Abstracts, 181

Internet resources
 buying guide for, 195–196
 vs. library resources, 12–13
 use of, 19–21

An Introduction to Chinese Sociology (Wu), 151

introductory texts. *See* reference (tertiary) sources

investment resources. *See* economics and business

ISI Emerging Markets, 164, 167

J

Japan
 imperialism of, 2–3
 photographs of, 99
 war with, xxii–xxiii

Jarman, Robert J., 123–124

Jefferies, Ian, 186
Jiang Zemin, 14, 127
Johns Hopkins University, 18, 26, 27*f*, 113, 121
Joseph, William, 185
Josephy, William A., 101
Journal of Asian Studies, 52
Journal of Chinese Cinemas, 114
Journal of Chinese Economic and Business Studies, 163
Journal of Chinese Economic and Foreign Trade Studies, 163
Journal of Chinese Entrepreneurship, 163
Journal of Chinese Law, 177
Journal of Chinese Philosophy, 136
Journal of Chinese Religions, 136
Journal of Contemporary China, 52
Journal of East Asian Studies, 52
Journal of Modern Chinese History, 121
Journal of Modern Literature in Chinese, 131
Journal of Women's History, 188
journals
    on economics and business, 161–164
    of English-language articles, 51–54
    on the humanities, 106–107, 113–115, 120–122, 131–132, 136
    on the social sciences, 144, 149, 153, 177, 182
    of translated articles, 59–62
    on women's and gender studies, 188–189
JSTOR, 18, 41–44, 103

K
keyword searches, 18, 26, 33, 47–48, 87, 111, 120
    See also search strategies
Kiang, Kang-hu, 3
King, Frank H., 128
Kirby, William C., 128
Kissinger, Henry, 124
The Kissinger Transcripts (Kissinger and Burr), 124
knowledge production, 14–15
Kramarae, Cheris, 191
Kuomintang (Guomindang), xxii, xxiii–xxiv
Kwong, Charles Yimtze, 133

L
Lan, Hua, 189
language, official, xvi, xvii

language options, in databases, 33, 50*f*
Late Imperial China journal, 121
Late Qing China, images of, 98
Late Qing Dynasty Database, 92, 202
Latham, Kevin, 117
Lau, Joseph S. M., 132
law
    core resources on, 175–177
    primary sources on, 178–179
    reference sources on, 179–180
    subject headings for, 160–161, 174–175
Law Yearbook of China, 177
LawInfoChina.com, 178
Lawrance, Alan, 124
Leaman, Oliver, 138
Lestz, Michael, 128
Leung, Edwin, 185
LEXIS (Taiwan company), 195
Lexis/Nexis, 175
Lhalungpa, Lobsang Phuntshok, 96
Li, Guannan, 147
Li, Jianming, 97
Li, Wenhai, 145
Liang, Bin, 179
Liberthal, Kenneth G., 12–13
library catalogs, searching, 18–19, 25–28, 30–31, 33, 35, 76
library resources *vs.* Internet resources, 12–13
Life of Empress in Forbidden City (Meng, Wu and Yu), 98
Lin, Julia, 133
Lin, Justin Yifu, 170
literature
    core resources on, 131–132
    primary sources on, 132–134
    reference sources on, 134–135
    subject headings for, 130
Literature Criticism Online, 131
literature review
    locating articles for, 65–73
    preparing for, 64–65
    as second step in research process, 10–11
Liu, Dalin, 189
Liu, Guoli, 185
Liu, Heung Shing, 96
Liu, Hong, 171
Liu, Joan, 180, 192n2
Liu, Jucai, 190
local gazetteers, 89, 137, 145, 150, 201

Lopez, Manuel D., 135
The Lost Boat: Avant-Garde Fiction (Zhao), 132
Louie, Kam, 134
Louie, Reagan, 96
Lovell, Julia, 132
Lu, Yiyi, 185
Lubman, Stanley B., 179
Luo, Wei, 180, 192n2

M

M. E. Sharpe, 59–61, 144, 149, 153
Mackerras, Colin, 147, 185
magazines, as popular source, 39–40
    See also periodicals
*Mahjong: Contemporary Art from the Sigg
    Collection,* 109
Major Education Documents of China (He), 154
Mak, Grace, 154
Mandarin Chinese, xvi, xvii
Mao Zedong, xxiii, xxiv, 83, 89, 124, 125, 184
Mao Zedong and China's Revolutions (Cheek),
    125, 184
Marion, Donald J., 117
market economy, xxv–xxvi, 90, 170
MarketLine Advantage, 167
MarketResearch.com, 166–167
mass media. *See* media
May Fourth Women Writers (Ng and Wickeri),
    133
McMillen, Donald H., 185
media
    core resources on, 93–94, 112–115
    government control of, 85, 89–90
    primary sources on, 115–116
    reference sources on, 116–117
    subject headings for, 111
*Media: Chinese Literature and Culture Resource
    Center,* 116
Menager-Xu, Michelle Yuan, 171
Meng, Zi, 98
Mergent Online, 169
Metzger, Thomas, 5
The Middle Kingdom (Williams), 2
Ming Dynasty, xx–xxi, 86, 121
Minglu, Gao, 108
missionaries, accounts of, 1–2, 95, 100, 140
MLA International Bibliography, 112, 131
Modern Asian Studies, 53
Modern China: A Guide (Hutchings), 127

Modern China journal, 53, 121, 182
Modern China Studies
    lack of reference resources for, xi–xii
    in the United States, 1–8
Modern Chinese Artists (Sullivan), 110
Modern Chinese Literary Thought (Denton), 133
Modern Chinese Literature and Culture, 131, 134
Modern Chinese Stories and Novellas (Lau), 132
Morse, Horsea Ballow, 127
Myers, Ramon, 5

N

National Bureau of Statistics of China, 165–166
National Digital Library of China, 108
*National Index to Chinese Newspapers and
    Periodicals,* 92, 120, 202
National Library of China, 33, 93
National People's Conference (NPC), 79
Neftci, Salih, 171
New Chinese Art website, 108
New York Times, 24
newspapers
    from contemporary China, 89–91
    English-language, 93–95
    from Late Qing and Republic Era, 91–93
    as popular source, 39–40
Ng, Janet, 133
Ng, Man Lun, 189
North China Herald, 95, 125
NWSA Journal, 188

O

Old Photos, 96
Olson, James, 146
On Chinese Studies (Kiang), 3
one-child policy, xxv, 14, 191
online resources. *See* Internet resources
Oriprobe databases, 82–83, 183, 199
Oriprobe Information Services, 199
*The Oxford Handbook of Business and
    Government* (Coen, Grant and Wilson), 171

P

painting, resources on. *See* arts
PAIS (Public Affairs Information Service), 181
PAJ: A Journal of Performing Arts, 113
Passport GMID, 167
peer review process, 22, 40, 43
Peerenboom, R. P., 179

Peng, Lu, 110–111
People's Bank of China, 166
People's Daily, 14, 83, 90, 122, 178, 183, 199
People's Liberation Army (PLA), 90, 97, 198
People's Republic of China
  buying books from, 194
  economic growth in, xi, xxv, 7, 170
  facts and figures on, xvi–xviii
  governmental control in, 13–15, 78, 85–86,
    89–90
  history of, xxii–xxvi
  map of, xv
  vendors in, 200–203
periodicals
  from contemporary China, 89–91
  English-language, 93–95
  from Late Qing and Republic Era, 91–93
  as popular source, 39–40
The Philosopher's Index, 136
philosophy
  sources on, 136–140
  subject headings for, 135
photographic images, locating, 95–101
*Photographical Impressions of Beijing in the
  1980s* (Li and Qian), 97
Picturing Hong Kong: Photography 1855–1910
  (Wue), 97
Picturing Power: Posters of the Cultural
  Revolution, 107–108
PLA Daily, 90, 122, 198
poetry, xx, 133
Policies and Laws of China (PLOC) database,
  178, 201
Policing the Shanghai International Settlement, 126
PolicyFile, 181–182
*Political, Economic, and Military Conditions in
  China*, 126
Political Developments in Contemporary China
  (Jefferies), 186
Political Leaders of Modern China (Leung), 185
political power, of Chinese government, 13–14,
  78, 89–90
*Political Relations and Conflict between
  Republican China and Imperial Japan*, 126
Political Risk Services Group (PRS), 164
politics
  core resources on, 181–182
  primary sources on, 182–184
  reference sources on, 185–186

  subject headings for, 180–181
  women and, 173, 187, 189, 191
  See also government
Politics and Government in China (Liu), 186
Politics in China (Joseph), 185
The Politics of Lawmaking in Post-Mao China
  (Tanner), 179
Politics of Modern China (Zheng, Lu and
  White), 185
Pong, David, 146
Ponzetti, James J., 151
Pop Culture China! (Latham), 117
popular sources, *vs.* scholarly, 39–41
population statistics, xvi–xvii, 150, 158, 164
Porter, Eliot, 96
Porter, Jonathan, 96
Positions: East Asia Cultures Critique, 52
Postiglione, Gerard A., 59, 154
prejudice, in sources, 1–3
Press Freedom Index, 89
primary sources
  on economics and business, 164–170
  on education, 153–155
  on the humanities, 107–109, 115–116,
    122–127, 132–134, 136–138
  search strategies for, 76–79
  vs. secondary sources, 11–12, 75–76
  on the social sciences, 144–145, 151,
    153–155, 178–179, 182–184, 189–191
  tools for locating, 79–83
  See also government documents
print reference sources, locating, 18–19
Project Muse, 43–44t
ProQuest Dissertations and Theses, 38
PsycINFO, 148, 153

Q

Qi, Wenyi, 191
Qian, Yu, 97
Qin Dynasty, xvi, xix
Qing Dynasty, xxi–xxii, 86, 92, 98, 121, 202

R

racism, 2–3
The Rape of Nanking: An Undeniable History
  (Shi), 97
The Real Story of Ah-Q (Lovell), 132
*Records of the National Council for United States-
  China Trade*, 123

Reel China: A Collection of Chinese
  Documentaries, 115
Reference Guide to Christian Missionary Societies
  (Tiedemann), 140
reference (tertiary) sources
    on the arts and film, 109–111, 116–117
    Chinese-language sources, locating, 21–22
    on economics and business, 59, 128,
      170–172
    on education, 153–155
    as first step in research process, 10, 17
    on history, 127–128
    on law, 179–180
    on literature, 134–135
    online databases, using, 19–21
    on politics, 185–186
    print sources, locating, 18–19
    on religion and philosophy, 138–140
    scholarly reviews, locating, 22–23
    on sociology and anthropology, 145–147,
      151
    on women and gender studies, 191–192
RefWorks, 49, 51, 52*f*
religion
    overview of, xvii
    sources on, 136–140
    subject headings for, 135
Religious Freedom in China (Chan), 139
Renditions, 132
Reports Without Borders (RWB), 89
Republic Era, 92–93, 119, 125, 145, 202
Republic Era Database, 92, 202
research papers, structure of, 63–64
research process
    digital environment and, 12–13, 34, 36
    effective *vs.* incomplete, 9–13
    unique aspects of, 13–15, 78, 85
research resources, lack of in China Studies, xi–xii
Review of Educational Research, 153
Review of Research in Education, 153
Reviews in Anthropology, 144
The Revolution Continues: New Art from China, 109
Roos, Maarten, 172, 179
Rosen, Stanley, 59
Roubini, Nouriel, 164–165
Roubini Global Economics, 164–165
Routledge Encyclopedia of Philosophy, 138
Routledge International Encyclopedia of Women,
  191

Routledge Religion Online, 138
Ryan, Janette, 155

S

Saatchi Gallery, 109
Sargent, William, 96
Saussy, Haun, 133
Schell, Orville, 124
scholarly articles, *vs.* popular, 39–41
scholarly research, conducting, 9–15
scholarly reviews, locating, 22–23
scholars, interaction between, 7–8
Schoppa, R. Keith, 124
Schwar, Harriet Dashiell, 184
Schwartz, Benjamin, 4
Scopus, 72
Search for Modern China (Spence), 128
search strategies
    for anthropology, 143
    for the arts, 105
    for economics and business, 157–161
    for education, 151–152
    for film and media studies, 111
    for history, 119–120
    for law, 160–161, 174–175
    for literature, 130
    for politics, 180–181
    for primary sources, 76–79
    for religion and philosophy, 135
    for sociology, 147–148
    for women's and gender studies, 186–187
    See also advanced search functions
search terms, 18, 26, 33, 47–48, 87, 111, 120
Second Historical Archives of China, 86
secondary sources, 10–11, 39–40, 75–76
Selected Stories by Mo Yan (Goldblatt), 132
Sexual Behavior in Modern China Report, 189
Shambaugh, David L., 124
Shanghia, 95, 100, 125, 126
Shanghia Library, 92, 120, 202
Shen, Kuiyi, 110
Shen Bao, 91–92, 125, 198
Shi, Yong, 97
Sidney D. Gamble Photographs Collection,
  98–99
Sigg, Uli, 109
Signs: A Journal of Women in Culture and Society,
  189
Sino-Japanese War, xxiii

Sinology, 3–4, 129
Smelser, Neil J., 151
Smith, Arthur, 2
social life, images of, 96
Social Politics: International Studies in Gender, State and Society, 189
social sciences, core resources for, 141–142
    See also specific subjects
Social Sciences Citation Index (SSCI), 66–71, 142
Social Sciences Full Text, 142
Social Sciences in China, 62
Social Surveys in Republic Era, 125
Social Surveys in Republic Era (Li), 145
socialism, xxiv–xxv, 13, 105
Socialist Era Database, 92, 202
SocINDEX, 148
Sociological Abstracts, 148
sociology
    sources on, 148–151
    subject headings for, 147–148
Sociology and Anthropology in Twentieth Century China (Dirlik, Li and Yen), 147
Sommer, Deborah, 138
Song Dynasty, xx
Soshoo, 202–203
A Sourcebook of Chinese Philosophy (Chan), 138
sources
    authoritative *vs.* inauthoritative, 13, 39–40
    core resources, 104, 105–107
    primary *vs.* secondary, 11–12, 75–76
    scholarly *vs.* popular, 39–41
Sources for Chinese Film Studies (Wu), 116
Sources in Chinese History (Atwill and Atwill), 125
Sources of Folk Culture (Ding), 145
South China Morning Post, 178
special economic zones, xxv
speeches, locating, 79, 82
Spence, Jonathan D., 96, 98, 128
Spencer, Jonathan, 146
Spender, Dale, 191
SSCI. *See* Social Sciences Citation Index (SSCI)
Standard and Poor's NetAdvantage, 167
Stanford Encyclopedia of Philosophy, 138
Starmark International, 193
statistical data, locating, 87–89
stereotypes, 2–3
students, in exchange programs, 7, 155

subject headings, overview of, 26–28
    See also search strategies
Sui Dynasty, xx
Sullivan, Lawrence R., 127
Sullivan, Michael, 110
Sun, Dajin, 186
Sung, Yongyi, 186
Super Star Digital Library, 36, 201
Svensson, Marina, 124
Sze, Arthur, 133

T

Taiwan, 116, 137, 195–196
Tang, Zhoumin, 97
Tang Dynasty, xx
Tanner, Murray S., 179
television. *See* film
tertiary sources. *See* reference (tertiary) sources
Thematic Database for Human-Earth System, 150
theses and dissertations
    government influence on, 15
    locating, 38, 201
Thomas H. Hahn Docu-Images Collection, 100
Thomson ONE, 170
Tiananmen Square and US-China Relations, 123, 184
Tiananmen Square demonstrations, xxv, 123, 124, 127, 184
Tianqiang, Gao, 97
Tibet, 96, 98, 101, 136–137
Tibet, the Sacred Realm: Photographs (Lhalungpa), 96
Tibet: From the Collections of American Geographical Society Library, 101
The Tibetan Album: British Photography in Central Tibet, 101
Tibetan Buddhist Resource Center, 136
Tibetan Women (Wu), 98
Tiedemann, R. G., 140
Tong, James, 60
Torgeson, Kristina M., 133
Toward a Truer Life: Photographs of China (Louie), 96
Tracking the Dragon (Hutchings), 124, 184
translated articles, 59–62
Trends of Recent Researches on the History of China, 121–122

Tsai, Kellee, 71
Tse-Tsung Chow Collection of Chinese Scrolls
    and Fan Paintings, 107
Twentieth Century China (Schoppa), 124
Twentieth Century China journal, 53, 121
Twenty-first Century journal, 121

U

United States
    buying Chinese books from, 193
    buying e-resources from, 197–200
    Modern China Studies in, xi, 1–8
University of Hawaii, 114, 136, 182
US Intelligence and China Collection, 123

V

vendors, 193–196, 197–203
verifiable sources, 13, 39–40
Virtual Shanghai, 100
visual arts resources. *See* arts
Visual Voices, 100 Photographs of Village China
    (Wu), 98
Visualizing China, 101

W

Wall Street Journal, 162
Wanfang Data, 38, 89, 201
Wang, Bin, 97
Wang, Chenglu, 171
Wang, Jing, 132
Wang, Peggy, 109
Wang, Q. Edward, 61
Wang, Xiufang, 154
war, images of, 97
Warlord Era, xxii–xxiii
Watson, Andrew, 185
Web of Science databases, 66, 71–72
websites. *See* Internet resources
West, Jackie, 191
White, Barbara Sue, 189
White, Lynn T., 185
white papers, locating, 79, 82
Wickeri, Janice, 133
Wide Angle, 113
Wikipedia, 11f, 12–13, 39–40
Wilkinson, Endymion, 128
Williams, Samuel Wells, 2
Wilson, Graham, 171
Wise Search, 91

women
    as authors, 133
    core resources on, 187–189
    images of, 98
    politics and, 173, 187, 189, 191
    primary sources on, 189–191
    reference sources on, 191–192
    subject headings for, 186–187
Women and Gender in Chinese Studies Review, 188
Women in China from Earliest Times to the
    Present (Yates), 191
Women in Republican China (Lan and Fong),
    189
Women of China: Economic and Social
    Transformation (West), 191
Women of Red Plain (Lin), 133
Women Writers in Modern China (Dooling and
    Torgeson), 133
Women Writers of Traditional China (Chang,
    Saussy and Kwong), 133
Women's Resources International, 187
Women's Studies: An Interdisciplinary Journal, 189
Women's Studies in China (Qi), 191
Women's Studies International Forum, 189
World Bank, 165
World Development Indicators, 165, 166
World News Connection, 93–94, 122, 183
World War II, impact of, 4
WorldCat
    for archives, 87, 128n2
    for books, 29–32f, 33–34, 140n1
    for government documents, 76–78f, 79–80
    for images, 95
Worldwide Political Science Abstracts, 181
Worswick, Clark, 98
Wu, Di, 116
Wu, Eugene W., 186
Wu, Kong, 98
Wu, Kunyi, 98
Wu, Xiaogang, 151
Wu, Xiaoxin, 138
Wu, Xinhua, 98
Wu, Yan, 98
Wue, Roberta, 97

X

Xi Jinping, xxvi
Xingjian, Gao, 129
Xu, Huiqi, 190

Xu, Xiushan, 97
Xu, Yuzhen, 190
Xun, Lu, 129, 132

Y

Yan, Mo, 129, 132, 140n2
Yang, Lixin, 179
Yang, Rae, 96
Yates, Robin D. S., 191
The Yearbook of Contemporary Art of China, 109
Yen, Hsiao-pei, 147
YesAsia.com, 196
Ying, Li-hua, 134
Yishu: Journal of Contemporary Chinese Art, 106
Yong, Cao, 170
Yu, Tianwei, 98
Yuan, Dongping, 96
Yuan Dynasty, xx

Z

Zhang, Eileen, 129
Zhang, Peitian, 178
Zhang, Xudong, 131
Zhang, Yingjin, 116, 117
Zhao, Yiheng, 132
Zheng, Yongnian, 185
Zheng He, xxi
Zhong, Fulan, 96
Zhou, Daming, 60
Zhou, Li Ping, 190
Zhou, Luo, 101n2, 117n1
Zhou, Xun, 125
Zhou Dynasty, xix
Zhu, Chengru, 98
Zhu, Wen, 132
Zimmerman, James M., 180